རྗེ་མཁས་ཞིང་གྲུབ་པའི་དབང་ཕྱུག་སྐལ་ལྡན་རྒྱ་མཚོ་

Journey to Distant Groves

Journey to Distant Groves

Profound Songs of the Tibetan Siddha Kälden Gyatso

Victoria Sujata

VAJRA
BOOKS

Published & Distributed by
Vajra Books
Jyatha, Thamel, P.O. Box 21779, Kathmandu, Nepal
Tel.: 977-1-4220562, Fax: 977-1-4246536
e-mail: bidur_la@mos.com.np, www.vajrabooks.com.np

Cover photos: Kälden Gyatso's main hermitage, the forested Rongbo Tashikhyil, in Amdo

ISBN 978-9937-9330-6-3

Printed in Nepal

Contents

Translator's Preface

My introduction to Tibet took place at the New England Conservatory of Music in the late 1970's, where I studied many kinds of non-Western music, one of which was the mysterious and profound chanting of the Tibetan Gyütö monks. In the 1980s, I began visiting a few countries in Asia, Africa, and the Middle East every year, in order to hear the outstanding music of each, within the context of its indigenous arts, religion, and healing traditions, on its own soil. This project first led me to the Tibetan cultural region in 1988, when I began what has turned out to be a long series of yearly summer visits, by staying in a number of monasteries in western Tibet and hiking for a month in the Himalayas.

Each time I visited the Tibetan cultural region—whether Ladakh in the west, the Himalayas to the south, Central Tibet, or Amdo to the northeast—my experiences were better. This consistent reinforcement of Tibet as a place of such richness kindled my enthusiasm to always try to do more there—visit more holy sites, and spend more time with more people, with whom I experienced a deep mutual connection and unconditional acceptance. I also met Michael Aris, an extremely charismatic visiting professor of Tibetan and Himalayan studies at Harvard University, and found myself irresistibly swept into doing graduate work, while my trips continued in the summer.

The quest to do more and more continually challenged me in terms of how to deal with demanding situations of altitude and weather, and how to supplement whatever food there was with things I could bring along to eat. On the one hand, the simple goal of my physical survival was a necessity around which a number of decisions had to be made. On the other hand, my spiritual life was so aglow that there was no question of the value of learning to deal with physical inconveniences. Traveling for three or more months at a time and always going farther led me to such exalted experiences as visiting the holy western snow mountain, Mt. Kailash,[1] where I slept and meditated by rushing streams and waterfalls of the holy waters rushing down from its glaciers at night, walked the circumambulation route and inner paths for days with nomads and yaks, and rode a horse for four days on the pilgrims' route around the radiant, aquamarine waters of its accompanying lake, Manasarovar.

There is no doubt that my experiences as a pilgrim in Tibet were priceless. But due to the high altitudes (I hiked up to 18,600 feet several times), the threat of snow and hailstorms even in the warmest months of summer, and the potential for physical problems in extremely isolated places, I did not feel I could linger in any one place. Though I took care to deal with and adjust to the physical challenges slowly, in order to preserve a sense of well-being that would allow me to have the inner experiences I wanted to have, it was a delicate sense of well-being that constantly needed to be protected and nourished. These pilgrimage trips were—and still are—exciting and deeply inspiring, and I learn lifelong lessons from them, but they are lessons to *bring back* with me. I have never stayed in a place in the middle of the Tibetan plateau where I could actually relax: the pilgrimages have always been *trips*, never something I could call real life.

My relationship with Tibet began to change from *traveling* to *residing* quite unconsciously, when I started visiting some of the monasteries in Amdo, a large area of the province of Qinghai.[2] I immediately felt more comfortable there than in other parts of Tibet, because it is slightly lower in altitude, milder in weather, and because I was near the edge of the Tibetan plateau, into which valleys cut deeply. It is always reassuring to know that I can walk down several thousand feet in a few hours for some extra oxygen, if needed, though

I never have. Even more importantly, Amdo has a milder, less agonizing political situation than Central Tibet, where my belief in a kind universe had been frequently challenged. Hence both the altitude, weather, and political scene are more nurturing in Amdo, and I actually felt I could relax more into daily life and even consider living somewhere there.

There were very few Western tourists in Rebgong[3] when I started visiting it in 1993 because it was not in any of the Western guidebooks, and because one really needs to speak some Chinese to use public transportation between villages and find a place to stay.

A friend in the States had spoken highly of a monastery that a friend of his had seen, and I thought I would visit it.[4] I found a guide to take me, and was given the choice of walking for three days, riding a horse for one day, or going by tractor for half a day. I chose the tractor since there would be no fruit or vegetables at the monastery three thousand feet up the steep wall of the valley, and I wanted to bring along a large cabbage, some apples, and some pears. Upon arriving up at the small monastery on the plateau I remember about ten monks encircling me, and gaping, with their mouths dropped open for about ten minutes, while my guide went to consult with the lama. Later, once enough of the ice between us had melted, I realized that those monks were usually very jovial. On my second visit there, we were able to bridge the difference in our dialects enough to converse more freely, and they told me that on that very first day of my arrival, they had been awestruck by my blue eyes and white skin, and had thought I was some sort of proto-human being.[5]

It was clear that my first visit to this small monastery was the key that opened the doors to a lifetime's worth of adventures. Looking outward in this lovely place at eleven thousand five hundred feet, I marveled at the almost three-hundred-and-sixty-degree panorama of steep valleys and distant mountain ranges. Incredibly, I was in an evergreen forest, even at this altitude, though when I looked out, the rest of the landscape was bare, with orange and pink mountainsides dotted with small shrubs. So the inner sense of expansiveness and joy that I felt and my meditation practices of looking inward resonated well with the periods of looking outward at the stunning landscapes and hearing the sonic delights of the songs and calls of the nomads far below echoing up between the steep valley walls. The two—inner life and external life—reinforced each other cyclically, and even blended at times into one continuous whole. I was touched by the joy of my hosts, which was at the same time well grounded, and I was convinced of their harmlessness and kindness. I felt so thoroughly understood and accepted; it was as if I had come home. I was in a place where Buddhism works perfectly.

Visiting this small monastery also became the key that opened a lifetime's worth of scholarship. My teacher at Harvard, Professor Leonard van der Kuijp, who is amazingly well-read, actually knew that its founder—Kälden Gyatso (1607–1677), the very scholar who had taken up residence there as a hermit—was also a great writer, and that his writings were practically unknown in the West. I chose to write my dissertation on his collection of *gur*, or songs of spiritual experience.

My thesis[6] was the first commentary in Western literature on the *Gurbum* (*Collected Songs of Spiritual Realization*), two hundred and forty-two songs attributed to Kälden Gyatso.[7] The thesis led to a subsequent publication in 2005 by Brill, entitled *Tibetan Songs of Realization*,[8] and an accompanying CD of the songs as they are sung today.[9] Reviews have praised this work as "an impressive achievement," "the most detailed treatment of formal and stylistic features of Tibetan songs to date... [that] will long serve as a major reference..." (JAS); and as "essential materials for students of Tibetan literature, poetics, and ethnomusicology" (JIATS). I had done this work largely in a place where all three aspects—wonderful meditations, scholarship, and enjoyment of the great beauties of nature—resonated together.

I next decided to expand my horizons by investigating the *gur* of some other songwriters of the last five centuries who had been born in Amdo or had lived there, or who had led a lifestyle similar to that of Kälden Gyatso in terms of receiving a substantial monastic education and later becoming siddhas and hermits.[10] Focusing on songwriters from Amdo made sense on a number of levels. Since it took several months to walk between there and Central Tibet, where the Tibetan government and huge monastic establishments were located, singers were more likely to be outspoken about their topics in Amdo—exactly the kind of *gur* I hoped to find. At the same time, continuing to study *gur* in Amdo suited my lifestyle perfectly, since I could approximate how the writer had lived in my own small way, and have a fuller experience of his life and his writing. A hermitage away from home is just the place for me to read the songs of hermits, who themselves had left their homelands behind.

After skimming through collections of songs by some ten authors who fit the description above, I found that I liked the *gur* of the author I had started with—Kälden Gyatso—and the *gur* of another songwriter, Shabkar Tshogdruk Rangdrol, the best because of their depth and richness of personal expression in very simple styles. Hence I had come full circle back to Kälden Gyatso's songs, now perceiving them within a larger context. Tshogdruk Rangdrol (1781–1851), or Shabkar—as many people call him—was already known in the West by the lovely translation of his autobiography by M. Ricard,[11] which has many songs in it. But another rich source of Shabkar's songs, his collection of songs, had not been translated,[12] and this became the source for my second book on *gur*, *Songs of Shabkar: The Path of a Tibetan Yogi Inspired by Nature,* published by Dharma Publishing in 2011.[13]

There were still plenty of Kälden Gyatso's songs that I had not dealt with, and other ones in *Tibetan Songs of Realization* whose translations I wanted to update. I thought it would be wonderful to publish a new work of more translations organized according to the phases of development he says he went through to attain the spiritual realization that he sought. I relished the idea of visiting his favorite hermitages again, in order to be right where he may have sung many of the same songs that I would be translating. While my first book on Kälden Gyatso involved a lot of commentary and analysis of his songs, my new one would focus on my translations, since the directness of the songs is so compelling that one can enjoy the experience of reading them by themselves. I would create a critical edition of the Tibetan texts based on as many extant versions as I could, and place it in Tibetan script on pages opposing my translations. Much could be written to supplement the songs in various ways, and this I would put in the back matter. And I would further enhance the translations with photographs so that the readers could see the environs of some of Kälden Gyatso's main hermitages, the vastness and power of the topography which is otherwise impossible to imagine. With these decisions, the seeds for this book were born.

Kälden Gyatso had spent nine years studying the usual curriculum in a large monastic establishment near Lhasa, and, largely under peer pressure, founded a large school of philosophy at Rongbo Monastery, had hundreds of disciples, and nurtured relationships with wealthy and powerful patrons for his school. He was also a prolific writer who wrote sixty-five texts, including biographies, eulogies, histories of Amdo, commentaries on philosophical works, and instruction manuals on meditation, tantric practices, and spiritual purification. He belonged formally to the Gelugpa school, and also had strong nonsectarian tendencies.

He seems to have been convinced that his busy life was standing in the way of his spiritual development, and eventually he was able to renounce his lifestyle as an important lama and founder to live a simple life in the high-altitude forest to the west above Rongbo valley[14] that I had visited more than three hundred years later. When he moved to this extraordinary place with its extraordinarily vast, nearly three-hundred-and-sixty-degree view, his preferred medium of communication became a style of song sometimes sung by hermits called *gur* (T: mgur)—songs of experience or realization—that he sang to himself, other mountain hermits, and sometimes wrote down. He excelled in singing *gur,* through which he expressed his concerns about themes such as the importance of confronting the inescapability of death and the spontaneous development of spiritual qualities and happiness that comes about when one renounces the world and lives in a delightful solitary place. And he was able to devote more time to his practices, one of which was the Ganden Oral Tradition of *Mahāmudrā*.

The songs of spiritual realization are a genre of unique importance for understanding the tradition of Tibetan Buddhism. They have religious themes but are at the same time more direct expressions of personal experience than classic monastic literature with its biographies, histories, philosophical instruction, and instruction on meditation and deities. *Gur* are sung largely by recluses in solitude or for other hermit-disciples away from monastic settings; their expression is often less formal and very personal. Because they show not only the highest levels that a saint attains but also the low points, bawdy humor, and inner struggles along the path, they provide road maps for others to follow that make enlightenment seem attainable by anyone who will renounce the world and do spiritual practices in solitude. Because *gur* are simple expressions of personal religious insights that aim to appeal to people in an accessible and pleasing way, they fill an essential role in Tibetan Buddhism.

Gur are also unique in terms of style. On the one hand, they can show considerable folk influence in metrics and figures of speech, and their melodies are probably related to folk melodies, like those of their forerunners, the songs of the *mahāsiddhas*, in India. Yet at the same time *gur* are not simply spiritually themed folk songs; they can also be influenced by very formal Indian classical verse, especially if their author at one time studied in a monastery. In that way, they can be an intriguing blend of classical and folk, formal and informal, foreign and indigenous.[15]

I have chosen less formal, more simple forms of *gur* for this collection of translations, songs that are outspoken in terms of opinions and feelings. Kälden Gyatso expresses criticism, often scathingly, of himself and the evils of his homeland and village monastery. He expresses feelings of sadness at the inescapability of impermanence, longing for his lama, and anger over the absence of virtue. He describes his life-style, and tells us why he chose to live in hermitages. And he expresses spiritual ideas in very simple, experiential ways. There is surely a place for gorgeous hagiographies of this realized master, but here one finds what he said about himself, and so we can see the stages he went through and learn that at many points in his life, this master was actually quite similar to us. While the more formal *gur*, characterized by rich styles adhering to the rules of poetics—or *kāvya*—that originated in the fifth century in India, are certainly beautiful in their ornateness, the *gur* I have translated here are less complex. I hope that readers will find them beautiful in their own right.

Kälden Gyatso's songs are often very rich in personal detail and have great depth of expression. Here he sings of the benefits one can gain from renouncing the world and living in solitary places, since they can lead one to great happiness in old age when those of us still in the world might be having our most anxious moments:

> I feared sickness, old age, and the Lord of Death,
> And never found the means to flee from these three enemies.
> But now I am sick, and a mountain peak is a happy place
> for being sick.
> Now I am growing old, and a mountain peak is a delightful place
> for aging.
> Now I am dying, and a mountain peak is a joyful place for dying.
> Whatever the circumstances of my karma, a mountain peak is
> a place of great bliss[16]

And we learn that he views old age and sickness as mere previous karma, and that with his body at ease, his spiritual practices flourish. I find that these simple, outspoken expressions by him cut right to the point in an unforgettable way. While there's unequivocally a place for the very valuable, long, complex philosophical commentaries that are the hallmark of much of Tibetan Buddhist literature, these simple songs fill another role and sometimes resonate very quickly and directly with the very core of our sense of truth.

I have organized the collection of twenty-four *gur* I present here around six topics. The central theme is the attainment of realization, but this is best done in a hermitage, and a hermitage is of no use if one has not renounced the world, which itself is inspired by confronting one's defects, impermanence, and death. So spiritual development involves layers, and I have ordered my themes around the process that Kälden Gyatso himself tells us he followed to attain experiences of realization.

I start with a chapter with songs about lamas, since in tantric Buddhism the lama is regarded as the essence of the Buddha, Dharma teachings, spiritual community, and as the gateway to one's spiritual practices. Chapter Two is devoted to the means one could employ to spur oneself on along the path towards realization. Recognizing how detrimental one's defects are to spiritual progress is an incentive to confront them and practice the Dharma. Kälden Gyatso sometimes bitterly criticizes himself, something rarely encountered in Tibetan literature. Although viewed as highly realized by others, he is quick to express his faults, sometimes with great humor, and sometimes with great disdain:

> When relatives look at me, they think I'm crazy.
> When monks look at me, they think I'm fickle.
> When I look at myself, I think I'm deceitful[17]

Moreover, the realization that things are always changing and lack inherent existence inspires one to take advantage of one's human body in youth and health to practice the Dharma. And confronting the reality of the inescapability of death will inspire one to the Dharma in this lifetime, while one has a human body.

Chapter Three is devoted to renunciation, because without renunciation, no matter what else one does—whether studying philosophy in a school or living as a hermit—the benefits will be small. In the West, we often view renunciation in the negative sense as something that would lead to a lack of things we may want or need, but Kälden Gyatso views it in a positive way:

> All renunciants become wealthy
> By living at the gates of the treasure-house
> Of contentment with few desires[18]

He concludes that he should get away from both the village and the monastery, where his behavior is poor, and go to a solitary grove.

Chapter Four focuses on what he tells us as he heads off to solitary hermitages—reasons for his departure, expectations that his spiritual practices will flourish from staying in solitude, and the inner joy he believes he will attain. His desire to go to a hermitage in order to focus on his spiritual practices is palpable when he compares himself to a bird, who can freely go wherever it desires.

Chapter Five is about the wonderful meditation experiences one can have in solitary places. We gain insight into some of the higher tantric Buddhist practices Kälden Gyatso performs at the hermitages, including a form of Gelugpa *Mahāmudrā* called the Ganden Oral Tradition of *Mahāmudrā* that by tradition was said to have been handed down from Tsongkhapa, the renowned founder of the Gelugpa school, but which may have been first systematized by the famed first Panchen Lama, the very lama from whom he had received ordination. Chapter Six is about the happiness that he says one will spontaneously feel, having renounced the world and being focused single-mindedly on the Dharma.

It is with pleasure that I present my third book on *gur*. All of my translations here were made from critical editions I created of each song. My translations are less literal than my previous ones, since my intention here is to communicate what the authors are telling us, so I go beyond a simple stringing together of definitions from the still highly limited dictionaries. On the other hand, I have not enhanced the language in an attempt to make the *gur* something that they are not. This was not out of an obsession with scholarship or blind faith on my part, but out of a recognition that the *gur* are already powerful expressions of spiritual experiences and realization.

I provide copious back matter, which is meant to supplement the songs in various ways. In my Notes, I address styles of writing, poetic figures, unusual metric patterns, ornithology, geography, biography, history; and I give definitions for some Tibetan terms that are not found in the main dictionaries, explanations of the meaning of lines and terms that are more obscure, and show how I translated some of the more intricate passages. My Table of Meters shows the meter of each song, and gives details on whatever variations occur within it.

The Glossary of Buddhist Terms defines all terms in the translations and notes. My aim is to give readers with little exposure to Buddhism a notion of the common usage of each term. My habitual quest for accuracy is challenged here, since I need to simplify what are in some cases truly complex concepts, and I regret that specialized scholarship about some of these terms is beyond the scope of my glossary.

Sources for the Songs gives the location of each song in six extant versions of the collected *gur* (T: mgur 'bum) of Kälden Gyatso. All spelling variants between the versions are also listed here. The Biography outlines briefly the main features of Kälden Gyatso's life. The Table of Tibetan Words lists the phonetic spellings I use throughout the book, and their respective spellings according to the Wylie system of transliteration. The maps show the geographical position of Amdo, and the places within Amdo found in the songs, respectively. Finally, I provide a copious index for those who want to trace one concept, name, or place from one *gur*, note, or glossary entry to another.

The Tibetan text I provide here is my critical edition based on the six extant versions of the text in Tibet.

I took the photographs between 1993 and 2017 in close proximity to where Kälden Gyatso lived in Amdo on the far northeast edge of the Tibetan plateau, and provide them here to enrich readers' experience of the songs. This powerful landscape, with its deep valleys that cut into the plateau resulting in striking patterns of erosion, is the context in which Kälden Gyatso lives his life and sings his *gur*. He sometimes uses similes and metaphors from nature to express his realizations, but beyond that, the steep valley walls of this dramatic landscape echo back his songs.

It is my hope that this book will be enjoyed by both scholars in Tibetan and Buddhist studies, and newcomers alike, so I have made my translations accessible to the novice reader by spelling the proper names and other Tibetan words in phonetics, and by explaining technical Buddhist terms in the glossary. Scholars in the field will realize that the rich Tibetan meters[19] cannot be duplicated in translation, but the Tibetan script of my critical editions is provided here alongside my translations, so that those with a knowledge of Tibetan can enjoy the songs in their original language.

Notes

1 For the location of Mt. Kailash, see map 1.

2 Qinghai is a large Chinese province to the northeast of what the Chinese call the Tibetan Autonomous Region, or T.A.R. These two provinces, about the same size, are parts of the Tibetan cultural area, since Tibetans live in each indigenously. For the approximate location of Amdo, see map 1.

3 For Rebgong, an area in eastern Amdo, see map 2.

4 Only after arriving did I learn that I had mistakenly ended up at a different place with the same name, but by then it did not matter, as will be clear by my story.

5 A friend clarified this many years later: "skra mi ni 'gro ba ma'i mes po red/". A *trami* (*skra mi*) is thought to be a progenitor of the Tibetan people—a link between the monkey, or first ancestor, and the first human being. While the monkey has a tail, the *trami* has no tail, though still lots of hair. Akhu Päljor, interview by author, notes, Rebgong, late summer, 2008.

6 V. Sujata, "A Commentary on the *Mgur 'bum* (*Collected Songs of Spiritual Realization*) of Skal ldan rgya mtsho, a Seventeenth-Century Scholar and Siddha from Amdo" (Ph.D. diss., Cambridge: Harvard University, 2003).

7 Skal ldan rgya mtsho, *Shar skal ldan rgya mtsho'i mgur 'bum* (Xining: Mtsho sngon mi rigs dpe skrun khang, 1994). For various woodcarvings and other editions of this work, please consult my Sources. I will henceforth refer to the author and 1994 edition of the text as Skal ldan, *Mgur 'bum* (1994).

8 V. Sujata, *Tibetan Songs of Realization: Echoes from a Seventeenth-Century Scholar and Siddha in Amdo* (Leiden: Brill, 2005). This will henceforth be referred to as *TSR*.

9 *Tibetan Songs of Realization: A Continuing Tradition from the Seventeenth Century*, recorded, compiled, translated and annotated by Victoria Sujata (Leiden: Brill, 2005). This CD is available with *TSR*.

10 My main source of references was a treatise on *gur* by one of the great twentieth-century scholars from Amdo, Döndrup Gyäl. For this, see Don

grub rgyal, *Bod kyi mgur glu byung 'phel gyi lo rgyus dang khyad chos bsdus par ston pa rig pa'i khye'u rnam par rtsen pa'i skyed tshal*, in *Dpal don grub rgyal gyi gsung 'bum*, vol. 3 (Beijing: Mi rigs dpe skrun khang, 1997), 316-601.

11 Zhabs dkar Tshogs drug rang grol, 1781–1851, *The Life of Shabkar: The Autobiography of a Tibetan Yogin*, trans. Matthieu Ricard, et al. (Albany: State University of New York Press, 1994). This is a translation of the first part of his autobiography. *See* Zhabs dkar Tshogs drug rang grol, *Snyigs dus 'gro ba yongs kyi skyabs mgon zhabs dkar rdo rje 'chang chen po'i rnam par thar pa rgyas par bshad pa skal bzang gdul bya thar 'dod rnams kyi re ba skong ba'i yid bzhin gyi nor bu bsam 'phel dbang gi rgyal po*, in *Rje zhabs dkar tshogs drug rang grol gyi gsung 'bum* by Zhabs dkar Tshogs drug rang grol, vol. 1 (Xining: Mtsho sngon mi rigs dpe skrun khang, 2002).

12 Zhabs dkar Tshogs drug rang grol, [*Bya btang tshogs drug rang grol gyis rang dang skal ldan gdul bya la mgrin pa gdams pa'i bang mdzod nas glu dbyangs dga' ston 'gyed pa rnams*], in *Rje zhabs dkar tshogs drug rang grol gyi gsung 'bum*, vols. 3–4 (Xining: Mtsho sngon mi rigs dpe skrun khang, 2002). Unfortunately, there is no title given for the collection of *gur* in this edition, but since the title is found in other editions (such as the Shechen Publication of 2003 in my bibliography), I have assumed that it is missing, and have inserted it here in brackets. I thank E.G. Smith for his advice in this regard.

13 V. Sujata, *Songs of Shabkar: The Path of a Tibetan Yogi Inspired by Nature* (Cazadero, Calif.: Dharma Publishing, 2011). This will henceforth be referred to as *S of SH*.

14 For the location of Rongbo, see maps 1 and 2.

15 For brief descriptions of the genre of *gur*'s predecessors in India, the *caryāgīti* and *dohā*, and the development of *gur* in Tibet up through the sixteenth century, see *TSR*, 78–85.

For a discussion of poetic figures that appear in *gur* that are influenced by very formal Indian classical verse, and ones that are indigenously Tibetan, see *TSR*, 162–246.

I thank Dharma Publishing for the contractual permission to freely reuse any portions of the forematter and endmatter in *S of SH*.

16 Skal ldan, *Mgur 'bum* (1994), 164.

17 Skal ldan, *Mgur 'bum* (1994), 207–208.

18 Skal ldan, *Mgur 'bum* (1994), 341.

19 For a detailed discussion of the Tibetan use of metrics, the backbone of verse, see *TSR*, 112–38.

Acknowledgments

I can never express enough gratitude to the many people who have either helped me arrive at the point of being able to compile and translate this collection of *gur*, or who have contributed to it more directly. A number of monks and lay people in the Rebgong area of Amdo, where I have been visiting for most summers since 1993, have contributed to this book in crucial ways. I could not have completed my translations without the consistent and expert assistance of one of the great scholars of Rebgong, Lobzang Chödrag (or Chidrag, in the local dialect), who patiently answered all the questions I posed regarding my translations, and tirelessly sorted out questions of spelling in the original manuscripts. There is perhaps no one who has personally explored Amdo step by step, cave to cave, peak to peak, as extensively as Gendun Döndrup, and I am so grateful to have been able to consult him about my maps. I would also like to thank Akhu Päljor (Whanjor), Lobzang Pälden (Whaden), Jamyang Chöphel (Chiphel), and the late Gendun Trinley for their wisdom, inspiration, hospitality, and laughter.

In the West, the late E. Gene Smith gave me both unfathomable inspiration and stern encouragement during my early years of exploration of the writings of Kälden Gyatso. Chris Leahy of the Massachusetts Audubon Society provided much crucial information regarding the names and songs of the birds in the *gur* translated here. K.E. Duffin, talented editor, artist, and poet, read the entire manuscript and offered many insightful suggestions that both elevated the quality of my writing and helped to bring out Kälden Gyatso's intentions. C. Scott Walker, of the Harvard Map Collection, worked with me meticulously to produce the maps that I wanted. Dan Lusthaus, Research Associate at Harvard University, generously read my entire Glossary of Buddhist Terms, and gave me gentle guidance so I could better maneuver between the many sources I was juggling to create definitions, and avoid certain pitfalls. Roger R. Jackson, Professor of Asian Studies and Religion, Emeritus, at Carleton College, kindly read the Glossary, and made many helpful recommendations. Robert Chilton helped work out issues of the Tibetan font for my critical edition printed here. Professor Leonard van der Kuijp of Harvard University, Erik Pema Kunsang of Rangjung Yeshes Publications, Geshe Tsultrim Chopel of the Kurukulla Center, Yael Bentor of The Hebrew University, Dan Martin, and Jann Ronis generously offered advice about lingering details. I owe much gratitude to my teachers of Tibetan language, culture, and history at Harvard from 1989 to 2003, the late Michael Aris, who fanned the embers of my fascination with Tibetology; and L. van der Kuijp, who offered many invaluable suggestions regarding my thesis on Kälden Gyatso. I am also grateful to Brill for permission to republish the songs in the appendix to *Tibetan Songs of Realization*, four of which are updated here. And I am so very thankful to Bidur Dangol of Vajra Books for having accepted to publish this work, and to Ram Krishna Dongol and other members of his staff for bringing it to fruition. Many other people in my life have contributed to the creation of this book in their own ways, especially Laurel McGregor, Gina Hosier, Yang Chengcai, Ann Wray, and the late Louis Belden, and I thank them all for their persistent encouragement and support. I accept responsibility for any remaining mistakes in this book.

Translations

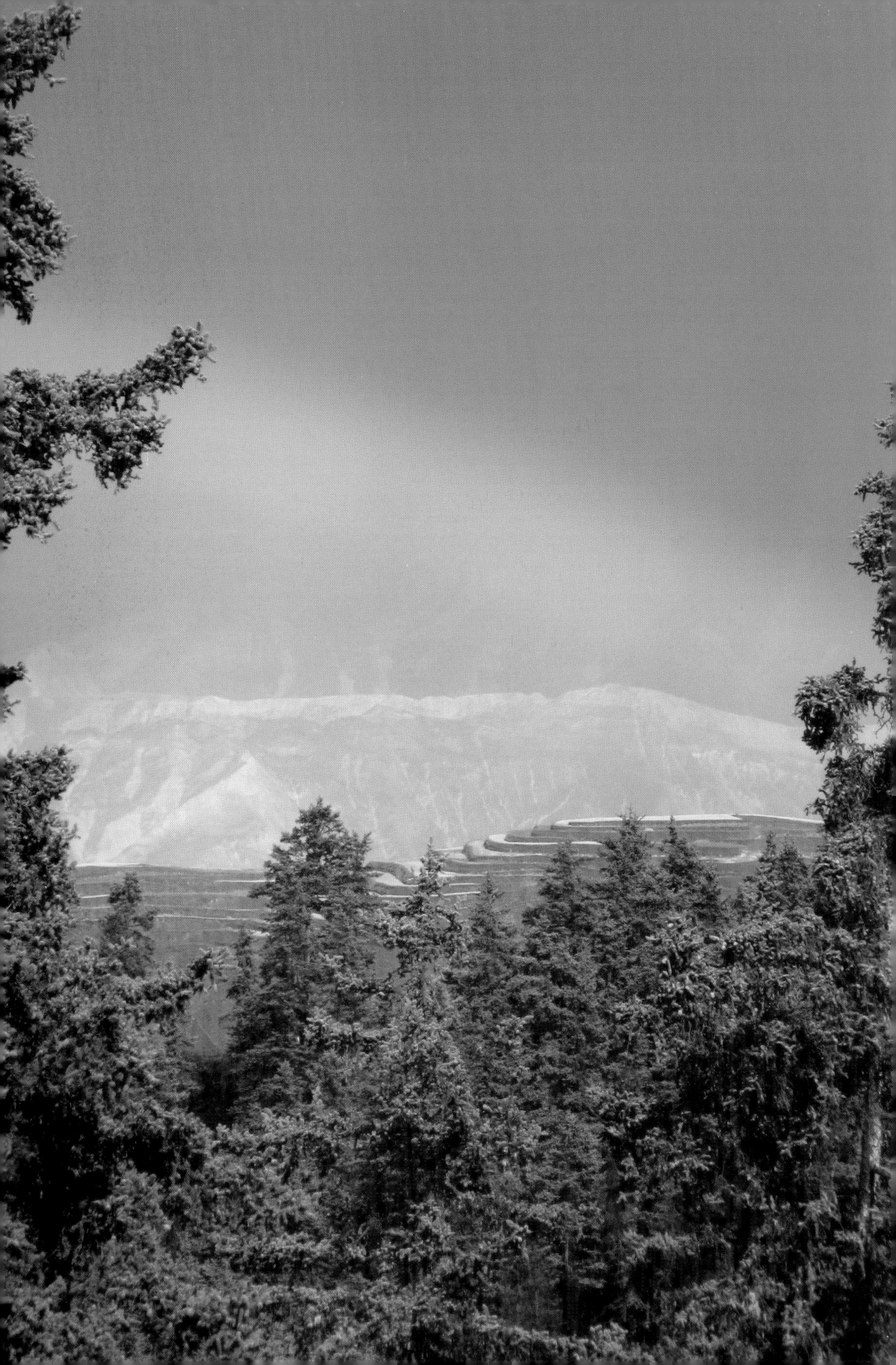

Chapter One

Homages to My Lamas

ཐུགས་བདེ་སྟོང་དང་ལས་མ་གཡོས་པར། །
སྒྱུ་ཅིར་ཡང་འཆར་བའི་རློལ་གར་གྱིས། །
གསུང་ལེགས་བཤད་ཆར་ཟིམ་འབེབས་མཁས་པའི། །
པ་བླ་མ་རྗེ་བཙུན་ཐམས་ཅད་མཁྱེན། །
ཁྱེད་ཐུགས་རྗེའི་སྤྱན་གྱིས་ཉེར་དགོངས་ནས། །
བུ་བདག་གི་སྤྱི་གཙུག་པད་ཟླའི་སྟེང་། །
ཞལ་འཛུམ་མདངས་ལྷམ་མེར་དགྱེས་བཞིན་དུ། །
མཆོག་ཐུན་མོང་དངོས་གྲུབ་སྩོལ་ཕྱིར་བཞུགས། །

རྗེ་གསུམ་ལྡན་བླ་མ་རིན་པོ་ཆེ། །
ཁྱོད་འོ་དོད་དྲག་པོས་རྒྱང་ནས་འབོད། །
འདི་གསན་ནམ་བླ་མ་བཀའ་དྲིན་ཅན། །
ཚེ་འདི་ཕྱིའི་འདུན་མ་ཁྱེད་རང་མཁྱེན། །

ཞིང་ཕྱོགས་བཅུར་བཞུགས་པའི་རྒྱལ་བ་དང་། །
སྲས་བྱང་ཆུབ་སེམས་དཔའ་མཐའ་དག་གིས། །
འབངས་བདག་བཤེས་ཁྱོད་ཀྱི་ཚུལ་བཟུང་ནས། །
རང་གང་འདོད་མདོ་སྔགས་ཆོས་ཆར་ཕབ། །

Father, lama, lord, omniscient one—
You who are skilled in causing a soft rain of eloquent explanations
to fall
By means of divine play in which bodily forms can manifest
everywhere,
Without moving your mind from the state of bliss-emptiness—
Please fully regard me, your son, with eyes of compassion,
And dwell on the lotus-moon at the crown of my head,
Joyfully radiant, with a smiling face
In order to bestow upon me the supreme and common *siddhi*s.

Precious lord, lama who possesses the three kindnesses,
I am calling out to you from afar, crying fiercely for your help.
Do you hear me, kind lama?
My hopes for this and future lives are in your hands.

All the Victorious Ones and their sons, the bodhisattvas,
Who dwell in the realms of the ten directions,
Have taken your form, my spiritual guide,
Causing a rain of sutras and tantras—whatever I, your subject,
have desired—to fall.

དོན་དེ་ཕྱིར་ཁ་ཙམ་མ་ཡིན་པས། །
སྙིང་རུས་པའི་གཉེར་ནས་བློ་གཏད་དེ། །
དུས་ཉིན་མཚན་ཀུན་ཏུ་མགོན་ཁྱོད་ལ། །
ངག་གདུང་ཤུགས་དྲག་པོས་གསོལ་བ་འདེབས། །

ཚེ་སྔོན་ཡང་ཁྱོད་ཀྱིས་རྗེས་བཟུང་བས། །
དུས་ད་ལན་དལ་ཐོབ་བསྟན་དང་མཇལ། །
ད་དེང་ནས་སངས་རྒྱས་མ་ཐོབ་བར། །
སྐྱབས་ཁྱོད་མིན་མ་མཆིས་བླ་མ་རྗེ། །

དབྱིངས་སྤྲོས་བྲལ་བདེ་ཆེན་ཆོས་ཀྱི་སྐུ། །
གདངས་འགག་མེད་ལོངས་སྤྱོད་རྫོགས་པའི་སྐུ། །
ཞིང་ཀུན་ཁྱབ་རྣམ་རོལ་སྤྲུལ་པའི་སྐུ། །
རྗེ་གསུམ་ལྡན་དབྱེར་མེད་རྡོ་རྗེ་འཛིན། །
མགོན་ཐུབ་དབང་སྲས་བཅས་ཉི་མ་དེ། །
ཞིང་གཞན་གྱི་ནུབ་རིར་གཤེགས་དུས་འདིར། །
ཁྱེད་ཐ་མལ་ཚུལ་གྱིས་བདག་དོན་མཛད། །
དྲིན་ལྷག་པར་ཆེའོ་ཆོས་ཀྱི་རྗེ། །

Therefore, without using mere words,
I have focused my mind single-pointedly upon you with intense
perseverance,
And I am praying to you, protector, in great anguish
Day and night.

Because also in former lives you accepted me with compassion,
This time I obtained a body complete with the freedoms, and
encountered the teachings.
From now on until I attain enlightenment
There will be no other refuge than you, lord lama.

At this time when the sun, the lord Buddha along with
his spiritual sons,
Has passed beyond the western mountain of another realm,
You have acted for my benefit in the guise of an ordinary man.
Your kindness is especially great, lord of the Dharma.
You, lord, who possess the three kindnesses,
Are in essence inseparable from Vajradhara,
The Dharma body, the realm of great bliss free from conceptual
elaborations;
The enjoyment body of unobstructed radiance,
And the emanation body, the display of manifestations pervading
all realms.

མར་ངན་སོང་གསུམ་དུ་ལྷུང་གྱུར་ཏམ། །
ཡར་མཐོ་རིས་ལྷ་མིའི་སར་སྐྱེས་ཀྱང་། །
མི་བདག་གིས་རེ་ལྟོས་བྱེད་ས་ནི། །
མགོན་ཁྱོད་ཞབས་མ་གཏོགས་གཞན་མ་མཆིས། །

ཕ་ཁྱོད་ཀྱི་བྱིན་རླབས་མ་ཞུགས་ན། །
ཉམས་རྟོགས་པ་སྐྱེ་ཐབས་མ་མཆིས་པས། །
རྒྱུད་ཀྱི་སྐམ་ལྟ་བུར་སོང་བ་འདིར། །
ད་སྒྱུར་དུ་བྱིན་རླབས་ཆར་ཐིམ་ཕོབ། །

ཚེ་འདི་ཕྱི་བར་གསུམ་བདེ་ལེགས་ཀུན། །
ཁྱོད་མཉེས་པར་བྱེད་ལ་རག་ལས་པར། །
བཀའ་མདོ་རྒྱུད་ཀུན་ལས་གསུངས་ལགས་པས། །
སྲོག་འདོར་ལ་ཐུག་ཀྱང་ཁྱོད་མི་སྤོང་། །

སྐྱབས་སངས་རྒྱས་ཆོས་དང་དགེ་འདུན་དང་། །
ལྷ་ཡི་དམ་མཁའ་འགྲོ་ཆོས་སྐྱོང་སོགས། །
མགོན་ཁྱོད་མིན་གཞན་ན་ཅང་མ་མཆིས། །
དོན་དེ་ཕྱིར་སྙིང་ནས་སྐྱབས་སུ་འཛིན། །

Although I tumbled down into the lower three realms
Or took birth in the higher realms of gods and humans,
There has been no reliable place for me
Other than at your feet, protector.

Father, since experience and realization
Only come about with your blessings,
Quickly bring a soft rain of blessings
Down upon my mind-stream, which is dry as an old hide.

All the scriptures, sutras and tantras,
Say well-being in this life, the next one, and the *bardo*
Depends fully on showing you esteem.
So even if I had to sacrifice my own life, I would not renounce you.

There is no protector other than you,
The essence of all refuges—Buddha, Dharma, Saṅgha,
Divine meditational deities, *ḍākinīs*, *dharmapālas*, and so forth.
Therefore, I take refuge in you with all my heart.

སྔོན་སྟོན་པས་སློབ་པ་ལམ་གྱི་ཚེ། །
ཆོས་ཤོ་ལོ་ཀ་ཙམ་གསན་ཕྱིར་དུ། །
མིའི་དོང་མཚོངས་ལྕགས་གཟེར་སྟོང་བཏབ་སོགས། །
བསྲན་དཀའ་བའི་དཀའ་སྤྱད་ཅི་ཙམ་མཛད། །

དུས་དེང་སང་འབད་རྩོལ་མི་དགོས་པར། །
དབང་རྫས་གནང་ཟབ་མོའི་མན་ངག་རྣམས། །
ཕ་ཕྲོད་ཀྱིས་ཇི་ལྟར་འདོད་འདོད་བསྩལ། །
དྲིན་སངས་རྒྱས་བྱང་སེམས་ཀུན་ལས་ལྷག །

རྒྱུ་དེས་ན་དཔལ་ལྡན་བླ་མ་ཕྲོད། །
དཔལ་སངས་རྒྱས་དངོས་སུ་མཐོང་བའི་བློས། །
ད་བློ་སྙིང་དབྲལ་གསུམ་ལིངས་གཏད་ནས། །
བཀའ་ཚུལ་བཞིན་སྒྲུབ་པའི་ཡི་དམ་བགྱིད། །

ཕྲོད་ཐུགས་རྗེའི་མཐུ་དཔུང་སྦྱར་སྐྱེད་ལ། །
དུས་གཏན་གྱི་ཕན་བདེ་མ་ལུས་དང་། །
སྒོས་ངེས་འབྱུང་བྱང་སེམས་ཡང་དག་ལྟ། །
ལམ་རིམ་གཉིས་རྒྱས་པར་མཛད་དུ་གསོལ། །

Long ago, when the Buddha was in training,
He performed austerities hardest to endure—
Such as jumping into a fiery pit, being pierced by one thousand
iron nails—
For the sake of hearing single stanzas of the teachings.

These days, I have no need to exert myself, father,
Because you have granted me whatever I have desired—
Initiations, textual readings, and ritual permissions.
Your kindness is greater than that of all Buddhas and bodhisattvas.

For that reason, with a mind which sees you, glorious lama,
Actually as the glorious Buddha, I have focused my attention
one-pointedly
On the three places—mind, heart, and forehead—
And now I vow to practice in accordance with your instructions.

Please generate your powerful compassion quickly,
And never abandon your concern for my spiritual and temporal
well-being.
Please develop both stages of the path in me—
The authentic views on renunciation and altruistic aspiration
to enlightenment.

ཞེས་རང་གང་མོས་ཀྱི་ཆོས་ཞུས་ཀྱི་བླ་མ་ལ་འོ་དོད་དྲག་པོས་རྒྱང་འབོད་ཀྱི་སྒོ་ནས་གསོལ་བ་
འདེབས་པ་འདི་ནི་དགེ་སློང་དགེ་འདུན་ཤེས་རབ་སོགས་ཀྱིས་བསྐུལ་བའི་ངོར་བླ་མའི་བཀའ་
འབངས་ཀྱི་ཐ་ཤལ་སྐལ་ལྡན་རྒྱ་མཚོས་སྦྱར་བའོ། ། ། །

"The anguished prayer that I am calling out fiercely to the lama from whom I request whatever teaching I desire," was composed by the lama's inferior subject, Kälden Gyatso, in response to a request by Gendün Sherab and other monks.

ས་པ་གི་ཞིག་ཉི་མ་བྱང་གི་ཕྱོགས། །
དཔལ་དགོན་ལུང་ཆོས་ཀྱི་སྡེ་ཆེན་ན། །
དྲིན་འཁོར་བར་དཀའ་བའི་ཐམས་ཅད་མཁྱེན། །
པ་བསྟན་འཛིན་བློ་བཟང་རྒྱ་མཚོ་བ། །
དབྱིངས་མི་མངོན་དག་པའི་ཞིང་ཁམས་སུ། །
དུས་ཚེ་འཕྲུལ་ཟླ་བའི་བཅོ་ལྔ་ལ། །
ལམ་འོད་གསལ་བརྒྱུད་ནས་གཤེགས་ཐོས་པས། །
ད་ཁོ་བོའི་བློ་གཏོད་སུ་ལ་ཞུ། །

ལམ་བླ་མའི་རྣལ་འབྱོར་བསྒོམ་པའི་ཚེ། །
ཕྱག་མཆོད་བསྟོད་སོགས་ཀྱི་ཚོགས་གསོག་རྟེན། །
དུས་གློ་བུར་ཞིང་གཞན་འབྱོན་ཐོས་པས། །
ད་ཁོ་བོའི་ཚོགས་ཞིང་སུ་ལ་ཞུ། །

རྟེན་དལ་འབྱོར་ཚང་བའི་མི་ཡི་ལུས། །
འདི་དོན་ཆེན་རྙེད་དཀར་བསམ་པའི་ཚེ། །
དོན་ཆོས་ཀྱིས་ལེན་པར་སྨོན་པའི་སྐྱབས། །
དགྲ་འཆི་བདག་ནམ་འོང་ཆ་མེད་པས། །
ད་ཁོ་བོས་བར་དོའི་འཇིགས་པ་ལས། །
སྐྱོབ་ནུས་པའི་སྐྱབས་གནས་གང་ནས་འཚོལ། །

ཞེས་པ་འདི་ཡང་རྗེ་སྐལ་ལྡན་རྒྱ་མཚོའི་གསུང་དྲི་མ་མེད་པའོ། ། ། །

Oh father, the one who holds the teachings, ocean of intelligence,
Whose kindness is so hard to repay,
Omniscient one in the great community of glorious Gönlung
Over there towards the sun's most northern point—
I have heard that you passed directly onto the path of clear light
And departed for an invisible, pure realm
On the fifteenth day of the first month.
So now who shall I beseech to be my trustworthy place of refuge?

When I practice guru yoga, I depend on the merit I accumulate
From making prostrations and offerings, giving praise, and so on.
I have heard that Tendzin Lobzang Gyatso suddenly departed
for another realm.
So now, through whom will I receive merit?

It is difficult to attain this great objective,
A human body complete with the freedoms and endowments.
And death strikes suddenly, without warning,
So I need a protector who will show me
How to attain another human body through the Dharma.
Now where can I find a source of refuge
Who will be able to protect me from the dangers of the *bardo*?

This is also an undefiled expression of Kälden Gyatso.

ན་མོ་གུ་རུ།

འཕགས་པ་ཀླུ་སྒྲུབ་ཉི་ཡབ་སྲས། །
མཉམ་མེད་བློ་བཟང་གི་གྲགས་པ། །
བློ་བཟང་ཆོས་ཀྱི་ཉི་རྒྱལ་མཚན། །
གསོལ་བ་སྙིང་ནས་རང་འདེབས་སོ། །
ཐུགས་རྗེའི་ལྕགས་ཀྱུ་ཡིས་དྲོངས་ཤིག །

རང་སེམས་སྒྲོས་མེད་ཀྱི་རྒོད་པོ། །
ཆོས་དབྱིངས་སུ་འཕུར་སྙིང་འདོད་ཀྱང་། །
བདག་འཛིན་གྱི་རྙི་ཐག་ཁྲ་བོས། །
དབང་མེད་དུ་འཁོར་བར་བཅིངས་སོ། །

ཟབ་ལམ་གྱི་མཚོན་ཆ་རྣོན་པོས། །
བདག་འཛིན་འདི་མྱུར་དུ་གྲོལ་ཅིག །
ཐུགས་རྗེའི་ལྕགས་ཀྱུ་ཡིས་དྲོངས་ཤིག །

བློ་བཟང་ཆོས་ཀྱི་ཉི་རྒྱལ་མཚན། །
རང་སེམས་ཐར་འདོད་ཀྱི་བུང་བ། །
ཐར་ལམ་དུ་འཕུར་སྙིང་འདོད་ཀྱང་། །
ཆོས་བརྒྱད་སྦྲང་རྩི་ཡི་དགའ་སྟོན། །
རྙེད་བཀུར་དོན་གཉེར་ལ་ཆགས་སོ། །

I prostrate myself before the lama.

Noble Nāgārjuna and disciples,
The unrivalled Lobzang Dragpa,
And Lobzang Chökyi Gyältsen—
I beseech you with all my heart.
Please guide me with the iron hook of compassion.

Although the eagle of my nonconceptual mind
Longs to fly to the *dharmadhātu,*
It has been entangled helplessly
In the colorful ropes of the trap of clinging to reality.

Please annihilate this grasping at reality quickly
With the sharp lance of the profound path.
Please guide me with the iron hook of compassion.

Lobzang Chökyi Gyältsen,
Although the liberation-seeking bee of my mind
Longs to fly on the path of liberation,
I am attached to the feast of honey—the eight worldly concerns—
And to striving for personal gain and esteem.

འདོད་ཡོན་བཙན་དུག་ཏུ་ཞེས་པའི། །
གདམས་ངག་ཟབ་མོ་ནི་སྩོལ་ཅིག །
ཐུགས་རྗེའི་ལྕགས་ཀྱུ་ཡིས་ཟུངས་ཤིག །

བློ་བཟང་ཆོས་ཀྱི་ནི་རྒྱལ་མཚན། །
འགྲོ་དྲུག་ཕ་མ་ཡི་དོན་དུ། །
སངས་རྒྱས་འཐོབ་འདོད་ལ་ཞུགས་ཀྱང་། །
ཉན་ཐོས་སེམས་བསྐྱེད་ཀྱིས་བཅིངས་སོ། །

གཞན་ཕན་ཐུགས་རྗེ་ཡི་ལྕགས་ཀྱུས། །
ཐེག་ཆེན་ལམ་བཟང་ལ་དྲོངས་ཤིག །
ཐུགས་རྗེའི་ལྕགས་ཀྱུ་ཡིས་ཟུངས་ཤིག །

བློ་བཟང་ཆོས་ཀྱི་ནི་རྒྱལ་མཚན། །
མི་རྟག་སྒྱུ་མ་ཡི་ནོར་རྫས། །
ཕྱུགས་མེད་དུ་སྒྲིན་པར་འདོད་ཀྱང་། །
ལན་དང་རྣམ་སྨིན་ལ་རེ་བས། །
ཐེག་དམན་རང་འདོད་ཀྱིས་བཅིངས་སོ། །

Please teach me how to recognize
That sensory pleasures are deadly poisons.
Please grasp me with the iron hook of compassion.

Lobzang Chökyi Gyältsen,
Although I embarked upon a path to attain Buddhahood
For the benefit of the six levels of sentient beings—my fathers
and mothers—
I have been bound by a śrāvaka motivation for enlightenment.

Please lead me on the good *Mahāyāna* path for the benefit of others
With the iron hook of compassion.
Please grasp me with the iron hook of compassion.

Lobzang Chökyi Gyältsen,
I want to give my wealth and goods impartially,
And be mindful that they are impermanent and illusory.
But because I hope for both compensation and ripening,
I have been bound by my desires to the lower path.

འདོད་ཡོན་སྒྱུ་མ་རུ་ཤེས་པའི། །
ཉམས་ལེན་རང་རྒྱུད་ལ་སྦྱོལ་ཅིག །
ཐུགས་རྗེའི་ལྕགས་ཀྱུ་ཡིས་ཟུངས་ཤིག །

བློ་བཟང་ཆོས་ཀྱི་ཉི་རྒྱལ་མཚན། །
ལུས་སེམས་སོ་སོ་རུ་འབྲལ་བའི། །
མི་རྟག་འཆི་བ་དེ་བྱུང་ཚེ། །
ཆོས་མེད་བྱ་བྲལ་ངའི་མདུན་དུ། །
འཇམ་དབྱངས་བླ་མ་ཁྱོད་བྱོན་ནས། །
རང་སེམས་འོད་ཀྱི་ཉི་ཐིག་ལེ། །
ཐུགས་རྗེའི་ལྕགས་ཀྱུ་ཉི་རྟོན་པོས། །
ཁྱོད་ཐུགས་བདེ་ཆེན་གྱི་ངང་དུ། །
དབྱེར་མེད་བྱིན་གྱིས་ཉི་རློབས་ཤིག །

བསླུ་མེད་སྐྱབས་ཀྱི་ཉི་དམ་པ། །
བླ་མ་ཁྱེད་ཉིད་ལས་མེད་དོ། །
འདི་ཕྱི་བར་དོ་ཡི་སྐྱེལ་མ། །
སངས་རྒྱས་ཁྱེད་ཉིད་ལས་མེད་དོ། །

Please bestow practical knowledge upon my mind-stream
So I apprehend sensory pleasures as illusory.
Please grasp me with the iron hook of compassion.

Lobzang Chökyi Gyältsen,
At the time of my death,
When I separate into a distinct body and mind,
You, lama, who are inseparable from Mañjuśrī,
Please appear before me, one lacking the Dharma and unable
to act decisively.
Please lift the *bindu*, the light of my mind,
With your sharp, iron hook of compassion,
And grant your blessings so I may be inseparable from your state
of great bliss.

Holy lama of infallible refuge,
There is no one other than you.
My guide through this life, later lives, and the *bardo*,
There is no Buddha other than you.

ཐུགས་རྗེའི་ལྕགས་ཀྱུ་ནི་རྣོན་པོ། །
དད་པའི་མགུལ་ཡོང་ལ་ཐོབ་ཅིག །

བླ་མ་ཁྱེད་དང་དབྱེར་མེད་དུ་གྱུར་ཅིག །

ཅེས་པ་འདི་ཡང་སྐལ་ལྡན་རྒྱ་མཚོས་སྨྲ་བའོ། ། ། །

Sharp iron hook of compassion,

Please hook onto and lift me—this vase—by its handle, my faith.

May I become inseparable from you, lama.

This also was composed by Kälden Gyatso.

ན་མོ་གུ་རུ། །

དང་པོའི་ཡོངས་འཛིན་བླ་མ་བཀའ་དྲིན་ཅན། །
བདག་ཅག་དད་པས་ལྷང་ལྷང་གསོལ་འདེབས་ན། །
བརྩེ་བའི་ཐུགས་ཀྱིས་དགོངས་ནས་འདིར་བྱོན་ལ། །
མདུན་གྱི་ནམ་མཁར་དགྱེས་བཞིན་བཞུགས་སུ་གསོལ། །

ཚེ་སྔོན་ངན་སོང་གནས་ལ་གཏན་ཡུལ་བྲལ། །
ད་ལན་མི་ལུས་ཐོབ་པ་ཁྱོད་ཀྱི་དྲིན། །
བཀའ་དྲིན་ཆེའོ་བླ་མ་རིན་པོ་ཆེ། །
ད་དུང་བདག་གི་སྙིང་སྡུག་ཁྱེད་རང་མཁྱེན། །

ལས་ཀྱི་དབང་གིས་མཐའ་འཁོབ་སར་སྐྱེས་ཀྱང་། །
སངས་རྒྱས་བསྟན་དང་མཇལ་བ་ཁྱོད་ཀྱི་དྲིན། །
བཀའ་དྲིན་ཆེའོ་བླ་མ་རིན་པོ་ཆེ། །
ད་དུང་བདག་གི་སྙིང་སྡུག་ཁྱེད་རང་མཁྱེན། །

ཁྱིམ་གྱི་མེ་འོབས་ནང་དུ་མ་ཚུད་པར། །
རབ་བྱུང་བསིལ་ཁང་ཐོབ་པ་ཁྱོད་ཀྱི་དྲིན། །
བཀའ་དྲིན་ཆེའོ་བླ་མ་རིན་པོ་ཆེ། །
ད་དུང་བདག་གི་སྙིང་སྡུག་ཁྱེད་རང་མཁྱེན། །

I bow to the guru.

When we pray clearly with faith
To you lamas, possessed of kindness, the first spiritual instructors,
I beseech you to regard us with compassion,
And appear here, dwelling joyfully before us in the sky.

In previous lives, I made the three lower realms my homeland.
I obtained a human body this time—this was your kindness.
Thank you, precious lamas.
Still now, my joy and sorrow are in your hands.

Although due to the power of karma I was born in the borderlands,
I came across the Buddha's teachings anyway—this was your kindness.
Thank you, precious lamas.
Still now, my joy and sorrow are in your hands.

Instead of being trapped in the fiery pit of a household,
I took ordination and obtained a cool, refreshing house—this was your kindness.
Thank you, precious lamas.
Still now, my joy and sorrow are in your hands.

དང་པོ་གཞོན་དུས་དགེ་སྡིག་ངོ་མི་ཤེས། །
ད་ནི་བླང་དོར་ཤེས་པ་ཁྱོད་ཀྱི་དྲིན། །
བཀའ་དྲིན་ཆེའོ་བླ་མ་རིན་པོ་ཆེ། །
ད་དུང་བདག་གི་སྐྱིད་སྡུག་ཁྱེད་རང་མཁྱེན། །

བླ་མ་གང་བཟང་ཞབས་ལ་ལེགས་གཏུགས་ནས། །
དམ་ཆོས་གང་འདོད་ཞུས་པ་ཁྱོད་ཀྱི་དྲིན། །
བཀའ་དྲིན་ཆེའོ་བླ་མ་རིན་པོ་ཆེ། །
ད་དུང་བདག་གི་སྐྱིད་སྡུག་ཁྱེད་རང་མཁྱེན། །

མཚན་ཙམ་ཐོས་པས་འཇིགས་པ་ཀུན་སྐྱོབ་པའི། །
སངས་རྒྱས་སྤྲུལ་སྐུ་མང་མཇལ་ཁྱོད་ཀྱི་དྲིན། །
བཀའ་དྲིན་ཆེའོ་བླ་མ་རིན་པོ་ཆེ། །
ད་དུང་བདག་གི་སྐྱིད་སྡུག་ཁྱེད་རང་མཁྱེན། །

ཚིག་རེ་ཙམ་ཡང་བསྐལ་བརྒྱར་རྙེད་དཀའ་བའི། །
གསང་སྔགས་ཆོས་དང་མཇལ་བ་ཁྱོད་ཀྱི་དྲིན། །
བཀའ་དྲིན་ཆེའོ་བླ་མ་རིན་པོ་ཆེ། །
ད་དུང་བདག་གི་སྐྱིད་སྡུག་ཁྱེད་རང་མཁྱེན། །

At first, when I was young I did not know virtue from evil.
Now I know what is to be accepted and rejected—this is
your kindness.
Thank you, precious lamas.
Still now, my joy and sorrow are in your hands.

Respectfully touching the feet of whatever fine lamas to my head,
I receive whatever I desire of the holy Dharma—this is your kindness.
Thank you, precious lamas.
Still now, my joy and sorrow are in your hands.

I have met many manifestations of Buddhas whose mere names
if heard
Could protect one from all dangers—this is your kindness.
Thank you, precious lamas.
Still now, my joy and sorrow are in your hands.

I encountered the teachings of the secret *Mantrayāna,*
Of which even a single word is difficult to find in a hundred eons—
this was your kindness.
Thank you, precious lamas.
Still now, my joy and sorrow are in your hands.

སངས་རྒྱས་ནས་བཟུང་བརྒྱུད་པ་མ་ཆད་པའི། །
དབང་ལུང་རྗེས་གནང་ཐོབ་པ་ཁྱོད་ཀྱི་དྲིན། །
བཀའ་དྲིན་ཆེའོ་བླ་མ་རིན་པོ་ཆེ། །
ད་དུང་བདག་གི་སྐྱིད་སྡུག་ཁྱེད་རང་མཁྱེན། །

ཞིང་ལས་སོ་ནམ་ཁེ་ཚོང་མ་བསྒྲུབས་ཀྱང་། །
ཡོ་བྱད་གང་འདོད་བྱུང་བ་ཁྱོད་ཀྱི་དྲིན། །
བཀའ་དྲིན་ཆེའོ་བླ་མ་རིན་པོ་ཆེ། །
ད་དུང་བདག་གི་སྐྱིད་སྡུག་ཁྱེད་རང་མཁྱེན། །

མགུལ་དུ་སྲུང་བའི་འཁོར་ལོ་མ་བཏགས་ཀྱང་། །
ལུས་སེམས་གནོད་གྱིས་མ་གཙེས་ཁྱོད་ཀྱི་དྲིན། །
བཀའ་དྲིན་ཆེའོ་བླ་མ་རིན་པོ་ཆེ། །
ད་དུང་བདག་གི་སྐྱིད་སྡུག་ཁྱེད་རང་མཁྱེན། །

འཆི་བས་རང་ལས་གཞོན་པ་མང་ཐོས་ཀྱང་། །
བདག་ནི་ད་དུང་གནས་པ་ཁྱོད་ཀྱི་དྲིན། །
བཀའ་དྲིན་ཆེའོ་བླ་མ་རིན་པོ་ཆེ། །
ད་དུང་བདག་གི་སྐྱིད་སྡུག་ཁྱེད་རང་མཁྱེན། །

I obtained initiations, textual readings, and ritual permissions
Whose lineage of transmission has been unbroken ever since
the Buddha—this was your kindness.
Thank you, precious lamas.
Still now, my joy and sorrow are in your hands.

Although I did not make a profit from farming,
Desired belongings came forth—this was your kindness.
Thank you, precious lamas.
Still now, my joy and sorrow are in your hands.

Although I did not fasten a protective mandala around my neck,
My body and mind were not harmed by demons—this was your
kindness.
Thank you, precious lamas.
Still now, my joy and sorrow are in your hands.

Although death has devoured the lives of many youths,
I am still living—this is your kindness.
Thank you, precious lamas.
Still now, my joy and sorrow are in your hands.

དུས་ཀྱི་དབང་གིས་ཆོས་དང་མཐུན་དཀའ་ཡང་། །
བློ་ཁ་ཆོས་ལ་ཕྱོགས་པ་ཁྱོད་ཀྱི་དྲིན། །
བཀའ་དྲིན་ཆེའོ་བླ་མ་རིན་པོ་ཆེ། །
ད་དུང་བདག་གི་སྙིང་སྡུག་ཁྱེད་རང་མཁྱེན། །

རྒྱུན་དུ་ཉེས་ལྟུང་ཆར་བཞིན་འབབ་ན་ཡང་། །
ཕྱིར་བཅོས་བཤགས་བསྡམས་བྱེད་པ་ཁྱོད་ཀྱི་དྲིན། །
བཀའ་དྲིན་ཆེའོ་བླ་མ་རིན་པོ་ཆེ། །
ད་དུང་བདག་གི་སྙིང་སྡུག་ཁྱེད་རང་མཁྱེན། །

རྒྱུད་ལ་འདོད་ཆགས་ཆུ་ལྟར་ཁོལ་ན་ཡང་། །
སོ་ཐར་སྡོམ་པ་མ་ཤོར་ཁྱོད་ཀྱི་དྲིན། །
བཀའ་དྲིན་ཆེའོ་བླ་མ་རིན་པོ་ཆེ། །
ད་དུང་བདག་གི་སྙིང་སྡུག་ཁྱེད་རང་མཁྱེན། །

ཞེ་སྡང་འབར་ནས་ཚིག་རྩུབ་སྨྲས་ན་ཡང་། །
དགེ་བའི་མྱུ་གུ་མི་བསྲེག་ཁྱོད་ཀྱི་དྲིན། །
བཀའ་དྲིན་ཆེའོ་བླ་མ་རིན་པོ་ཆེ། །
ད་དུང་བདག་གི་སྙིང་སྡུག་ཁྱེད་རང་མཁྱེན། །

Although it is difficult to be in accord with the Dharma because of
the negative power of the times,
My mind turned to it—this was your kindness.
Thank you, precious lamas.
Still now, my joy and sorrow are in your hands.

Although transgressions are falling continually like rain,
I have the remedies—making confessions and promises never
to repeat those offences—this is your kindness.
Thank you, precious lamas.
Still now, my joy and sorrow are in your hands.

Although passions have boiled like water in my mind,
I have not strayed from the Prātimokṣa vows—this is your kindness.
Thank you, precious lamas.
Still now, my joy and sorrow are in your hands.

Although I have spoken harsh words, burning with anger,
The reeds of virtue have not burned—this is your kindness.
Thank you, precious lamas.
Still now, my joy and sorrow are in your hands.

སེམས་ཉིད་གཏི་མུག་མུན་པས་ཁེབས་ན་ཡང་། །
ཆོས་ལ་བློ་གྲོས་རྒྱས་པ་ཁྱོད་ཀྱི་དྲིན། །
བཀའ་དྲིན་ཆེའོ་བླ་མ་རིན་པོ་ཆེ། །
ད་དུང་བདག་གི་སྙིང་སྡུག་ཁྱེད་རང་མཁྱེན། །

ང་རྒྱལ་དབང་གིས་སྐད་མགོ་མཐོ་ན་ཡང་། །
མཁས་གཞན་ཁྱད་དུ་མི་གསོད་ཁྱོད་ཀྱི་དྲིན། །
བཀའ་དྲིན་ཆེའོ་བླ་མ་རིན་པོ་ཆེ། །
ད་དུང་བདག་གི་སྙིང་སྡུག་ཁྱེད་རང་མཁྱེན། །

སེར་སྣའི་མདུད་པ་ཤིན་ཏུ་དམ་ན་ཡང་། །
ཕྱོགས་བཅུར་ལྟོ་ཕྱིར་མི་རྒྱུག་ཁྱོད་ཀྱི་དྲིན། །
བཀའ་དྲིན་ཆེའོ་བླ་མ་རིན་པོ་ཆེ། །
ད་དུང་བདག་གི་སྙིང་སྡུག་ཁྱེད་རང་མཁྱེན། །

ཆོས་དང་སེམས་གཉིས་ད་དུང་མ་འདྲེས་ཀྱང་། །
ཆོས་ལ་ཞེན་པ་མ་ལོག་ཁྱོད་ཀྱི་དྲིན། །
བཀའ་དྲིན་ཆེའོ་བླ་མ་རིན་པོ་ཆེ། །
ད་དུང་བདག་གི་སྙིང་སྡུག་ཁྱེད་རང་མཁྱེན། །

Although the nature of my mind has been veiled with the darkness
of delusion,
I have a vastly discriminating intellect with respect to the Dharma—
this is your kindness.
Thank you, precious lamas.
Still now, my joy and sorrow are in your hands.

Although my speech is lofty and head held high from pride,
I do not scorn other scholars—this is your kindness.
Thank you, precious lamas.
Still now, my joy and sorrow are in your hands.

Although the knots of greed are very tight,
I do not run in the ten directions for the sake of food—this is
your kindness.
Thank you, precious lamas.
Still now, my joy and sorrow are in your hands.

Although my mind has still not integrated with the Dharma,
I have not turned away from my conviction in it—this is
your kindness.
Thank you, precious lamas.
Still now, my joy and sorrow are in your hands.

ཞེ་རྒྱུད་འདུལ་བའི་གཉེན་པོར་འགྲོ་དཀའ་ཡང་། །
ཆོས་ལ་འབད་ལོ་བྱེད་འདི་ཁྱོད་ཀྱི་དྲིན། །
བཀའ་དྲིན་ཆེའོ་བླ་མ་རིན་པོ་ཆེ། །
ད་དུང་བདག་གི་སྙིང་སྡུག་ཁྱེད་རང་མཁྱེན། །

རང་གི་སྣ་ཐག་གཞན་ལ་མི་སྟེར་བར། །
རྟག་ཏུ་རང་གིས་འཛིན་འདི་ཁྱོད་ཀྱི་དྲིན། །
བཀའ་དྲིན་ཆེའོ་བླ་མ་རིན་པོ་ཆེ། །
ད་དུང་བདག་གི་སྙིང་སྡུག་ཁྱེད་རང་མཁྱེན། །

བདག་བློ་ཆོས་སུ་འགྲོ་བར་བྱིན་གྱིས་རློབས། །
དམ་ཆོས་ལམ་དུ་འགྲོ་བར་བྱིན་གྱིས་རློབས། །
ཆོས་ལ་བར་ཆད་མེད་པར་བྱིན་གྱིས་རློབས། །
བླ་མ་ཁྱེད་རང་ལྟ་བུར་བྱིན་གྱིས་རློབས། །

ཞེས་རང་གི་རྩ་བའི་བླ་མ་དང་པོར་ཆོས་ལ་འཇུག་མཁན་གང་ཡིན་པ་དེ་ལ་
གསོལ་བ་འདེབས་པ་འདི་ནི། རི་ཁྲོད་པ་སྐལ་ལྡན་རྒྱ་མཚོས་སྦྱར་བའོ། ། ། །

Although it is difficult to pursue antidotes for taming my
mindstream,
I make a pretense of striving toward the Dharma—this is
your kindness.
Thank you, precious lamas.
Still now, my joy and sorrow are in your hands.

Not giving my nose rope to others,
I continually grasp it myself—this is your kindness.
Thank you, precious lamas.
Still now, my joy and sorrow are in your hands.

Please bless me, that my mind may proceed towards the Dharma.
Please bless me, that I may progress along the path of the holy
Dharma.
Please bless me, that I may have no obstructions to the Dharma.
Please bless me, that I may be like you, lamas.

These devotional verses to my first root lamas, whomever established me on the Dharma path, were composed by the mountain hermit, Kälden Gyatso.

Chapter Two

Dreadful Defects

སྔོན་བསྐལ་བརྒྱར་ཚོགས་གཉིས་བསགས་པ་ལས། །
མགོན་དམ་པས་རྗེས་བཟུང་གཞུང་ཀུན་མཁྱེན། །
རྒྱུད་སྦྱངས་རྟོགས་ཡོན་ཏན་མཛོད་འཛིན་པ། །
པ་བསྟན་འཛིན་བློ་བཟང་ཞབས་ལ་འདུད། །

སྤྱི་ར་ཉོན་མོངས་དབང་གིས་འཁོར་བར་འཁྱམས། །
སྒོས་ཁོང་ཁྲིམས་དགེ་རྩ་དཔག་མེད་འཛོམས། །

ཁོང་བྱང་ཆུབ་སེམས་དཔའ་ནང་ཕན་ཚུན། །
ཐུགས་ཁྲིམས་ན་བསྐལ་བརྒྱའི་དགེ་འཛོམས་ཤིང་། །
ལར་གཞི་ནས་ལམ་ལ་སློབ་དགོས་གསུངས། །

གཞན་ཕལ་པས་རྒྱལ་བའི་སྲས་པོ་ལ། །
སེམས་ཞེ་སྡང་སྐད་ཅིག་སྐྱེས་གྱུར་ན། །
ཡུན་བསྐལ་བ་སྟོང་གི་དགེ་རྩ་འཛོམས། །

གྲོགས་ཕན་ཚུན་ཁྲིམས་པའི་ཞེ་སྡང་གིས། །
ས་ཆེན་པོའི་རྡུལ་གྱི་གྲངས་མཉམ་པའི། །
སྟོང་འཁོར་ལོས་སྒྱུར་རྒྱལ་ཐོབ་པ་ཡང་། །
དུས་སྐད་ཅིག་ཉིད་དུ་འཛོམས་ལ་ལྟོས། །

I bow at the feet of my father, Tendzin Lobzang,
Treasurer of the qualities of renunciation and realization,
Who understands all scriptures accepted by the holy protector,
Having gathered the two accumulations over the past hundred eons.

Afflicted by many disturbing emotions, I have been wandering
in samsara.
Anger, in particular, has been destroying countless roots
of my virtue.

It has been said that if bodhisattvas become angry with each other
It destroys the virtue of a hundred eons
And they need to train on the path again from the beginning.
Anger arising in ordinary people towards bodhisattvas,
Even for an instant,
Destroys the roots of the virtue of a thousand eons.
And wrathful aggression between friends destroys in an instant
The merit accumulated by thousands of universal monarchs
Equal in number to the grains of sand in the world. Look!

དགྲ་ཉོན་མོངས་ནང་ན་ཞེ་སྡང་གི །
དགྲ་འདི་ལས་འཇིགས་པ་གང་ནའང་མེད། །
འདིས་སྡུར་བྱས་དགེ་རྩ་ཐམས་ཅད་འཕྲོག །
ཚེ་ཕྱི་མར་ངེས་པར་ངན་འགྲོར་འཕེན། །

ཕལ་ཆེ་བ་དམྱལ་བའི་གནས་སུ་སྐྱུར། །
ལར་ཡི་དྭགས་གནས་སུ་སྐྱེས་ན་ཡང་། །
གཞན་སྲོག་འཕྲོག་རྒྱལ་འགོང་དྲི་གཤེད་སོགས། །
གདོན་ཆེན་པོ་འཇིགས་སུ་རུང་བར་སྐྱེ། །

དུས་སྐབས་རེར་དུད་འགྲོར་སྐྱེས་ན་ཡང་། །
སྦྲུལ་སྦལ་ལྗོང་སྦོམ་སྡིག་ལ་སོགས་དང་། །
སྟག་དྲེད་སོགས་གཅན་གཟན་འཇིགས་རུང་དང་། །
གླག་ཁྲ་སོགས་བྱ་ཚོགས་མ་རུངས་དང་། །
ཆུའི་ནང་གི་ཆུ་སྲིན་སོགས་སུ་སྐྱེ། །

མིར་སྐྱེས་ཀྱང་མདོག་ནི་མི་མཛེས་ཤིང་། །
སྡིག་སྤྱོད་པའི་ཧོར་སོག་ནང་དུ་སྐྱེ། །

Among all enemies, the disturbing emotions,
There is no danger greater than this—aggression.
It will plunder all the roots of virtue gathered in the past,
And will surely drive one into the lower realms in the next life.

Nearly everyone is cast into hell.
But even if you were born in the realm of hungry ghosts,
Other beings—frightful, large, evil spirits
Such as life-force plunderers, demonic spirits, and impure enemies—
could emerge.

Even if you were born as an animal,
Sometimes snakes, frogs and tadpoles, spiders, scorpions;
Frightful carnivorous beasts such as tigers and bears;
Scores of ferocious birds such as eagles and hawks;
And water dragons, and so on, in the rivers, could sneak forth.

Even if you are born as a human, your color might not be beautiful,
And you could be born among Mongols who engage in evil.

ལྷར་སྐྱེས་ཀྱང་ལྷ་མིན་དང་འཐབ་ཅིང་། །
ཡུལ་ལྷ་མིན་སྐྱེས་ཀྱང་ལྷ་དང་འཐབ། །

ལར་གང་དུ་སྐྱེས་ཀྱང་སྔོན་གོམས་ཀྱི། །
ཁོང་ཁྲོས་པའི་བག་ཆགས་འཁྲུག་པོ་དེས། །
གར་སྐྱེས་ཀྱང་སེམས་དང་ཞེ་སྡང་འགྲོགས། །
དུས་ནམ་ཡང་བདེ་བའི་གོ་སྐབས་མེད། །

དགྲ་ཞེ་སྡང་འདྲ་བའི་ཉོན་མོངས་མེད། །
ཆོས་བཟོད་པ་འདྲ་བའི་དཀའ་ཐུབ་མེད། །
བཟོད་གོ་ཆ་གྱོན་པའི་སྐྱེས་བུ་ལ། །
ཚིག་རྩུབ་མོའི་མདའ་མདུང་ཅི་བྱར་ཡོད། །

གཟུགས་ཡིད་འོང་སྒྲུབ་པའི་བྱེད་པོ་ཡང་། །
རྒྱུན་བཟོད་པ་འདི་ཉིད་གཅིག་པུར་གསུངས། །

འདིར་ཙུང་ཟད་འབད་པའི་དགེ་བ་དེས། །
ཀུན་མཁྱེན་པའི་ཡེ་ཤེས་མྱུར་ཐོབ་ཤོག །

ཅེས་པ་འདི་ཡང་སྐལ་ལྡན་རྒྱ་མཚོས་སྦྱར་བའོ། ། ། །

And if you are born as a god, you will fight with demigods,
And if you are born in the realms of demigods, you will fight
with gods.

Whatever the realm into which you were born,
If you have strong habitual tendencies to wrathful habits,
Wherever you are born next, your mind will be associated
with aggression.
You will never have the chance to be happy.

There is no disturbing emotion like the enemy, hatred.
There is no tolerance like accepting the truth of suffering.
What can the arrows and spears of harsh words do
To a noble wearing the armor of forbearance?
It has been said that anyone who attains a distinctively
beautiful body
Must endure his form as well.

Through the merit of this little endeavor,
May all beings quickly attain supreme, all-knowing wisdom.

This, also, was composed by Kälden Gyatso.

ན་མོ་གུ་རུ།

གཏི་མུག་ཁོ་བོ་ཅི་ཐེ་ཆེ་རེད། །
ཤེས་རབ་ཁྱོད་ཉལ་ནས་འདུག་ཡོད་དམ། །

འདོད་ཆགས་ཁོ་སྒྲུ་སྒྲོད་ཐེ་རྩིང་རེད། །
མི་སྡུག་ཁྱོད་གང་གི་འདམ་དུ་འགྱེལ། །

ཞེ་སྡང་ཁོ་སྒྲུ་བརྫིད་ཐེ་ཆེ་རེད། །
བྱམས་པ་ཁྱོད་ས་ཆ་གང་དུ་བྲོས། །

ང་རྒྱལ་ཁོ་ངར་སྐད་ཐེ་ཆེ་རེད། །
ཁེངས་སྐྱུངས་ཁྱོད་རྣ་བ་འོན་ནམ་ཅི། །

ཕྲག་དོག་ཁོ་ཟུག་རྔུ་ཐེ་རགས་རེད། །
དག་སྣང་ཁྱོད་གར་སོང་རྩར་མ་རྙེད། །

I prostrate myself before the guru.

Stupidity's senseless jokes are always increasing.
Primordial wisdom, do you dare dwell out there, asleep?

Desire's actions are growing cruder.
Contemplations of the repulsive, which swamp did you fall into?

Anger's brute force is always increasing.
Loving kindness, where have you fled?

Pride's roaring is louder and louder.
Humility, are you deaf, or what?

Envy's torments are grosser and grosser.
Pure perception, wherever you went, you did not penetrate to
the root.

ཡོག་ལྷ་ཁོ་བསླུ་བྲིད་ཧེ་མཁས་རེད། །
དད་གུས་ཁྱོད་རྨང་ནས་ཡལ་ལམ་ཅི། །

འདད་ཟས་ཁོ་ཁ་ལ་ཧེ་ཞིམ་རེད། །
དགེ་སྦྱོར་ཁྱོད་སྟོང་ཡལ་འགྲོ་ལ་ཁད། །

ཉེས་ལྷུང་ཁོ་ཆར་བཞིན་ཧེ་འབབ་རེད། །
བསླབ་སྡོམ་ཁྱོད་ཨེ་ཡོད་ངས་མ་ཤེས། །

སེར་སྣ་ཁོ་མདུད་པ་ཧེ་དམ་རེད། །
སྦྱིན་པ་ཁྱོད་ལག་པ་འཁྱུམས་སམ་ཆག །

ཅེས་པ་འདི་ནི་རོང་སྐྱེས་སྐལ་ལྡན་རྒྱ་མཚོས་སྤྱང་གཉེན་འབྱེད་ཕྱིར་དབྱེན་ཚིག་གི་ཚུལ་དུ་བྲིས་པའོ། ། ། །

False views are increasingly skilled in deception.
Faith and respect, are you vanishing from the foundation, or what?

Funeral repasts are more and more delicious to the mouth.
Spiritual practice, you are on the verge of dwindling into emptiness.

Transgressions are pouring down, heavier and heavier, like rain.
Vows and precepts, are you there? I don't know.

Greed is a tighter and tighter knot.
Patron, did your hand shrink or break?

Rongbo-born Kälden Gyatso wrote these words of dissension to distinguish between renunciation and attachment.

དུས་ཉིན་ཞིག་སྐྱེད་གསུམ་མཐོན་པོའི་རྩེར། །
ཕུ་སེ་ཀུའི་ཛ་རྒྱུད་བལྟ་རུ་ཕྱིན། །
རི་གངས་དཀར་ཚར་དུ་དངར་བ་རྣམས། །
ཕྱི་མིག་ཡུལ་སྣང་ཚེ་བླ་མ་དྲན། །

རྗེ་མཚུངས་མེད་བསྟན་འཛིན་བློ་བཟང་གི།
དྲིན་བཟང་པོ་དྲན་ཏེ་གླུ་འདི་ལེན། །
ཁྱེད་དད་བརྩོན་ལྡན་པའི་མཆེད་གྲོགས་རྣམས། །
དབྱངས་འདི་ལ་དར་ཅིག་གསན་པར་ཞུ། །

ཞིང་རབ་འབྱམས་བཞུགས་པའི་རྒྱལ་བ་ཀུན། །
འབངས་དད་ལྡན་བདག་སོགས་སྣང་ངོ་རུ། །
མགོན་སྡེ་པ་ཆོས་ཀྱི་རྒྱལ་པོ་ཞེས། །
མཚན་འབྲུག་སྒྲ་ལྷ་བུར་ཡོངས་སུ་གྲགས། །

པ་ཐུགས་རྗེ་ཅན་དེའི་བཀའ་དྲིན་ལས། །
སྤྱིར་དབང་ལུང་རྗེས་གསུམ་གང་འདོད་དང་། །
སྒོས་བཅོམ་ལྡན་འཁོར་ལོ་བདེ་མཆོག་གི།
དབང་ཟབ་མོ་ལུང་དང་མཐུན་པར་ཐོབ། །

One day I went to view the clay range of Phu Seku
From the tall peaks of Gyesum.
When the well-proportioned row of white snow mountains
Appeared as an outer object of my eye, I recalled my lama.

Reflecting on the sincere kindness of the unrivalled lord,
Tendzin Lobzang, I sing this song.
You faithful and diligent spiritual friends—
Please listen awhile to this tuneful melody!

As for the protector named Depa Chökyi Gyälpo,
Through whom all the Victorious Ones dwelling in the infinite realms
Appear to faithful disciples such as me,
His name resounds boundlessly, like the sound of thunder.

Due to the kindness of that compassionate father,
I obtained whatever tantric initiations, textual readings, and
authorizations I wanted,
In particular the profound initiation of Bhagavan Cakrasaṃvara,
In accordance with textual transmission.

ཆོས་མདོ་སྔགས་ཀྱི་གནད་དོན་དུ་མ་ཞིག །
ནང་སེམས་ཉིད་སྟེང་དུ་སྒྲོར་ཚུལ་ཤེས། །
དེ་ཤེས་ཀྱང་ཉམས་ལེན་མ་ནུས་པས། །
དུས་ད་དུང་ཉམས་རྟོགས་འབྲས་མ་སྨིན། །

ཆོས་མདོ་སྔགས་སྒྲོམ་ཁྲིད་ཟབ་ན་ཡང་། །
བདག་སྒྲོམ་མཁན་ལེ་ལོ་ཆེ་བ་དེས། །
ཁྲིད་ཟབ་མོ་ཞུས་ནས་ལོ་མང་ཡང་། །
དུས་ད་དུང་སེམས་དང་ཁྲིད་མ་མཛལ། །

ལྷ་བདེ་མཆོག་བྱིན་རླབས་ཆེ་ན་ཡང་། །
ཐུགས་སྐྱུལ་བྱེད་ཀྱི་བཟླས་པ་མ་ནུས་པས། །
ལྷ་གཅིག་ཕུར་བཟུང་ནས་ལོ་མང་ཡང་། །
དུས་ད་དུང་རྨི་ལྟས་ཙམ་མ་བྱུང་། །

ཁོང་དད་ལྡན་སློབ་མའི་ཚོགས་རྣམས་ལ། །
ཆོས་གང་འདོད་བཤད་ནས་ཡུན་རིང་ཡང་། །
མི་རང་ལ་ཉམས་མྱོང་མེད་པ་དེས། །
དུས་ད་དུང་གཞན་ལ་ཕན་མ་ཐོགས། །

I came to know how to apply the essential teachings
In sutras and tantras to benefit my innermost mind,
But because I was unable to practice,
The fruits of experience and realization have not yet matured.

Meditation instructions of the teachings, sutras and tantras, are deep,
And I received them many years ago.
But because I am a very lazy meditator,
My mind and the instructions have not yet met.

The blessing of the deity Cakrasaṃvara is great
And I have taken him as my sole deity for many years.
But since I have not been able to do the recitations for inducing
    the presence of his enlightened mind,
The merest sign of him in my dreams has not yet emerged.

I have explained whatever is desired of the Dharma
To gatherings of faithful disciples for a long time.
But because I have had no real experience
I have yet to bring benefit to others.

ལམ་བསླབ་པ་གསུམ་གྱི་ཉམས་ལེན་ལ། །
དྲན་ཤེས་བཞིན་བསྟེན་ཚུལ་ཤེས་ན་ཡང་། །
རྒྱུད་ཉེས་ལྟུང་དྲི་མས་ཆེར་སྦགས་པས། །
དུས་ད་དུང་བསླབ་སྡོམ་ཕྱོགས་ལས་གཡེལ། །

མཚན་ཡོངས་གྲགས་བླ་མ་མང་ན་ཡང་། །
གཞི་དམ་ཚིག་ཚུལ་བཞིན་མ་བསྲུངས་ཤིང་། །
དུས་ཉིན་བཞིན་གསོལ་བ་མ་བཏབ་པས། །
དུས་ད་དུང་བྱིན་རླབས་རྟགས་མ་ཤར། །

ཚིག་སྐམ་བཤད་ཀྱི་སྦྲུན་པ་འཕྱུར་མཁས་ཀྱང་། །
ནང་སེམས་ཉིད་ཀྱི་ས་གཞི་ཡངས་པ་རུ། །
དོན་ཉམས་ལེན་གྱི་འབྲུ་ཆར་མ་བབ་པས། །
དུས་ད་དུང་རྒྱུད་སྣོད་སྟོང་པར་ལུས། །

གནས་རི་ཁྲོད་བསྟེན་ལོ་བྱས་ན་ཡང་། །
འཕྲལ་ཕལ་བ་དང་བྱ་སྤྱོད་ཁྱད་མེད་ཅིང་། །
ཚེ་འདི་ལ་ཞེན་པ་མ་ལོག་པས། །
དུས་ད་དུང་ཆོས་པའི་གྲལ་མ་ཐོབ། །

I know how to rely with mindfulness
On the practice of the path of the three trainings.
But since my mind has been stained greatly by the excrement of transgressions,
I am still careless about vows and precepts.

I have studied with many renowned lamas,
But because I have not observed the *samaya* commitments correctly
And have not been praying daily,
Still now, not even a trace of their blessings has appeared.

I am skilled at brandishing a mixture of meaningless words.
But because the seasonal rains of beneficial practice
Have not fallen on the spacious, fertile soil of my inner mind,
The vessel of my mind-stream still remains empty.

I have been going through the motions of relying on mountain retreats.
But because there is no difference between my own behavior and that of a common, worldly person
And I have not yet grown disgusted with the concerns of this life,
I have not yet attained the rank of a Dharma practitioner.

གཏམ་འདི་ལས་བྱུང་བའི་དགེ་བ་དེས། །
ཚིག་ཁ་བཤད་ཀྱི་དབྱུ་བས་མི་ངོམས་པར། །
དོན་ཉམས་ལེན་གྱི་བདུད་རྩི་འཐུང་བཞིན་དུ། །
མཆོག་སངས་རྒྱས་ཀྱི་ས་རུ་བགྲོད་པར་ཤོག །

ཅེས་པ་འདི་ནི་རི་ཁྲོད་པ་སྐལ་ལྡན་རྒྱ་མཚོས་མཁར་གོང་གི་ནགས་ཁྲོད་དུ་བྲིས་པའོ། ། །།

By means of the merit which has arisen from this speech,
May you drink the nectar of beneficial practice
Without being quenched by the froth of empty talk,
And journey to the supreme level of Buddhahood.

This was written by the mountain hermit, Kälden Gyatso, in the dense forest dwelling of Khargong.

སྐྱབས་གནས་བླ་མ་དམ་པའི། །
ཞབས་ལ་གུས་པས་བཏུད་ནས། །
ཡིད་འོང་དབེན་པའི་གནས་སུ། །
སྙན་པའི་གླུ་འདི་ལེན་ནོ། །

དབྱར་དུས་ལྷུང་སྤྲོའི་སྤྱང་གཤོང་། །
འཛུམ་ཞིང་རྒོད་པའི་པད་གཞོན། །
ཤིང་ལོ་སར་བའི་རྩེད་འཛོ། །
ད་ལྟ་བལྟས་ཚེ་མཛེས་པ། །
ནམ་ཟླ་དུས་བཞིའི་འགྱུར་བས། །
སྟོན་དུས་ཁ་དོག་སྐྱ་ཞིང་། །
དགུན་དུས་མེད་པར་འགྱུར་བའི། །
གནས་ཚུལ་བསམས་ཤིང་སྐྱོ་བ། །

ཤ་ཁྲག་རྒྱས་པའི་ལུས་དང་། །
འཇམ་མཉེན་མཛེས་པའི་གོན་པ། །
ནད་མེད་རྒུད་མེད་བདེར་གནས། །
ད་ལྟ་འཛོམ་པ་དགའ་ཡང་། །
ནམ་ཞིག་མི་རྟག་འགྱུར་བའི། །
གནས་ཚུལ་བསམས་ཤིང་སྐྱོ་བ། །

Having bowed respectfully at the feet
Of the holy lama, the place of refuge,
I am singing this melodious song
In a beautiful, solitary place.

When I look now
At the lush, blue-green, summer meadows,
The youthful lotuses smiling and laughing,
And all the leaves on the trees dancing,
They are lovely.
But due to the changes of the four seasons,
In autumn the colors will be muted,
And in winter they will be gone.
I have thought about these conditions, and I feel sad.

My body, brimming with flesh and blood,
And wearing soft, smooth, lovely clothes,
Is free from disease and decline, and dwells at ease.
I am pleased with this abundant well-being,
But one day my body will change, because of impermanence.
Thinking about these inevitable changes I feel sad.

བྱ་རྒྱལ་ཁུ་བྱུག་དེ་ཡང་། །
ད་ལྟ་སྐད་སྙན་སྒྲོགས་ཀྱང་། །
སྤུར་དུ་ཡུལ་གཞན་འགྲོ་བའི། །
གནས་ཚུལ་བསམས་ཤིང་སྐྱོ་བ། །

བདག་ཅག་སྙིགས་དུས་ཚེ་ཡང་། །
ད་ལྟ་རིང་རིང་འདྲ་ཡང་། །
སྤུར་དུ་ཕ་རོལ་འགྲོ་བའི། །
གནས་ཚུལ་བསམས་ཤིང་སྐྱོ་བ། །

དེས་ན་སྐལ་ལྡན་རས་པ། །
ཚེ་འདི་བློ་ཡིས་ཐོངས་ལ། །
དམ་པའི་ལྷ་ཆོས་ཟབ་མོ། །
ཚུལ་བཞིན་ཉམས་སུ་ལོངས་ཤིག །

ཤ་ཉེས་བལྟས་ཚེ་སྨྲོན་པ། །
གྲྭ་པས་བལྟས་ཚེ་བློ་མང་། །
རང་གིས་བལྟས་ཚེ་ཟོག་པོ། །

Moreover, the cuckoo, king of birds,
Is calling out melodiously
But soon it will go elsewhere.
Thinking about this I feel sad.

Our lives in this Degenerate Age
Seem very long at present,
But soon we will pass away.
Thinking about this I feel sad.

Therefore, Kälden Repa,
Renounce the concerns of this life
And practice in accordance
With the profound, holy, divine Dharma.

When relatives look at me, they think I'm crazy.
When monks look at me, they think I'm fickle.
When I look at myself, I think I'm deceitful.

སྐལ་ལྡན་རས་པ་ཁྱོད་ལ། །
ང་ཡིས་བཏབ་པའི་གྲོས་འདི། །
རང་གཞན་ཀུན་ལ་ཕན་པར། །
དཀོན་མཆོག་གསུམ་གྱིས་མཛོད་ཅིག །

བཀྲ་ཤིས། ། །།

Kälden Repa—

May this advice I have given you

Benefit yourself and all others

Through the blessings of the Three Precious Jewels.

Good fortune!

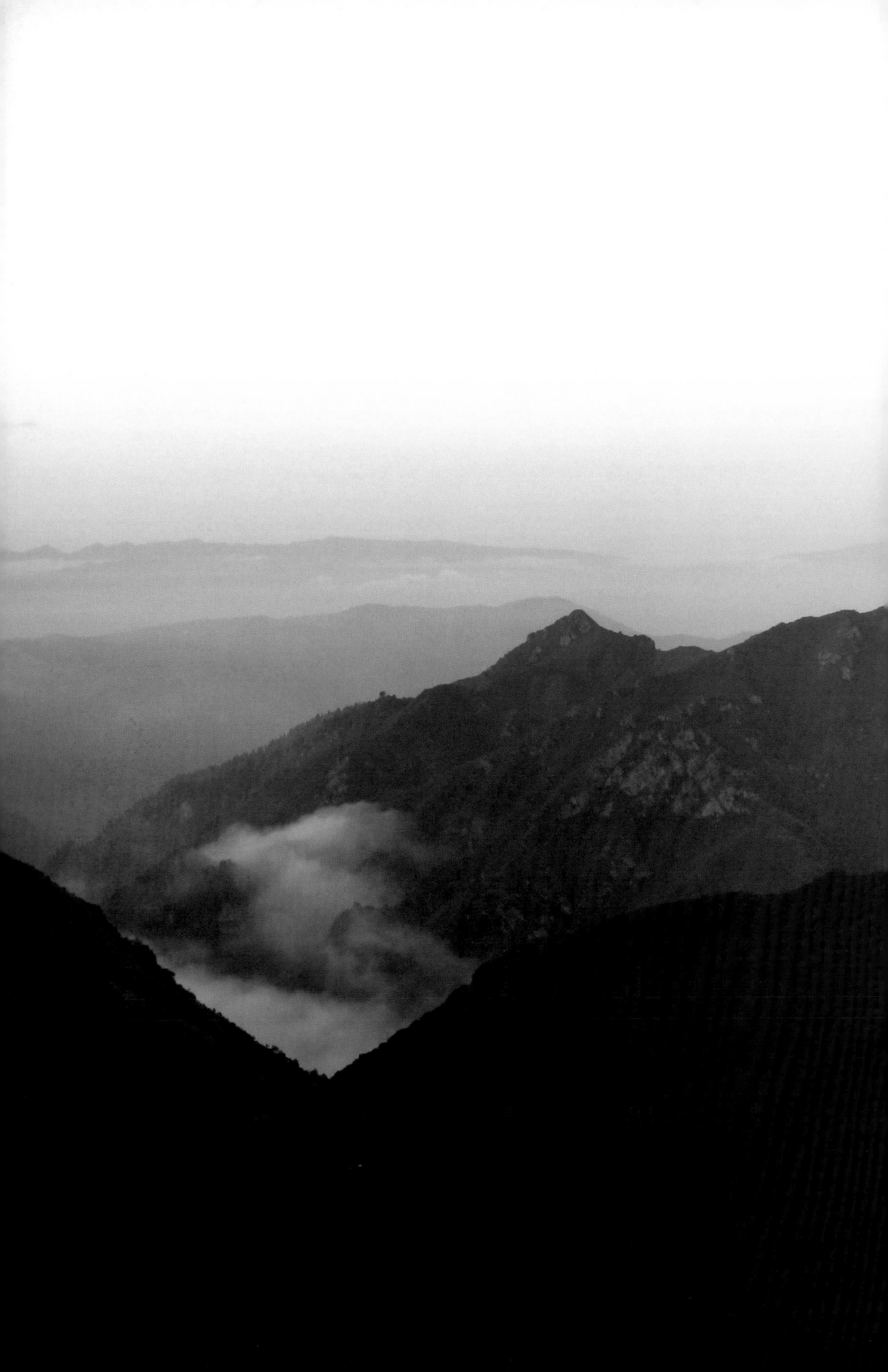

Taken in Western Tibet

Chapter Three

Aspirations for Renunciation

ལྷ་ཆོས་ཤིག་ནུས་ན་དགའ་བ་ལ། །
མི་ཆོས་འདི་དོར་ན་སྐྱིད་པ་ལ། །

རང་ཉིད་ལ་བལྟས་ཀྱང་འཇིག་རྟེན་པ། །
གཞན་དག་ལ་བལྟས་ཀྱང་འཇིག་རྟེན་པ། །
མཚན་ཉིད་ལ་སྦྱངས་ཀྱང་འཇིག་རྟེན་པ། །
རི་ཁྲོད་ལ་སོང་ཡང་འཇིག་རྟེན་པ། །
གང་ལྟར་བྱས་ཀྱང་འཇིག་རྟེན་པ། །
འཇིག་རྟེན་སྤངས་ན་དོ་མཚར་ཆེ། །

ཞེས་པ་འདི་གཉིས་ཀྱང་མཁས་ཤིང་གྲུབ་པའི་དབང་ཕྱུག་ཆོས་ཀྱི་རྗེ་སྐལ་ལྡན་རྒྱ་མཚོའི་གསུང་དྲི་མ་མེད་པའོ། ། ། །

If you are able to practice the divine Dharma—Oh joy!
If you are able to abandon concern for worldly things—
Oh happiness!

Regarding yourself, you are a worldly person.
In relation to others, you are a worldly person.
Even if you have studied philosophy, you are a worldly person.
Even if you have gone to a mountain retreat, you are a worldly
person.
No matter what you've done, you are still a worldly person.
But when you abandon the world—How wondrous!

This is the flawless speech of the sovereign of scholars and practitioners, lord of the Dharma, Kälden Gyatso.

བླ་མ་སངས་རྒྱས་ཀྱི་རྣམ་པར་ཐར་བ་ལ། །
ཉིན་མཚན་ཁོར་ཡུག་ཏུ་ལེགས་པར་འབད་པར་ཤོག །

ཡུལ་བྱང་ཕྱོགས་ཨ་མདོའི་ས་ཕྱོགས་འདིར། །
གནས་བཀྲ་ཤིས་འཁྱིལ་གྱི་རི་རྩེ་ན། །
ང་རྒོད་པོས་ཁ་པོ་འབྲུག་བཞིན་ལྡིར། །

ཡུལ་ཨ་མདོའི་ཕྱོགས་ན་ཧ་ནོར་མོད། །
ང་རྒོད་པོ་གཉོམ་ཆུང་གཅིག་ཕྱུར་འདུག །
དོན་དེ་ཕྱིར་ཧ་ནོར་འཚོ་སྐྱོང་དཀའ། །
ནོར་ཧ་ཕྱིར་ཐག་རིང་སར་མི་འགྲོ །

མི་ཕལ་ཆེར་ཕྱུག་པོ་ནོར་ལ་སློན། །
མི་ང་ནི་གཅིག་ཕྱུར་སྤྱོད་ལ་སློན། །
སེམས་འདོད་ཆུང་ཆོག་ཤེས་ཀྱི་མཛོད་ཁང་སྒྲོར། །
མི་བྱ་བཏང་ཕྱུག་པོ་ཐམས་ཅད་གནས། །

ལོ་ལོན་ཀྱང་བློ་རྩེ་ཆོས་ལ་གཏོད། །
མི་དེ་ལ་བདེ་སྐྱིད་སྣན་གསུམ་འབྱུང་། །

May I strive continually day and night
To follow the enlightened example of my lama.

I, an old man on the mountain peak at Tashikhyil
In this northern part of Amdo,
Am roaring boastfully like thunder.

In the Amdo region, horses and yaks abound.
I, a weak old man, am alone,
So it would be difficult to look after animals.
I am not going far away for their sake.

Most people aspire to abundance and wealth.
As for me, I aspire to live alone.
All renunciants become wealthy
By living at the gates of the treasure-house
Of contentment with few desires.

Although I am old, I focus single-pointedly on the Dharma.
Happiness, well-being, and homage come naturally to such a person.

ཆོས་བྱ་བ་ནང་གི་སེམས་ལ་ཐུག །
སེམས་བསམ་པ་བཟང་ན་ཐེག་ཆེན་ཆོས། །
མཆོག་སངས་རྒྱས་ཐག་རིང་ཡུལ་ན་མེད། །
བློ་ལིངས་ཀྱིས་གཏད་ན་རང་མདུན་བཞུགས། །

ཁམས་བདེ་གཤེགས་སྙིང་པོ་ཆོས་ཀྱི་སྐུ། །
རྒྱུད་མཐའ་གཉིས་སྤངས་པའི་ཁྲི་རྩེར་བཞུགས། ། ། །

Religious activities depend on the inner mind.
When one's motivations are pure,
The Dharma of *Mahāyāna* and supreme enlightenment
Are not in some far-off place.
When one focuses completely,
They remain in one's presence.

Dharmakāya, the realization of enlightened essence,
Resides on the mind's throne, beyond the two extremes.

ཨོཾ་སྭ་སྟི།

ཕ་བླ་མའི་རྒྱལ་པོ་ཆོས་ཀྱི་རྗེ། །
རྗེ་བླ་མ་ཆོས་པ་རིན་པོ་ཆེ། །
དྲིན་བསམམས་ཤིང་རྣམ་ཐར་དྲན་ཙ་ན། །
སེམས་གདུང་བའི་མོས་གུས་ཆེས་ཆེར་འཕེལ། །

མགོན་ཁྱོད་ཀྱི་དྲིན་ལན་འཁོར་ཐབས་མེད། །
དུས་ཡང་ཡང་དྲན་ཞིང་གསོལ་བ་བཏབ། །
ཐུགས་བཞེད་པའི་དགོངས་པ་རྫོགས་ཕྱིར་དུ། །
བསྟན་བཤད་སྒྲུབ་བྱ་བ་གང་ནུས་བསྒྲུངས། །

ལུས་རྒྱས་ཀྱང་སེམས་ཀྱི་ཁྱུར་མ་དོར། །
འདི་དགོངས་སམ་བླ་མ་ཐུགས་རྗེ་ཅན། །
ལར་སྐྱེ་འཆི་འདི་ལ་འཛད་མཐའ་མེད། །
ཁོ་འཆི་བདག་སླེབས་ན་ཅི་ཙུག་བྱེད། །

Oṃ swa sti!

When I think of the kindness
Of the lord lama, Chöpa Rinpoche,
The father, king of lamas, lord of the Dharma,
And recall your life story,
Devotion surges in my anguished mind.

Protector, I have no means of repaying your kindness.
I have recalled you again and again, and prayed.
In order to fulfill your wishes I have attended to the duties
Of the schools of teaching and practice as much as I could.

Even though my body was aged, I did not abandon
those responsibilities.
Do you realize this, lama imbued with kindness?
Yet this cycle of birth and death is inexhaustible.
When the Lord of Death arrives, what shall I do?

ཆོས་ཟང་མ་ཞིག་བྱེད་ན་ད་ནི་རན། །
གདོན་འབྱུང་པོ་འདི་ལ་སྙིང་རྗེ་མེད། །
སྒྲོག་ནམ་གཅོད་ཀྱི་ངེས་པ་མ་མཆིས་པས། །
སྐྱབས་དཀོན་མཆོག་གསུམ་ལ་བློ་གཏོད་ལ། །
ཚེ་འདིར་ལྟོས་ཀྱི་ཆགས་ཞེན་འཁྲི་བ་ཆོད། །

རྒྱུ་ཟས་ནོར་གྱི་འཛིན་ཆགས་མ་དོར་ན། །
ལམ་ཟབ་ཀྱང་འཆི་ཁར་ཕན་པ་ཆུང་། །

ཚེ་འདི་ལ་མ་ཆགས་མ་ཞེན་ན། །
སེམས་གང་འདོད་ཀྱི་བདེ་བའི་ཞིང་དུ་འགྲོ །

རང་སྐྱེས་པའི་ཡུལ་ལ་ཆགས་ཞེན་འབྱུང་། །
ཆོས་བྱེད་ན་ཕ་ཡུལ་རྒྱབ་ཏུ་སྐྱུར། །

ཡུན་རིང་འགྲོགས་ཀྱི་གྲོགས་ལ་གདུང་སེམས་འབྱུང་། །
ཆོས་བྱེད་ན་གྲོགས་ལ་ཞེན་པ་སྤོངས། །

ནོར་ཟང་ཟིང་གི་སྟེང་ནས་སེར་སྣ་འབྱུང་། །
ཆོས་བྱེད་ན་འདོད་ཆུང་ཆོག་ཤེས་གྱིས། །

It is now time to practice in order to experience the Dharma directly.
Demons and evil spirits have no affection for this.
Uncertain when my life will be cut off,
I must rely on the refuges, the Three Jewels,
And stop clinging to and craving this life.

Though my path is deep, if I do not abandon my attachments
To wealth, food, and possessions, the benefit at death will be small.
But if I don't cling to and crave this life,
I will go to whatever blissful realm I desire.

I am attached to my birthplace.
When I practice the Dharma, I must cast my homeland behind me.

I feel affection for old friends.
When I practice the Dharma, I must renounce any desire for friends.

I feel greedy around material wealth.
When I practice the Dharma, I must be satisfied, and have only
a few small desires!

གཉེན་ཉེ་དུ་འཁོར་བའི་འཛིན་ཐག་ཡིན། །
ཆོས་བྱེད་ན་འདི་ལ་ལྷག་པ་སྟོན། །

གཞི་དགོན་གོག་འདི་དྲི་ཟའི་གྲོང་ཁྱེར་ཡིན། །
ཆོས་བྱེད་ན་བསྐྱུར་ཏེ་བྲོས་ན་བཟང་། །

གནས་དབེན་པ་དེ་སྐྱིད་པའི་གྲོང་ཁྱེར་ཡིན། །
ཆོས་བྱེད་ན་དེ་རུ་བསྟེགས་ན་བཟང་། །

ཕ་བླ་མ་དེ་བཤད་དང་སྒྲུབ་པས་མཉེས། །
ཆོས་སྒྲུབ་བརྒྱུད་ཀྱི་རྒྱལ་མཚན་བསྒྲེངས་ན་ལེགས། །

ཞེས་པ་འདི་ཡང་སྐལ་ལྡན་རྒྱ་མཚོ་རང་ཉིད་ལ་གྲོས་སུ་བཏབ་པའོ། ། ། །

Kinsmen and relatives are a leading rope which entangles me.
When I practice the Dharma, I must show them the nape of my neck.

Dilapidated village temples and small monasteries are the towns
of scent eaters.
When I practice the Dharma, I must abandon them: it's best to flee!

The place of solitude is the village of happiness.
When I practice the Dharma, it's so good to pursue it!

Father lama took delight in expounding the Dharma and
practicing it.
It is fitting to hoist the victory banner of the Practice Lineage.

Kälden Gyatso also gave himself this advice.

རྗེ་གསུམ་ལྡན་གྱི་བླ་མ་ཐམས་ཅད་མཁྱེན། །
ཕ་བསྟན་འཛིན་བློ་བཟང་རྒྱ་མཚོ་ལ། །
བདག་གསོལ་བ་འདེབས་སོ་ཐུགས་རྗེས་གཟིགས། །
བློ་ཆོས་སུ་འགྲོ་བར་བྱིན་གྱིས་རློབས། །

དུས་ཉིན་གཅིག་སྐྱོ་ཤས་ཐན་ཐུན་གྱིས། །
གནས་ཤིན་ཏུ་དབེན་པར་འགྲོ་འདོད་ནས། །
ཕུ་སེ་ཀུའི་གངས་ལ་བལྟས་པའི་ཚེ། །
གླུ་ངག་གི་ལམ་ནས་འདི་ལྟར་བླངས། །

སྔོན་བསོད་ནམས་བསགས་པའི་འབྲས་བུ་ལས། །
རྟེན་དལ་ཐོབ་དམ་པའི་ཆོས་དང་མཇལ། །
འདི་ཡིད་བཞིན་ནོར་བུ་ལས་ཀྱང་དཀོན། །
ད་ཆུད་ཟོས་ཕོད་འདི་ཁྲོད་སྙིང་ལྷུགས། །

སྤྱིར་ཆོས་སྒོར་ཞུགས་ནས་ཡུན་རིང་ཞིང་། །
སྒོས་རི་ཁྲོད་བསྟེན་ནས་ལོ་མང་ཡང་། །
དུས་ད་དུང་སེམས་དང་ཆོས་མ་འདྲེས། །
འདི་བསམས་ཤིང་འགྱོད་པ་གཏིང་ནས་སྐྱེས། །

I pray to the father, Tendzin Lobzang Gyatso,
Lord lama omniscient in the teachings of the three vehicles.
Please look after me with compassion.
Please bless me, that my mind may go towards the Dharma.

I was a bit sad one day
And wanted to go to a very solitary place.
When I saw the snow of Phu Seku,
I sang a song in this way from the path of my voice.

Because of merit accumulated in former lives,
I obtained a human body complete with freedoms, and encountered the holy Dharma.
This human life is even rarer than a wish-fulfilling jewel.
But now I actually have the nerve to waste it—my heart is as hard as iron!

Although I entered the door of Buddhism long ago
And have stayed in mountain hermitages for many years,
Up to now my mind has not integrated with the Dharma.
I thought about this and regret arose from my depths.

སྤྱིར་བླ་མ་གྲྭ་པ་ཡོན་བདག་ལ། །
ཚེ་བློས་གཏོང་སྒྲུབ་པ་ལྷུར་ལེན་ཞེས། །
ཚིག་མང་གཏམ་དམ་བཅའ་མང་ཕྱུལ་ཡང་། །
དུས་ད་དུང་ཚེ་འདི་བློས་མ་ཐོང་། །

སྔོན་རི་ཁྲོད་མ་བསྟེན་གནས་སྐབས་སུ། །
དུས་ནམ་ཞིག་སྒྲུབ་པ་བྱེད་པའི་ཚེ། །
རྗེ་མི་ལ་ལྟ་བུར་བྱེད་སྙམ་ཡང་། །
ད་སྒྲུབ་ལ་ཞུགས་ཚེ་རེ་མ་བྱུང་། །

རྗེ་མི་ལ་ལྟ་བུ་ཕར་ལ་ཞོག །
དུས་ད་ལྟའི་སྒོམ་ཆེན་ཐ་མ་ལའང་། །
མིག་ཡར་བལྟས་འགྲན་པར་མི་བཟོད་ན། །
ཉམས་རྟོགས་པའི་ཡོན་ཏན་ག་ལ་སྐྱེ། །

ས་དབེན་ཞིང་ཉམས་དགར་མི་འགྲོ་ན། །
མིང་རས་པར་བཏགས་པས་ཅི་ལ་ཕན། །
གཏམ་འདི་ལས་བྱུང་བའི་དགེ་བ་དེས། །
ཀུན་མཁྱེན་པའི་ཡེ་ཤེས་མྱུར་འཐོབ་ཤོག །

ཅེས་པ་འདི་ཡང་སྐལ་ལྡན་རྒྱ་མཚོས་སྦྱར་བའོ། ། ། །

Although I previously offered many words and made many promises
To lamas, monks, and patrons,
Saying "I earnestly apply myself to renouncing this life and
its concerns,"
Until now I have not renounced this life completely.

At times when I was not relying on mountain hermitages,
I would imagine I could do my practices like Milarepa.
But when I actually entered into practice,
My hopes were not fulfilled.

Dismiss the notion of practicing like Milarepa!
Today's common siddhas have set their aims too high.
If they cannot bear comparison with Milarepa,
How can the qualities of experience and realization arise?

If I don't go to a solitary and pleasing place,
What good would it do to call myself "*repa*"?
Through the merit that has arisen from this discourse,
May all sentient beings quickly attain the wisdom of omniscience.

This also was composed by Kälden Gyatso.

Chapter Four

Setting Off for Solitary Hermitages

རྗེ་བློ་བཟང་ཆོས་ཀྱི་རྒྱལ་སྲིད་ལ། །
དབང་འདོད་དགུར་བསྐྱུར་བའི་འགྲོ་བའི་མགོན། །
པ་བསྟན་པའི་རྒྱལ་མཚན་ཞབས་ལ་འདུད། །
ཉམས་རྟོགས་པའི་ཡོན་ཏན་རྒྱས་པར་མཛོད། །

མགོན་ཁྱོད་ཀྱིས་རྗེས་སུ་བཟུང་བ་ལས། །
དཔལ་ཐུབ་དབང་བསྟན་པའི་སྒྲོ་རུ་ཞུགས། །
གཞུང་ལེགས་བཤད་མང་ལ་ཐོས་བསམ་བྱས། །

ཆོས་གང་ཤེས་བློ་གསལ་ཚོགས་རྣམས་ལ། །
སེམས་གཡོ་སྒྱུ་མེད་པར་ལེགས་པར་བཤད། །

ད་མགོན་ཁྱོད་རྣམ་ཐར་རྗེས་ཞུགས་ནས། །
གནས་དབེན་པའི་དགའ་ཚལ་ཉམས་དགར་འགྲོ །

མི་སྐྱུ་སེར་མང་པོ་སྤོན་ཚད་ངས། །
ནོར་ཞབས་ཏོག་ཙམ་གྱི་ཆེད་དུ་བསླུས། །
ད་མི་མགོ་ནོར་ཕྱིར་མི་སྐོར་ཆེད། །
བདག་སྐལ་ལྡན་རི་ཁྲོད་དགོན་པར་འགྲོ །

I bow at the feet of the lord, my father Lobzang Tenpai Gyältsen,
Ruler over the dominion of the Dharma,
And protector of beings who have transformed all desires.
Please cause the qualities of my experience and realization
to flourish.

Protector, because you received me as a disciple,
I entered the door of the glorious Buddha's teaching,
And studied and contemplated numerous eloquent elucidations
of scriptures.

I explained whatever teaching I knew honestly and carefully
To gatherings of clear-minded disciples.

Now, following your example, protector,
I am going to the delightful grove of a hermitage.

I used to deceive monks and lay people
To gain mere wealth and servants.
Now, so I will not waver for the sake of wealth,
I, Kälden, am going to a mountain hermitage.

ཕུར་རྙེད་ཕྱིར་ཕྱོགས་བཅུར་འཁྱམས་འཁྱམས་པས། །
དུས་ད་ལྟ་ཟོག་པོའི་ཁྱུ་རུ་ཆུད། །
ད་ཆོས་པའི་གྲལ་ཞིག་ཨེ་འཐོབ་ཕྱིར། །
ང་རང་སྐྱེས་སྐལ་ལྡན་དབེན་པར་འགྲོ། །

རྒྱུད་ཞི་དུལ་ཆོས་དང་རྒྱང་རིང་བས། །
དུས་ད་ལྟ་ཆུ་དང་ཆུ་ཇེ་བཞིན། །
ད་ཆོས་སེམས་རྒྱབ་འགལ་མི་གཏོང་ཕྱིར། །
མིང་སྐལ་ལྡན་སྐལ་དམན་དབེན་པར་འགྲོ། །

ཁྱེད་དགོན་པོ་གྲྭ་པ་ཡོན་བདག་རྣམས། །
བློ་ཆོས་ལ་གཏོད་ལ་བདེ་བར་བཞུགས། །
ང་སྐལ་ལྡན་དབེན་པའི་དགའ་ཚལ་དུ། །
སེམས་ཐེ་ཚོམ་མེད་པར་སྒྱུར་དུ་འགྲོ། །

སྒོས་ཆོས་ཀྱི་གྲྭར་ཞུགས་བློ་གསལ་རྣམས། །
སྤྱོད་དབུས་གཙང་ཕྱོགས་སུ་ད་སོང་ལ། །
ཆོས་ཐོས་བསམ་གཉིས་ལ་ནན་ཏན་འཚལ། །
ང་ཡིད་གཉིས་མེད་པར་དབེན་པར་འགྲོ། །

Because I wandered and wandered in the ten directions
For the sake of getting stuff, I joined in with a bunch of frauds.
Now, hoping to attain the rank of a Dharma practitioner,
I, Kälden, born in Rong, am going to a solitary place.

Because my mind has been very far from the gentle Dharma,
Like water from the dry core of hollow pebbles,
I am anxious not to stray from my intention to practice.
I, Kälden, of poor fortune, am now going to a solitary place.

You nephew-disciples, other monks, and patrons—
Direct your minds to the Dharma, and dwell contentedly.
I, Kälden, am going soon, without any doubt,
To a delightful grove of a hermitage.

In particular, you clear-minded ones who have entered schools
 for Dharma study—
Go now to the upper region of Ütsang,
And be diligent in both studying and contemplating the Dharma.
I am not of two minds. I am going to a solitary place.

ན་གཞོན་པས་ཐག་རིང་མི་བགྲོད་པའི། །
ལོ་གཞོན་ནུ་ཐོས་བསམ་འདོད་པ་རྣམས། །
ཡུལ་མདོ་སྨད་ཀྱི་ཆོས་གྲྭ་གང་དགར་སོང་། །
ང་ཐག་རིང་གི་རི་ཁྲོད་དགོན་པར་འགྲོ །

སྤྲང་བདག་ལ་བློ་གཏད་སློབ་མ་རྣམས། །
སྐྱབས་དཀོན་མཆོག་གསུམ་ལ་བློ་གཏོད་ལ། །
བཀའ་དྲི་མེད་དགོངས་དོན་ཚོལ་ལ་འབོད། །
ང་སྐལ་ལྡན་རྒྱ་མཚོ་དབེན་པར་འགྲོ །

བྱ་ཁྲ་བྱུག་སྙེ་མ་མཆུར་བཟུང་ནས། །
ཡུལ་ཐག་རིང་གནས་སུ་འགྲོ་བ་ལྟར། །
ང་ལེགས་བཤད་ཟབ་མོ་བཟུང་བྱས་ནས། །
ས་དབེན་ཞིང་ཉམས་དགར་སྦྱུར་དུ་འགྲོ །

རྒོད་ཧེ་མཐོ་ཧེ་མཐོར་ལེགས་འཕུར་ནས། །
རང་གང་འདོད་ས་རུ་འགྲོ་བ་ལྟར། །
ང་ཡུལ་ལས་ཧེ་རིང་ཧེ་རིང་ཐོས། །
གནས་དབེན་པའི་དགའ་ཚལ་གང་དགར་འགྲོ །

བཀྲ་ཤིས། ། ། །

You younger ones who want to study and contemplate the Dharma
But feel too young to travel far away,
Go to any pleasing school for Dharma study in Domey.
I am going to a distant mountain hermitage.

You disciples—have confidence in me, a beggar.
Depend on refuge in the Three Jewels
And strive to find the intended meaning of the Buddha's
  flawless words.
I, Kälden Gyatso, am going to a solitary place.

Just as a cuckoo goes off to live in a distant place,
Grasping a stalk of grain in its beak,
So I, grasping the deep *Eloquent Explanations*,
Am going soon to a solitary and delightful place.

Just as an eagle skillfully flies higher and higher,
And goes wherever it desires,
I am going farther and farther from the gate of my home,
To whatever delightful grove of a hermitage.

Good fortune!

དཔལ་བཀྲ་ཤིས་དཔལ་འབར་ལྷ་ཡི་ལྷ། །
མགོན་བླ་མ་སངས་རྒྱས་སྤྱི་བོར་བཞུགས། །

ཁྱེད་རྒྱང་ནས་བྱོན་པའི་དགེ་བའི་བཤེས། །
མཚན་བློ་བཟང་དག་དབང་ཤེས་རབ་གཉིས། །
ཕྱོགས་ཐག་ཉེའི་རི་ཁྲོད་ཚུ་བཟང་བར། །
དུས་དབྱར་སོས་བར་དུ་བཞུགས་ན་བཟང་། །

མི་ང་ནི་ཚེ་ལྷག་རི་ལ་སྐྱེལ། །
ཉམས་རྟོགས་པ་མེད་ཀྱང་ཞེ་རེ་བྲོད། །
ཆོས་སེམས་དང་མ་འདྲེས་སོ་སོར་སོང་། །
ཆོས་བྱེད་པོའི་ངང་ལས་མི་ཚེ་རྒས། །

ནད་རྒས་པ་འཆི་བདག་ཞེད་ན་ཡང་། །
དགྲ་འདི་གསུམ་ལ་འབྲོས་པའི་ཐབས་མ་རྙེད། །

ད་ན་རུང་ན་ས་རི་རྩེ་སྐྱིད། །
ད་རྒས་རུང་རྒས་ས་རི་རྩེ་སྐྱིད། །
ད་འཆི་རུང་འཆི་ས་རི་རྩེ་སྐྱིད། །
ལས་ཅི་ལ་ཐུག་ཀྱང་རི་རྩེ་སྐྱིད། །

Oh protector, lama—splendid deity of deities, blazing glory
of goodness, Buddha—
Please dwell on my crown *cakra*.

As for you spiritual friends who have come from afar—
Lobzang and Ngawang Sherap—
It would be good if you stayed until summer
In a nearby mountain hermitage with good water.

I myself am going to live for the rest of my life in the mountains.
My mind has gone its own way separately from the Dharma
And I have grown old, while pretending to practice well.
But though I have had no profound experiences or realizations,
I feel joyful.

I feared sickness, old age, and the Lord of Death,
And never found the means to flee from these three enemies.
But now I am sick, and a mountain peak is a happy place
for being sick.
Now I am growing old, and a mountain peak is a delightful place
for aging.
Now I am dying, and a mountain peak is a joyful place for dying.
Whatever the circumstances of my karma, a mountain peak is
a place of great bliss.

རི་ན་བུན་འཁྲིགས་པའི་དབེན་གནས་ན། །
ང་བན་རྒན་གྱིས་གླུ་དབྱངས་འབྲུག་བཞིན་སྒྲོགས། །

རྗེ་བྱ་བཏང་གོང་མའི་རྣམ་ཐར་ལ། །
མིག་ཡར་ཡར་བལྟས་ནས་རྗེས་སུ་སློག །

ལུས་བདེ་ན་དགའ་སྐྱེ་དགེ་སྦྱོར་འཕེལ། །
ལུས་ན་རྒས་ནོན་ཡང་སྔོན་གྱི་ལས། །
ད་སྐྱིད་སྡུག་རེས་མོས་གང་བྱུང་ཡང་། །
བློ་གཏོད་ས་བླ་མ་དཀོན་མཆོག་གསུམ། །

ང་རྒད་པོ་སྐལ་ལྡན་རྒྱ་མཚོ་འདི། །
འཕྲལ་གང་བྱུང་གི་འདུན་མའི་ངང་ནས་གནས། །
ཐུགས་བློ་རྩེ་ཆོས་ལ་གཏད་པ་དེས། །
དུས་སྐབས་རེ་འདུན་མ་ལེགས་སོ་སྙམ། །

ཁྲིད་གཞི་བྱེས་ཀྱི་བྱ་བཏང་དགེ་འདུན་རྣམས། །
ཆོས་ཆོས་བཞིན་བྱས་ན་གཏན་འདུན་འགྲུབ། །

བཀྲ་ཤིས་པའི་དགེ་མཚན་རྒྱས་གྱུར་ཅིག །
དགེའོ། །

In solitude on a mountain in thick mist,
I, an old monk, am calling out a song like thunder.
Having looked up to and respected the life-stories of the lords,
Renunciants of former times, I am following their example.

When my body is at ease, I am joyful and my spiritual practices
flourish.
Although my body is overcome by illness and old age, that is
previous karma.
Now no matter what is arising—happiness or suffering, in turns—
I rely on the lama and the Three Jewels.

I, this old man, Kälden Gyatso,
Am motivated by whatever arises in the present.
Because I have focused my innermost mind single-pointedly
on the Dharma,
I think that at each moment my inclinations are good.

You renunciant monks, both at home and far away,
If you practice the Dharma according to the teachings, your
intentions will always be realized.

May auspicious signs flourish!
Good fortune!

ཨོཾ་སྭ་སྟི།

མཚོ་ཁྲི་ཤོར་རྒྱལ་མོའི་ཚབ་རྩ་ན། །
རྟོར་སོག་པོའི་ཡུལ་སྡེ་མང་གནས་ཀྱང་། །
དུས་རྟག་ཏུ་མི་དགེ་སྡིག་ལ་སྤྱོད། །
དགེ་གང་ནུས་ཀྱིས་དང་བོད་སྡེ་རྣམས། །

མཚོ་དེ་དཀྱིལ་རི་གླིང་ཆགས་པ་ལ། །
དུས་དེང་སང་མ་ཧཱ་དེ་བ་ཟེར། །
སྔོན་ཆོས་རྒྱལ་སྲོང་བཙན་སྒམ་པོ་དང་། །
དཔལ་ཨུ་རྒྱན་པདྨས་ལུང་བསྟན་ཅིང་། །
ཀླུ་བྱང་ཆུབ་སེམས་དཔའ་གནས་པའི་ས། །
རྗེ་གྲུབ་ཐོབ་མང་པོ་བཞུགས་པའི་གནས། །
གནས་དེ་རུ་འགྲོ་འདོད་འདུན་པ་སྐྱེས། །

ཡུལ་སྡེ་དགོན་བདུད་ཀྱི་བཙོན་ར་ཡིན། །
དབོན་གྲྭ་སློབ་དགེ་བའི་བར་ཆད་ཡིན། །
ནོར་རྫིད་བཀུར་འཆིང་བྱེད་ཐག་པ་སྟེ། །
ཆོས་འདོད་ན་དབེན་གནས་དེ་འདྲ་སྙེན། །

Oṃ swa sti!

Near the waters of Lake Trishor Gyälmo
Live many communities of Mongols,
But they are always engaged in evil deeds.
Practice virtue as much as possible, Tibetan communities!

There is a mountain island which rises in the center of that lake,
Now called Mahādeva,
About which the king of the Dharma, Songtsen Gampo,
And the glorious Pema of Ugyen made prophesies in former times.

This is where the Nāga Bodhisattva
And many lord *siddhas* dwell.
A desire has arisen in me to go there!

My homeland and its local monastery are demonic prisons.
My nephews and other disciples are obstacles to my virtue.
Obtaining riches and homage are ropes which ensnare me:
If I desire the Dharma, I must rely on a solitary hermitage
like Mahādeva.

ཧོར་སོག་པོ་ཐག་ཉེར་གནས་ན་ཡང་། །
ཕར་ངོ་བསྲུང་གི་བྱ་བ་མ་བྱེད་དང་། །
ཚུར་འོང་མི་མེད་ཅིང་འོངས་ཀྱང་བླ། །
ཆོས་དགེ་བའི་བར་ཆད་བྱེད་མི་མེད། །

སྐད་མི་གཅིག་མི་རིགས་སྣ་ཚོགས་པས། །
ཕྱོགས་གཅིག་འཚོགས་གཅིག་གཏམ་གཅིག་མི་གོ །
དེའི་དབང་གིས་མཉམ་དུ་འདུག་མི་འདོད། །
ཆོས་དགེ་སྦྱོར་གང་བྱེད་བསམས་བཞིན་འགྲུབ། །

མ་མཁའ་འགྲོ་མི་མེད་ས་ཆར་འབྱོན། །
ཆོས་གང་བྱེད་དེ་ལ་མགོན་སྐྱབས་བྱེད། །
དཔལ་ཆོས་སྐྱོང་སྲུང་ཚོགས་སྤྲིན་བཞིན་འདུ། །
ཆོས་བྱེད་མཁན་དེ་ཡི་བར་ཆད་སྲུང་། །

དགུང་ཉི་མ་ཟེར་ཟེར་བྱུང་ཙ་ན། །
སྐྱོ་ཕྱོད་དེ་ཟློ་སྣ་དུང་དུང་འབྱུང་། །
ནང་སྤུ་བར་ཡར་ལ་ལངས་ཙ་ན། །
ལྷ་བླ་མ་ཡི་དམ་ཞ་ལེར་འཆར། །
དགེ་སྒྲུབ་འདོད་ཀྱི་འདུན་པ་ལྷང་ལྷང་སྐྱེ། །

Mongols stay nearby,
But I should not do crowd-pleasing deeds over there,
And no one comes over here, though it would usually be proper.

We are of different ethnic groups, and speak different languages
So don't understand each other and don't want to be together.
Therefore no one will interfere with my Dharma practices
And whatever spiritual rituals I have considered, I will carry out.

Mother *ḍākinī*s appear in uninhabited places,
And they will protect my practices.
Hosts of glorious protectors, guardians of the Dharma, gather
like clouds,
And protect religious practitioners from any hindrances.

When the rays of the noon sun shine down,
Wavering feelings of sadness emerge.
But if I rise early in the morning
When the essence of my divine lama and *yidam* appears most vividly,
The intention to cultivate virtue will clearly arise.

ཚོས་གང་བྱེད་ཀྱི་འདུན་པ་བཏང་བཞིན་འགྲུབ། །
སྡིག་ལྟུང་བའི་ཕྱོགས་ལ་འགྱོད་ཅིང་སྡོམ། །
ཉིན་ཕལ་ཆེར་དགེ་སྦྱོར་བྱ་བས་འདལ། །
མཚན་གཉིད་ཆུང་དགེ་སྦྱོར་རིམ་པ་སྐྱོང་། །

ལས་དེ་འདྲས་དལ་འབྱོར་དོན་ལྡན་བྱེད། །
མི་དེ་ལ་སྐྱིད་པའི་ཉི་མ་འཆར། །

ཨ་ལ་ལ་བསམ་པ་འདི་འགྲུབ་ན་དགའ་བ་ལ། །
འོ་ན་ལ་འདུན་པ་འདི་འགྲུབ་ན་སྐྱིད་པ་ལ། །

ཞེས་པ་འདི་ཡང་སྐལ་ལྡན་རྒྱ་མཚོས་ཡིད་ལ་ཇི་ལྟར་བསམས་པ་ལྟར་དབེན་གནས་བཀྲ་ཤིས་འཁྱིལ་བར་བྲིས་པའོ། ། ། །

Whatever Dharma practices I have aspired to will be realized.
I will repent and retake vows in areas in which I have transgressed,
And pass most of the day performing spiritual practices.
With just naps at night,
I will sustain a succession of virtuous acts.

Through karmic action like that,
One makes a free and well-favored human birth worthwhile,
And the sun of happiness will shine from within.

A la la, if I carry out my intention to stay on Mahādeva, I will rejoice.
O na la, if I carry out this aspiration, I will be happy.

This was written by Kälden Gyatso in the hermitage, the center of good fortune, in accordance with whatever thoughts came to mind.

བྱང་ཆུབ་ལམ་གྱི་རིམ་པ། །
ཡིད་འོང་རི་ཁྲོད་ཉམས་དགའ། །
སྐྱོང་བཙུན་འཇམ་དཔལ་རྡོ་རྗེ། །
ལྷན་ཅིག་འགྲིགས་པའི་རྟེན་འབྲེལ། །
མྱུར་དུ་འགྲིགས་ན་དགའ་བ། །
མྱུར་དུ་འགྲིགས་ན་སྐྱིད་པ། །

རྡོ་ལ་ཡང་བའི་གོས་ཧྲུལ། །
དཀོར་དང་མ་འདྲེས་དམན་ཟས། །
སྔོ་ལྡང་རྩྭ་ཡི་གདན་གསུམ། །
སྐྱོང་བཙུན་འཇམ་དཔལ་རྡོ་རྗེའི། །
ཡོ་བྱད་ཡིན་ན་དགའ་བ། །
ཡོ་བྱད་ཡིན་ན་སྐྱིད་པ། །

སྐད་སྙན་འབྱིན་པའི་བྱ་དང་། །
ལུས་མཛེས་ཡིད་འོང་རི་དྭགས། །
འཇམ་དཔལ་རྡོ་རྗེ་ང་ཡི། །
གྲོགས་པོ་ཡིན་ན་དགའ་བ། །
གྲོགས་པོ་ཡིན་ན་སྐྱིད་པ། །
མྱུར་དུ་འགྲོག་པར་སྨོན་ནོ། །

The Stages of the Path to Enlightenment,
A delightful, lovely mountain hermitage,
And the beggar-monk Jampel Dorje—
If the conditions for their simultaneity
Are auspicious soon—Oh joy!
If they are auspicious soon—Oh happiness!
If the conditions for simultaneity
Are favorable soon—Oh joy!
If they are favorable soon—Oh happiness!

Warm and light tattered clothing,
Lowly food not associated with religious offerings,
And a mat of blue-green grass—
If they are the belongings of the beggar-monk
Jampel Dorje—Oh joy!
If they are my belongings—Oh happiness!

Birds emitting eloquent tunes
And delightful hoofed animals with beautiful bodies—
If they are the friends
Of Jampel Dorje—myself—Oh joy!
If they are my friends—Oh happiness!
I wish to befriend them soon.

རབ་དཀར་བྲག་གི་ཤུག་ཏུ། །
སྤྲང་བཙུན་འཇམ་དཔལ་རྡོ་རྗེ། །
སྒུར་དུ་སོང་ན་དགའ་བ། །
སྒུར་དུ་སོང་ན་སྐྱིད་པ། །

བྱང་ཆུབ་ལམ་རིམ་ཁུར་ནས། །
གཡའ་སྤང་མཚམས་སུ་སོང་ན། །
འཇམ་དཔལ་རྡོ་རྗེ་དགའ་བ། །
འཇམ་དཔལ་རྡོ་རྗེ་སྐྱིད་པ། །

གོན་པ་ཧྲུལ་པོ་གྱོན་ནས། །
ཡིད་འོང་དབེན་པའི་རི་ལ། །
རི་དྭགས་ལྷ་བུར་སྤྱོད་པའི། །
དུས་ཞིག་བྱུང་ན་དགའ་བ། །
དུས་ཞིག་བྱུང་ན་སྐྱིད་པ། །

If the beggar-monk, Jampel Dorje,
Goes soon
To a cave with glittering rocks—Oh joy!
If I go soon—Oh happiness!

If I go to the juncture of slate crags and meadows
Carrying *The Stages of the Path to Enlightenment,*
Jampel Dorje is joyful.
Jampel Dorje is happy.

If a time arises in which
I cover myself with ragged clothes
And live like the hoofed animals
On delightful, solitary mountains—Oh joy!
If a time like that arises—Oh happiness!

གྲྭ་བ་གཉེན་བཤེས་ཀུན་གྱིས། །
གར་བསྡོད་ཞེས་པར་དཀའ་བའི། །
མི་མེད་ལུང་པ་སྟོང་པར། །
གཅིག་པུར་འཇིགས་མེད་གནས་པའི། །
དུས་ཞིག་བདག་ལ་བྱུང་ན། །
ཨ་ལ་ལ་དགའ་བ་ལ། །
ཨ་ལ་ལ་སྐྱིད་པ་ལ། །

ཉམས་དགའི་རི་ཁྲོད་གནས་སུ། །
འགལ་རྐྱེན་བར་ཆད་མེད་ཅིང་། །
མཐུན་རྐྱེན་ཚང་བའི་སྒྲོན་ནས། །
དམ་པའི་ལྷ་ཆོས་བྱེད་པའི། །
རྟེན་འབྲེལ་ལེགས་པར་འགྲིགས་ཚེ། །
ཉམས་དགའི་གླུ་དབྱངས་ལེན་ནོ། །
སྐྱིད་པའི་རྐང་བྲོ་བྱེད་དོ། །

ཨ་ལ་ལ་འདི་འདྲའི་ཡིད་སྨོན། །
ཨོ་ན་ལ་མྱུར་དུ་འགྲུབ་ན། །
ཨ་ལ་ལ་རྫོང་སྐྱོན་དགའ་བ། །
ཨོ་ན་ལ་ང་ཡི་སྐྱིད་པ། །

ཞེས་པ་འདི་ཡང་སྐལ་ལྡན་རྒྱ་མཚོས་གྲུང་རིས་སུ་རང་དགར་བྲིས་པའོ། ། །།

If a time arises for me
To live alone, without fear,
In secluded, uninhabited valleys
Where it would be hard for any monk or relative
To find me—
A la la—Oh joy!
A la la—Oh happiness!

When the occasion becomes suitable
For me to practice the holy, divine Dharma
In a delightful, mountain hermitage
By means of all favorable conditions
And no obstructions or hindrances,
I will sing a joyful song.
I will dance a happy dance.

A la la! If a desire like this
O na la! is quickly fulfilled,
A la la! The madman of Rongbo will be joyful!
O na la! I will be happy.

This also was written by Kälden Gyatso, casually on a wall.

Chapter Five

Emptiness and Mahāmudrā

དོན་དམ་ལ་ཡེ་ནས་མེད་ན་ཡང་། །
མིང་ཙམ་ལ་འདི་ཙམ་གྲུབ་པ་ཡི། །
གནས་ཚུལ་ཆོ་རིག་པའི་བླ་མ་དེས། །
རང་ཉིད་ཀྱིས་གང་གཟིགས་བདག་ལ་སྩོལ། །

སྩོལ་རྒྱུ་ཡི་ཆོས་ཀྱང་རང་ངོས་ནས། །
ཡེ་མེད་ནི་ཡིན་ན་ཇི་ལྟར་སྩོལ། །
འོན་ཀྱང་ནི་མིང་ཙམ་བརྡ་ཙམ་དུ། །
ཕྱར་ཞུས་ཀྱི་དོན་དེ་བསྩལ་དུ་གསོལ། །

སྟོང་ཉིད་ནི་མཐོང་འདོད་མང་ན་ཡང་། །
མཐོང་རྒྱུ་ཡི་སྟོང་ཉིད་སུ་ཡིས་མཐོང་། །
མ་མཐོང་དེ་སྟོང་ཉིད་ཡིན་པས་ན། །
འོ་སྐོལ་ཆོས་མཐོང་རྒྱུ་རེ་བ་མཚར། །

འོ་ན་ནི་དེང་སང་སྣང་བ་ལ། །
མི་གནོད་པར་སྟོང་ཉིད་ལྟ་བ་ནི། །
ལག་པ་ལ་མིག་གིས་ཕར་བལྟས་པས། །
ནམ་མཁའ་ནི་མཐོང་བར་རེ་བ་བཞིན། །
སྟོང་ཉིད་ནི་ཟེར་བ་གཞན་ནས་མེད། །

Oh lama, you are aware that conditions
Exist only just this much—in mere name.
At the same time, you realize that
None exist from the very beginning in ultimate truth—
Please grant me the ability to see what you yourself see.

If a thing to be bestowed is, in its own right, nonexistent
    from the beginning,
How does one bestow it?
Nevertheless, I pray that you bestow what I just requested
With the mere conventional designation of words.

Although there are many who want to see emptiness,
Who has seen the emptiness of a visual object?
Since emptiness is not to be seen,
Our hope of it being visible is astonishing.

Nevertheless, the view of emptiness
In terms of everyday appearances is free of contradictions—
So-called emptiness is not elsewhere,
And the view of it is not like some vision of the sky
One mistakenly hopes to have by looking at one's hand.

ད་ལྟར་གྱི་སྣང་ཚུལ་འདི་བཀག་པའི། །
སྟོང་སང་དེ་ཟབ་མོ་སྟོང་ཉིད་དུ། །
ལྟ་ཁྲིད་ཀྱི་ཡིག་ཆར་བཤད་ནས་སྣང་། །

འདི་ཡང་ནི་བླ་མའི་བཀའ་དྲིན་ལས། །
རང་ཉིད་ལ་རང་གིས་གྲོས་སུ་བསྟད། །
དགེ་བ་ཀུན་དོན་དམ་ཡེ་མེད་ཀྱི། །
རང་ཞལ་ལ་ཧྲེན་པར་ལྟ་ཕྱིར་བསྒོ། །

ཞེས་པ་འདི་ཡང་བན་གཟུགས་ཀྱི་རྒྱལ་འགོང་སྐལ་ལྡན་རྒྱ་མཚོས་སྦྱར་བའོ། ། ། །

An explanation of emptiness
As that completely empty, deep vacuum
Through which one refutes the way things seem in the present
Appears in the instruction manuals.

Due to the kindness of the lama,
I have related this song as counsel to myself.
I dedicate it for the sake of looking freshly
At the genuine face of all virtue,
Which lacks real existence in ultimate truth from the very beginning.

This also was composed by Kälden Gyatso, a demon in the body of a monk.

ཨོཾ་སྭ་སྟི།

ཉི་མ་དབུས་གཙང་གི་བྲ་བཏང་ཚོ་ལ། །
མིག་ནི་ཡར་ལྷ་བྲུས་ནས་གཅིག་ཕྱུར་སྤྱོད་དོ། །

རྩ་རླུང་ཐིག་ལེ་སྒོམ་པའི་བྲ་བཏང་མིན་ཡང་། །
བློ་ཁ་ཆོས་ལ་ཕྱོགས་པའི་བན་རྒན་ལགས་སོ། །
གཏུམ་མོའི་སྟོབས་ཀྱིས་སྐྱེས་པའི་ཕྱུག་ཆེན་སྒོམ་མཁན་མིན་ཡང་། །
སེམས་ཀྱི་རང་ཞལ་ལྟ་འདོད་འདུན་པ་དྲག་པོ་མཆིས་པས། །
བསམ་གཏན་ཁང་བུར་བླ་མ་ལྷ་ལ་གསོལ་བ་བཏབ་ནས། །
གདམས་ངག་ཡང་ཡང་སེམས་སྟེང་བསྒྲོར་ནས་ཉམས་སུ་ལེན་པའི་
བན་རྒན་ལགས་སོ། །

Oṃ swa sti!

I have looked up to renunciants who are the sun of Ütsang,
And am living alone.

Although I was not a renunciant who meditates on *nāḍī, prāṇa,*
and *bindu,*
I was indeed an old monk whose mind turns to the Dharma.
I was not one who meditates on *Mahāmudrā*—
Born through the power of *caṇḍālī*—
But an intense desire to see the nature of mind arose in me.
So I petitioned lamas and deities in small meditation huts
And applied the oral instructions to my mind again and again.
And I am now an old monk who practices *Mahāmudrā.*

ཕྱག་རྒྱ་གྲོགས་སུ་ཁྲིད་ནས་གསང་སྔགས་སྨུར་ལམ་ཉམས་སུ་ལེན་པའི་བྱ་བཏང་
མིན་ཡང་། །
དངོས་གྲུབ་རྩ་བ་དམ་ཚིག་སྡོམ་པ་གང་ནུས་ལེགས་པར་བསྲུངས་ནས། །
ཐུན་དྲུག་ཐུན་བཞིའི་རྣལ་འབྱོར་སྒོ་ནས་ཚོགས་གསོག་སྒྲིབ་སྦྱོང་ལ་འབད་ཅིང་། །
གསང་སྔགས་སྨུར་ལམ་བསྐྱེད་རྫོགས་ཕྱོགས་ལ་དད་པ་བརྟན་པའི་བན་རྒན་
ལགས་སོ། །

ཏིང་འཛིན་སྒོ་བརྒྱ་ཕྱེ་ནས་དག་པའི་སྣང་བ་སྣ་ཚོགས་མཐོང་བའི་བྱ་བཏང་མིན་ཡང་། །
སེམས་ཉིད་གྱོང་པོ་འདི་ལ་དུལ་བའི་དུས་ཤིག་ཨེ་འོང་བསམས་ནས་གདམས་ངག་གང་
ཟབ་ཞུས་ཏེ། །
དབེན་གནས་བརྒྱ་ཕྲག་བསྟེན་ནས་དགེ་སྦྱོར་གང་ནུས་བསྐྱངས་ཤིང་ལྷོད་མོ་ཡང་ཡང་
སེམས་ལ་བལྟས་ཏེ། །
ད་ལྟ་རང་ལ་དགེ་སློབ་འདུན་པ་མ་དོར་གཞན་ལ་འང་ཕན་ཐོགས་ལེགས་པོ་བྱུང་བའི་བན་
རྒན་ལགས་སོ། །

ཞེས་པ་འདི་ཡང་སྐལ་ལྡན་རྒྱ་མཚོས་རང་ལོ་རེ་གཉིས་པ་ལ་ཉམས་དགར་བྲིས་པའོ། ། ། །

Although I was not a renunciant who practices the quick path
  of mantras,
I was led to *mudrā* friends.
So I guarded as best I could the commitments and vows—
The foundation of the spiritual powers—
And strove for the attainment of merit and the cleansing of obscurations
By doing yogic practices in four or six sessions.
And I am now an old monk with firm faith
In the areas of the quick mantra path: the Generation
  and Completion Stages.

Although I was not a renunciant who opens a hundred doors
  of *samādhi*
And sees a variety of pure perceptions,
I did used to wonder whether the time would come
For this coarse mind itself to be tamed.
So I requested oral instructions of whatever depth,
And stayed in a hundred solitary places,
Sustaining spiritual practice as much as possible.
And I have now looked at the displays of the mind again and again.

I have still not abandoned the aims of a virtuous mind.
I am an old monk through whom benefits have been arising for others
  as well.

Kälden Gyatso wrote this joyfully, at the age of sixty-two.

ན་མོ་གུ་རུ་ལོ་ཀེ་ཤྭ་ར་ཡ།

གསེར་བཟང་པོ་འདྲ་བའི་སེམས་ཀྱི་དབྱིངས། །
དེ་གཅེར་མཐོང་དམ་པ་ཕྱག་གི་ཡུལ། །
སེམས་རང་ངོ་མ་ཤེས་འཁོར་བར་འཁྱམས། །

སེམས་རང་ངོ་ཟིན་ན་གཏན་དུ་བདེ། །
འདི་འཕགས་པ་རྣམས་ཀྱིས་རྗེན་པར་གཟིགས། །
འདི་སོ་སྐྱེ་རྣམས་ཀྱིས་ངོ་མ་ཤེས། །

ལར་ཀུན་གཞིའི་སེམས་དང་སྟོང་པ་ཉིད། །
དོན་མཐུན་པར་བཀའ་བརྒྱུད་གོང་མ་བཞེད། །

དཔལ་ས་ར་ཧ་བའི་ཐུགས་ཀྱི་བཅུད། །
རྗེ་ཀླུ་སྒྲུབ་ཡབ་སྲས་ལེགས་བཤད་དོན། །
མགོན་ནཱ་རོ་མཻ་ཏྲིའི་བཞེད་པ་གང་། །
རྗེ་མར་མི་ཡབ་སྲས་ཐུགས་དམ་མཐིལ། །
སེམས་མི་རྟོག་ཁྱབ་གདལ་ཆེན་པོའི་ངང་། །
དུས་རྒྱུན་དུ་འཛོག་ལ་ཕྱག་ཆེན་ཟེར། །

I bow to the guru, Lokeśvara.

As for seeing the realm of mind directly,
That holy object of reverence like fine gold,
I have not perceived its natural face,
And have been wandering in samsara.

If you apprehend the very essence of mind, you will be happy
forever.
The exalted ones have looked at it directly,
But ordinary people do not recognize it.

The Kagyüpa forefathers have asserted that
There is compatibility in general between the mind—
The basis of all things in samsaric experience—and emptiness.

The essence of the intentions of glorious Saraha,
The purpose of the eloquent explanations of the lord Nāgārjuna
and his disciples,
All the orientations of the protectors, Nāropa and Maitrīpa,
And the central practice of the lords Marpa and Milarepa—
Were to rest the mind continually
In the state of great, all-pervading, nonconceptual thought.
This is called *Mahāmudrā*.

དཔལ་ཀླུ་གྲགས་ཇོ་འབྲོམ་རྗེ་ཡབ་སྲས།།
སེམས་གཞི་རྩ་གཅོད་འདོད་དགག་བྱ་འཚོལ།།

དེ་ངེས་ཚེ་ཁྱབ་དང་ཕྱོགས་ཆོས་དགོས།།
ལར་དགག་བྱ་ལྟར་དུ་མེད་པ་ལ།།
དུས་དང་པོར་དཔྱད་སྒོམ་གཙོ་བོར་བྱེད།།
དུས་བར་དུ་དཔྱད་འཇོག་མཉམ་པར་སྐྱོང་།།
དུས་ཐ་མར་འཇོག་སྒོམ་གཙོ་བོར་མཛད།།

དེའི་སྟོབས་ཀྱིས་ཞི་གནས་བརྟན་པའི་ཚེ།།
སྒོམ་དཔྱད་འཇོག་གཉིས་ཀ་སྤེལ་མར་སྐྱོང་།།

ལར་དང་པོར་དཔྱད་པ་གཙོ་ཆེར་བྱེད།།
དེའི་སྟོབས་ཀྱིས་གནས་པ་སྐྱེད་པའི་ཚེ།།
སྒོམ་ཞི་ལྷག་གཉིས་པོ་ཟུང་དུ་འབྲེལ།།

The glorious Candrakīrti, Atiśa, Dromtön, and Tsongkhapa
and his chief disciples
Wanted to sever the root of the grasping mind,
And sought precisely what was to be refuted.

When ascertaining the conventional existence of something,
That existence needs to be determined by valid reason.
However, in the case in which things are to be negated,
One simply sees that they have no inherent existence.

In the beginning, one makes analytic meditation the principal focus.
Next, one sustains analytic and resting meditations equally.
Finally, one makes stabilizing meditation the principal focus.

Through that process, when peaceful calm is stable,
One sustains both analytic and resting meditations together.

Again, first one makes analysis the main process.
By means of that, when one develops calm abiding,
Both meditations—peaceful calm and insight into emptiness—
Will be integrated.

འདི་ཞྭ་སེར་ཡོངས་ཀྱི་ལྷ་སྒོམ་སྟེ། །
སྒོམ་ནུས་ན་བྱིན་རླབས་གཞན་ལས་མྱུར། །

འདི་ལེགས་པར་སྐྱོངས་དང་བྱ་བཏང་ཚོ། །
འདི་གོ་བས་ཐར་པའི་ས་བོན་འཛོག །

འདི་ཐུན་རེ་སྒོམ་པའི་མི་དེ་ལ། །
དགྲ་བདག་ཏུ་འཛིན་པ་ཕར་ཕར་འགྲོས། །
མཆོག་ཐར་པའི་གོ་འཕང་ཚུར་ཚུར་འདུ། །

སྒོམ་ནུས་ན་དཔའ་བོ་ཁྲོམ་ཤོག་ཡིན། །

ཏ་ཏ་རང་ལ་མེད་ཀྱང་ཀུ་རེ་རྩེ། ། ། །

If one is able to meditate, one's progress will be quicker than through
other blessings.
This is the view and meditation of all Yellow Hats.

Sustain this practice well, renunciants!
As you listen to this song, seeds of liberation are being planted
in you.

The enemy, clinging to self, will flee farther and farther
From whomever does these meditations at each shift,
And one will come nearer and nearer to merge with the supreme
level of liberation.

Someone able to meditate is a warrior
Who can cleave right through the midst of an enemy army,
Divide them, and fight them single-handedly.

Ha ha, although I have no intrinsic existence, I am jestfully playing!

རྒྱལ་བའི་བསྟན་པའི་ཉིང་ཁུ། །
རྟེན་འབྱུང་སྟོང་པའི་དོན་དུ། །
ལམ་ལམ་གཟིགས་པའི་བླ་མ། །
སྙིང་གི་པདྨོར་རྟག་བཞུགས། །

བདག་གཞན་ཀུན་གྱི་སྣང་ཚུལ། །
འདི་ལས་གཞན་པའི་དགག་བྱ། །
གཞན་དུ་བཙལ་བས་མི་རྙེད། །

རང་གི་ཉམས་ལ་ལྟོས་ཤིག །
གཅིག་དང་དུ་བྲལ་རིགས་པས། །
ཡོད་མེད་ལེགས་པར་དཔྱད་ཚེ། །
ནམ་མཁའི་པདྨོ་ཇི་བཞིན། །
ཡེ་ནས་མེད་པར་འཆར་རོ། །

ཤར་བའི་དང་དུ་སེམས་ཉིད། །
སྤྲོས་པ་ཀུན་དང་བྲལ་བར། །
གཡོ་མེད་རྩེ་གཅིག་ཞོག་དང་། །
མྱུར་དུ་ལྟ་བ་རྙེད་འགྱུར། །

Oh lama, who perceives clearly
The meaning of interdependent origination and emptiness,
The quintessence of the teaching of the Victorious Ones,
Please dwell continually on the lotus at my heart.

By searching elsewhere
For what is to be negated,
Other than how all things seem to be to myself and others,
I do not find anything.

Look at your own experiences!
When you have examined closely whether they exist independently
or not
Through the logic of whether they are single entities
Or can be separated into however many parts,
They will appear as primordially non-existent,
Just as there are no lotuses in the sky.

Place your unwavering attention single-pointedly
On the nature of mind in its shining manner,
Which has no conceptual elaboration whatsoever.
You will quickly attain the direct view of its nature.

ངེས་ཤེས་ཞན་དུ་སོང་ན། །
སྤྱར་གྱི་རིགས་པ་དྲན་ལམ། །
བྲུས་ལ་ངེས་ཤེས་ཇེ་ཆེར། །
ཡང་དང་ཡང་དུ་གཏང་ངོ། །

དེ་ལྟའི་མཉམ་བཞག་རྣལ་འབྱོར། །
གནད་དུ་སོང་ན་རྗེས་ཐོབ། །
འཁོར་འདས་སྣང་བ་གང་ཤར། །
རྟོག་བཏགས་རོལ་བར་འཆར་རོ། །

འདི་སྐྱུར་རྣམ་དཀར་དགེ་བས། །
རིགས་ཤེས་གཞོན་ནུ་མིག་ཡངས། །
སྟོང་ཉིད་མཛེས་མ་ལྷན་ཅིག །
སྨུར་དུ་མཇལ་བར་གྱུར་ཅིག །

ཅེས་པ་འདི་ནི་བཙུན་པའི་གཟུགས་བརྙན་སྐལ་ལྡན་རྒྱ་མཚོས་སྦྱར་བའོ། ། ། །

If your determinate awareness becomes weak,
Incorporate recollections of the preceding logic into your path,
And it will become stronger again and again.

When the yoga of meditative equipoise like that
Strikes its essential point,
In between meditation sessions,
Both cyclic existence and its transcendence
Will appear as the play of conceptual labeling,
No matter how they have seemed in the past.

By means of the virtuous merit of this composition,
May everyone quickly encounter
That knowledgeable youth, rational cognition,
Together with that beautiful woman, emptiness.

This was composed by the manifestation as a monk, Kälden Gyatso.

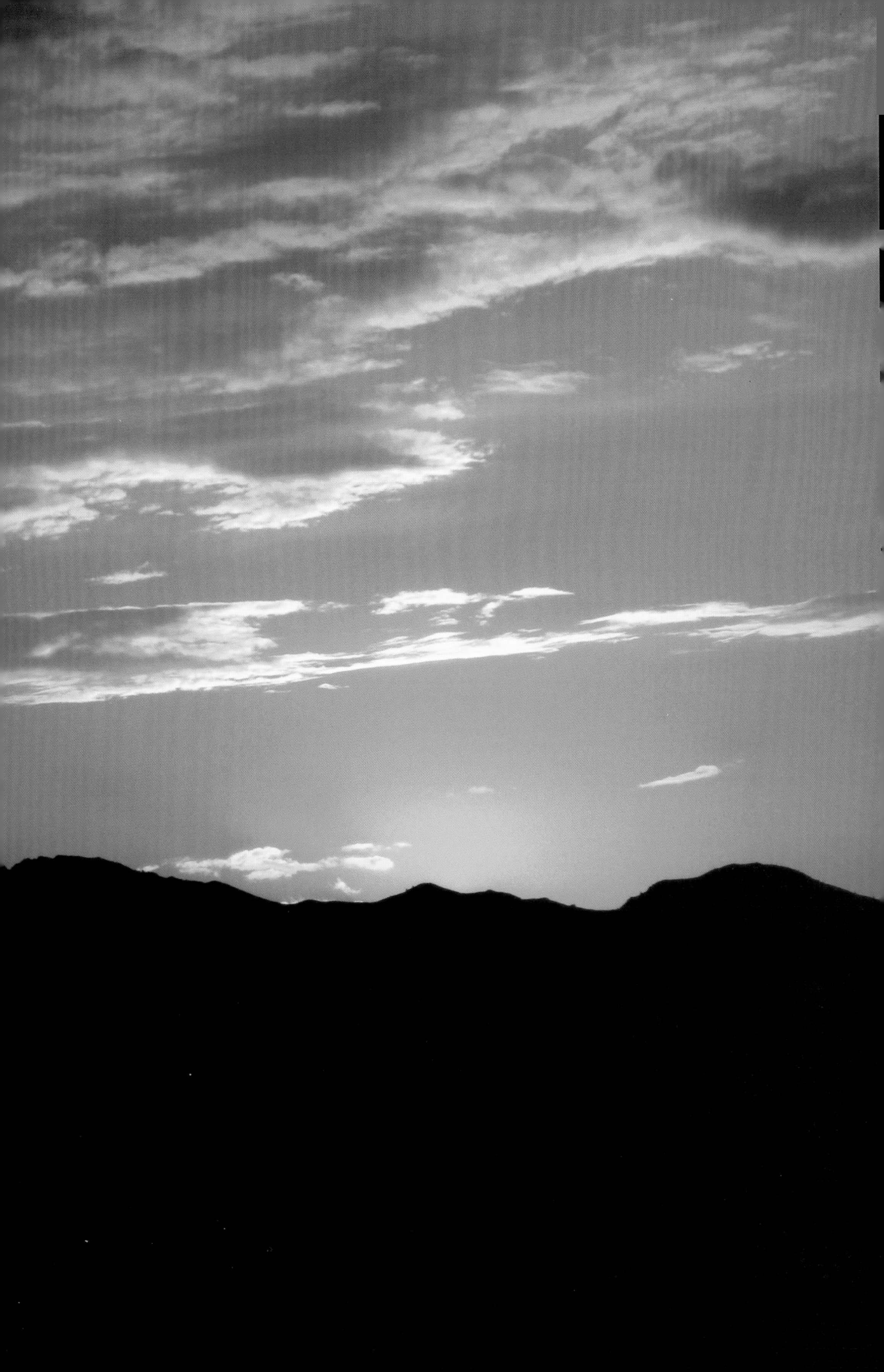

Chapter Six

Mountain Retreats and Happiness

ན་མོ་གུ་རུ་ཏ་ས་བཛྲ་ཡ། །

བླ་མ་མི་ལ་བཞད་པའི་རྡོ་རྗེ་དྲན་བྱུང་། །
རྗེ་ཁྲིད་ཉམས་དགའ་དབེན་པའི་དགའ་ཚལ་དྲན་བྱུང་། །
དམ་པའི་ལྷ་ཆོས་སྒོམ་ཁྲིད་ཟབ་མོ་དྲན་བྱུང་། །
རྣམ་ཐར་བཟང་པོ་ཆེ་འདི་བློས་བཏང་དྲན་བྱུང་། །

ཨ་ལ་ལ་རྒྱལ་ཁམས་འཁྲིམ་པའི་བན་རྒན་ང་ནི། །
གོང་གི་མི་ཆེན་རྣམས་ལ་ངོ་འཛིན་མི་དགོས། །
ཐད་ཀའི་མཆེད་གྲོགས་རྣམས་ལ་རེ་ལྟོས་མི་བྱེད། །
དམའ་བའི་སྐྱ་སེར་ཀུན་ལ་སྐྱོང་དྲིན་མེད་ཀྱང་ཆོག་གོ།

ཨ་ལ་ལ་རྒྱལ་ཁམས་འཁྲིམ་པའི་བན་རྒན་ང་ནི། །
གོང་དུ་བཀུར་གནས་བླ་མ་དཀོན་མཆོག །
བར་དུ་རེ་ས་དམ་པའི་ལྷ་ཆོས། །
ཐ་མར་སྐྱོང་དགོས་ཆོས་མཐུན་གཉེར་ཆུང་། །

I bow to the guru, Hāsa Vajra.

The lama Mila Shepai Dorje has come to mind.
Delightful mountain hermitages—solitary, pleasant groves—
have come to mind.
Deep meditation instructions for the holy, divine Dharma
have come to mind.
Fine life-stories about renouncing the concerns of this life
have come to mind.

A la la, as for me, an old monk who wanders around the country,
I don't need to flatter leaders up above.
I don't depend on Dharma brothers around me.
And although I don't have the kindness to care for all the lesser
monks and lay persons, it's all right.

A la la, as for me, an old monk who wanders around the country:
First, objects of veneration—the lama and the Three Jewels;
Later, hope—in the holy, divine Dharma;
Finally, what to sustain—good behavior in accordance with
the Dharma.

ཨ་ལ་ལ་རྒྱལ་ཁམས་འཁྲིམ་པའི་བན་རྒན་ང་ནི། །
དང་པོ་ལྷ་ས་རྣམ་ཐར་མགུར་མ། །
བར་དུ་སྡོད་ས་མི་མེད་ལུང་སྟོང་། །
ཐ་མར་ལྡོམ་ས་ཕྱོགས་མེད་རྒྱལ་ཁམས། །

ཨ་ལ་ལ་རྒྱལ་ཁམས་འཁྲིམ་པའི་བན་རྒན་ང་ནི། །
དང་པོར་གཞུང་ལུགས་ཐོས་པ་མང་བྱས། །
བར་དུ་གཞུང་དོན་བརྟགས་ཤིང་དཔྱད་པས། །
ཐ་མར་གོ་བ་བཟང་པོ་ཤར་བྱུང་། །

ཨ་ལ་ལ་རྒྱལ་ཁམས་འཁྲིམ་པའི་བན་རྒན་ང་ནི། །
སྔོན་གྱི་ལས་འཕྲོས་ན་རྒྱུ་མང་བྱུང་། །
སྒྱུ་མའི་ལུས་པོ་རྒས་ཤིང་རྒུད་རུང་། །
ནང་གི་བློ་ཁ་ཆོས་ལ་ཕྱོགས་སོ། །

ཨ་ལ་ལ་རྒྱལ་ཁམས་འཁྲིམ་པའི་བན་རྒན་ང་ནི། །
ཕྱི་བལྟས་འདོད་ཡོན་སྣང་བ་ཆེ་ཡང་། །
ནང་བལྟས་འདོད་སྲེད་ཆགས་ཞེན་ཆུང་ལ། །
བླ་མའི་དྲིན་ལས་སྐབས་སྐབས་གཉེན་པོ་སླེབས་བྱུང་། །

A la la, as for me, an old monk who wanders around the country:
First, objects to read—songs of realization and stories of liberation;
Later, residence—empty, uninhabited valleys;
Finally, almshouse—the country, without direction.

A la la, as for me, an old monk who wanders around the country,
First, I studied the scriptural tradition a lot.
Next, I examined and analyzed the meaning of the texts.
Ultimately, a fine understanding arose in me.

A la la, as for me, an old monk who wanders around the country,
Because of residual karma from the past, many illnesses emerged in me.
But the aging and decline of this illusory body are all right:
I have turned my inner mind towards the Dharma.

A la la, as for me, an old monk who wanders around the country,
When others look at me from the outside, my interest in desirable objects seems intense,
But when I look within, craving and attachment are weak,
And due to the kindness of lamas, from time to time antidotes come to me.

ཨ་ལ་ལ་རྒྱལ་ཁམས་འཁྲིམ་པའི་བན་རྒན་ང་ནི། །
ད་ལྟ་སྙིགས་མའི་དུས་ཀྱི་བསྐལ་བར། །
བླ་མ་སངས་རྒྱས་དངོས་དང་མཇལ་ནས། །
དམ་ཆོས་བུ་རམ་རོ་མཆོག་སྤྱོང་ངོ་། །

ཨ་ལ་ལ་རྒྱལ་ཁམས་འཁྲིམ་པའི་བན་རྒན་ང་ནི། །
མཐའ་འཁོབ་ཨ་མདོའི་ས་ཕྱོགས་འདི་རུ། །
བཤད་དང་སྒྲུབ་པའི་བསྟན་པ་སྐྱོང་འདི། །
ལེགས་པར་བསམས་ན་འདུན་མ་བཟང་འདུག །

ཨ་ལ་ལ་རྒྱལ་ཁམས་འཁྲིམ་པའི་བན་རྒན་ང་ནི། །
སྒྲུབ་པ་བྱས་ན་ཁ་ནི་སོས་འདུག །
གཅིག་པུར་བསྡད་ན་སེམས་ཉིད་བདེ་འདུག །
རྒས་པའི་སྐབས་འདིའི་དགའ་སྐྱིད་ཆེའོ། །

ཨ་ལ་ལ་རྒྱལ་ཁམས་འཁྲིམ་པའི་བན་རྒན་ང་ནི། །
བློ་རྒྱ་ཆེ་རུང་ཕལ་ཆེར་འགྲུབ་བོ། །
ད་ནི་ལུགས་གཉིས་བྱ་བ་མི་མང་། །
བླ་མའི་བཀའ་བཞིན་སྒྲུབ་ལ་འབད་དོ། །

A la la, as for me, an old monk who wanders around the country,
Now, during this Degenerate Age,
I have encountered the lama—the Buddha in person—
And am savoring the sublime raw-sugar taste of the holy Dharma.

A la la, as for me, an old monk who wanders around the country,
When I consider carefully
The way I have sustained the teachings of explanation and practice
Here in this borderland region of Amdo, my aims have been good.

A la la, as for me, an old monk who wanders around the country,
When I practice the Dharma, I can sustain myself.
When I stay alone, my mind itself is at ease.
At this time of old age, my joy and happiness are great.

A la la, as for me, an old monk who wanders around the country,
Although my plans were immense, they have generally been fulfilled.
As for now, my activities regarding the secular and religious traditions are few.
I am diligent in practicing according to the lama's instructions.

ཨ་ལ་ལ་རྒྱལ་ཁམས་འཁྱིམ་པའི་བན་རྒན་ང་ནི། །
འདོད་ཡོན་དངོས་པོ་ཚར་བཞིན་བབས་བྱུང་། །
ཟང་ཟིང་ནོར་ལ་ཞི་སྤྲར་མ་འཐམས། །
དགེ་བའི་ཕྱོགས་སུ་གང་འགྲོ་བྱས་སོ། །

ཨ་ལ་ལ་རྒྱལ་ཁམས་འཁྱིམ་པའི་བན་རྒན་ང་ནི། །
བླ་ཆེན་ཁུར་དེ་དུས་སྐབས་བབ་ཀྱང་། །
ཁུར་དེ་མ་བཟུང་བྱ་བཏང་ཚུགས་བཟུང་། །
རང་ཚུགས་འདི་ཡང་ཆོས་དང་མཐུན་བྱུང་། །

ཨ་ལ་ལ་རྒྱལ་ཁམས་འཁྱིམ་པའི་བན་རྒན་ང་ནི། །
ཀུན་དང་བསྟུན་ཀྱང་ཆོས་དང་མ་འགལ། །
ཆོས་དང་བསྟུན་ཀྱང་ཀུན་དང་མ་འགལ། །
ཀུན་མཐུན་ཆོས་མཐུན་གཉིས་པོ་བྱུང་ངོ། །

A la la, as for me, an old monk who wanders around the country,
Desirable objects and wealth have fallen upon me like rain,
But I have not been clutched in the death grip of material possessions
or riches.
For the sake of virtue, I have gone to any lengths.

A la la, as for me, an old monk who wanders around the country,
When the time once came for me to take on the responsibilities
of a great lama,
Although I neither fully accepted this burden, nor fully let it go,
Even this pretense I made of renouncing it was still in harmony
with the Dharma.

A la la, as for me, an old monk who wanders around the country,
Although I was in accord with everyone, that was not in conflict
with the Dharma.
And although I was in accord with the Dharma, that was not
in conflict with anyone.
Both harmony with everyone and harmony with the Dharma
came to be.

ཨ་ལ་ལ་རྒྱལ་ཁམས་འཁྲིམ་པའི་བན་རྒན་ང་ནི། །
དབུས་སུ་སློབ་གཉེར་གང་ནུས་བགྱིས་ནས། །
ཁམས་ཀྱི་ཕྱོགས་སུ་བསྟན་པ་སྤེལ་བས། །
ད་ལྟ་སྐྱེན་པའི་གྲགས་པ་འབར་རོ། །

ཨ་ལ་ལ་རྒྱལ་ཁམས་འཁྲིམ་པའི་བན་རྒན་ང་ནི། །
ད་ལྟ་རི་ཁྲོད་འཁྲིམ་པའི་འཕོར་མང་། །
དེ་ཀུན་ཁ་ལོ་ཆོས་ལ་སྒྱུར་དང་། །
ནམ་ཞིག་རང་དང་གཞན་ལ་ཕན་ནོ། །

ཨ་ལ་ལ་རྒྱལ་ཁམས་འཁྲིམ་པའི་བན་རྒན་ང་ནི། །
ད་ལྟ་གྲྭ་ཚང་འཁྲིམ་པའི་གྲྭ་ཚོགས། །
ཆོས་དང་ཟང་ཟིང་གཉིས་ཀས་སྐྱོངས་དང་། །
བསྟན་དང་འགྲོ་ལ་ཕན་མཁན་འབྱུང་ངོ། །

ཨ་ལ་ལ་རྒྱལ་ཁམས་འཁྲིམ་པའི་བན་རྒན་ང་ནི། །
དགེ་བའི་ལས་ལས་འབྲས་བུ་བདེ་འབྱུང་། །
གཞན་ལ་འཕྲུལ་ཕྱུགས་ཕན་ཐབས་བྱས་ན། །
རང་ཉིད་འཕྲུལ་ཕྱུགས་གཉིས་ཀར་བདེའོ། །

A la la, as for me, an old monk who wanders around the country,
Because I studied as much as I could in Ü,
And promoted the teaching in the region of Do Kham,
My "glorious" fame is now ablaze.

A la la, as for me, an old monk who wanders around the country,
Now my "entourage" which roams the mountain hermitages is large.
Steer the prow of their ship to the Dharma!
I will eventually benefit myself and others.

A la la, as for me, an old monk who wanders around the country,
Sustain the congregations of monks now journeying to the seminaries
With both the Dharma and material offerings!
Those who benefit the teaching and beings are emerging.

A la la, as for me, an old monk who wanders around the country,
The fruits of well-being arise from virtuous deeds.
When I look after the temporary and ultimate concerns of others,
I myself achieve both present and ultimate happiness.

ཨ་ལ་ལ་རྒྱལ་ཁམས་འགྲིམ་པའི་བན་རྒན་ང་ནི། །
ནོར་ཡང་མང་སྐྱེ་ཚོགས་སུ་བསྔོས་སོ། །
ཆོས་ཀྱང་ཤེས་ཏེ་མི་ལ་བཤད་དོ། །
ལོ་ཡང་ལོན་ཀྱང་བདེ་ཞིང་སྐྱིད་དོ། །

ཨ་ལ་ལ་རྒྱལ་ཁམས་འགྲིམ་པའི་བན་རྒན་ལགས་སོ། །

ཞེས་པ་འདི་ཡང་རོང་པོའི་བཀའ་བཅུ་བ་སྐལ་ལྡན་རྒྱ་མཚོ་རི་བོ་འཕན་འཛང་གསེར་ཁྲབ་ཅན་གྱི་ལྷ་མདུན་སྤང་ལྗོངས་ཉམས་དགའ་བ་ཞིག་ནས་བྲིས་པའོ། ། ། །

A la la, as for me, an old monk who wanders around the country,
I am very wealthy too. I have dedicated offerings to the *Saṅgha* community.
I understand the Dharma as well. I have explained it to people.
Although my years are passing, I am peaceful and happy.

A la la, I am indeed an old monk who wanders around the country.

This also was written by the Kachuwa of Rongbo, Kälden Gyatso, in a delightful meadow in front of the deity with a coat of gold mail, Ribo Phendzang.

དབྱིངས་ཀུན་ཁྱབ་ཆོས་སྐུའི་ནམ་མཁའ་ལ། །
བྱམས་བརྩེ་བའི་སྤྲིན་ཕུང་ཆེར་འཁྲིགས་ནས། །
གསུང་ལེགས་བཤད་ཆར་ཟིམ་འབེབས་མཁས་པ། །
པ་བསྟན་འཛིན་བློ་བཟང་ཞབས་ལ་འདུད། །

བདག་པ་ཡུལ་བཞག་ནས་རི་ལ་འོངས། །
རི་བག་ཕེབས་ཉམས་དགའི་རྩེ་མོ་ནས། །
ཆོས་ཁ་ཧོན་ཅི་ནུས་བགྱིས་པའི་ཚེ། །
སེམས་སྐྱིད་པའི་སྣང་བ་འདི་ལྟར་བྱུང་། །

བྱ་ཁྲ་བྱུག་རི་སྐེགས་འཛོལ་མོ་དང་། །
བྱི་འུ་འཛིན་མ་བྱ་ཤང་གོང་མོ་སོགས། །
སྐད་ཀུར་ཀུར་སྙན་པའི་སྒྲ་འབྱིན་པས། །
སེམས་རང་དབང་མེད་པར་སྐྱིད་དུ་བཅུག །

མདོག་རབ་མཛེས་མེ་ཏོག་ཚོགས་རྣམས་ལ། །
ཁང་དྲུག་ལྡན་སྦྲང་མའི་ཚོགས་འདུས་ནས། །
སྒྲ་དིར་དིར་ཟེར་ཞིང་གླུ་བླངས་པས། །
སེམས་རང་དབང་མེད་པར་སྐྱིད་དུ་བཅུག །

I bow at the feet of the father Tendzin Lobzang,
Who is skilled in gathering ever more rain clouds of loving kindness
In the sky of the all-pervading expanse of the *dharmakāya,*
And causing a fine rain of eloquent explanations to fall.

I left my homeland behind and came to the mountains.
When I was doing as much practicing and chanting as possible
On restful, delightful mountain peaks,
Feelings of happiness arose in my mind like this:

I became spontaneously happy
Because cuckoos, grouse, thrushes,
Crows, cranes, partridges, and other birds,
Were uttering pleasing sounds such as *kyur kyur*.

I became spontaneously happy
Because swarms of six-legged bees gathered
On clumps of flowers blazing with color,
And buzzed and sang.

ཤིང་ལྗོན་པའི་ཚོགས་རྣམས་གར་བསྒྱུར་ནས། །
རེས་མགོས་འདུད་ཤུབ་བུའི་སྤུགས་འདྲེན་ཞིང་། །
སྐབས་ཕལ་ཆེར་ཟེམ་མེར་འདུག་པ་དེས། །
སེམས་རང་དབང་མེད་པར་སྐྱིད་དུ་བཅུག །

སྤང་ལྗང་སེར་སྐྱེང་དུ་རི་དྭགས་ཚོགས། །
ཡིད་བག་ཕེབས་ལམ་ལམ་འགྲོ་བཞིན་དུ། །
བང་ཕན་ཚུན་རྩེ་རིགས་ཆེར་བྱེད་པས། །
སེམས་རང་དབང་མེད་པར་སྐྱིད་དུ་བཅུག །

ཚུ་རྒྱ་ཅང་མི་ཆེ་མི་ཆུང་བ། །
སྒྲ་མི་མཐོ་མི་དམའ་རན་ཙམ་དུ། །
ཐག་ཉེ་རིང་འཚམ་པར་འབབ་པ་དེས། །
སེམས་རང་དབང་མེད་པར་སྐྱིད་དུ་བཅུག །

བྲག་ཕྱི་དབྱིབས་རི་ལ་ནང་ཁང་པ། །
ཆར་ཁ་བ་བབས་ཚེ་ཆེར་སྲ་ཞིང་། །
དབྱར་ཉི་མས་གདུངས་ཚེ་བསིལ་སྐྱེར་བས། །
སེམས་རང་དབང་མེད་པར་སྐྱིད་དུ་བཅུག །

I became spontaneously happy
Because groves of trees were dancing back and forth,
At times bowing with their heads and drawing out whispered
    mantras,
And because most of the time it was quiet.

I became spontaneously happy
Because herds of deer were going about here and there,
Carefree on the light green meadows
Racing back and forth playing a medley of games.

I became spontaneously happy
Because the rivers were neither very large nor small,
And flowed at appropriate distances
With noises neither loud nor soft.

I became spontaneously happy
Because my home inside the rock mountain
Was completely sheltered from rain or snow,
And when the sun was oppressive in summer, it provided coolness.

དྲི་བཟང་པོ་འཐུལ་བའི་ཤུག་ཤུན་ལ། །
སྙན་སྔས་འབོལ་ལ་སོགས་ལེགས་བྱས་ནས། །
ས་སྲ་རླན་འཛིགས་ལས་བསྐྱབས་པ་དེས། །
སེམས་རང་དབང་མེད་པར་སྐྱིད་དུ་བཅུག །

ཀུན་ཕར་འགྲོ་ཚུར་འགྲོའི་གཡེང་བ་མེད། །
རི་མཐོ་ཞིང་ལ་ཡང་ཆེར་གཟར་བས། །
སྒྲ་འར་ཙུར་མེད་པའི་འགོལ་བ་དེས། །
སེམས་རང་དབང་མེད་པར་སྐྱིད་དུ་བཅུག །

ཛ་ཚྭ་མར་གཉིས་ཀྱི་སྦྱོར་ལྡན་པས། །
བཞིན་རབ་དཀར་འོ་མའི་དོན་ཆེད་དུ། །
ཉོར་མཛོ་འབྲིའི་སྐྱུ་གཡོག་མི་དགོས་པས། །
སེམས་རང་དབང་མེད་པར་སྐྱིད་དུ་བཅུག །

མི་གཞན་ལ་རེ་ལྟོས་མི་དགོས་པར། །
གཉེར་རང་གིས་བྱས་ནས་ནམ་འདོད་དུས། །
ཟས་བཙུང་བ་ཅི་བདེར་སྤྱོད་པ་དེས། །
སེམས་རང་དབང་མེད་པར་སྐྱིད་དུ་བཅུག །

ཅེས་པ་འདི་ཡང་སྐལ་ལྡན་གྱིས་ཇོང་ཉིན་བྲག་ཕུག་ནས་བྲིས་པའོ། ། ། །

I became spontaneously happy
Because I had no anxieties about sitting on the hard, wet ground,
Having made the floor of the cave comfortable
By arranging mats and cushions on top of sweet-smelling
juniper bark.

I became spontaneously happy
Because I wasn't distracted by anyone going back and forth—
The mountains were high and the passes very steep—
And because I was relaxed in the absence of clamor.

I became spontaneously happy
Because I already had both salt and butter for tea,
Which are like very white milk,
And did not need attendants for yaks.

I became spontaneously happy
Because food or drink were easily at hand,
Whenever I wanted them, and I could provide for myself
Without expecting anything from anyone else, or relying upon them.

Kälden wrote this at the cave of Dzongnyin.

རྗེ་བླ་མ་རྣམས་ལ་ཕྱག་འཚལ་ལོ། །
ལྷ་དཀོན་མཆོག་གསུམ་ལ་སྐྱབས་སུ་མཆི། །
མི་ང་དང་དབེན་པའི་དགའ་ཚལ་གཉིས། །
ལྷན་གཅིག་ཏུ་གནས་པར་བྱིན་གྱིས་རློབས། །

ཡུལ་རེ་བ་གོང་སྨུང་བའི་མ་ཐུ་རྩལ་ཙན། །
གཉན་ཆེན་པོ་སེ་ཀུ་བྲུ་ཁྲུང་གི །
གཡས་རྫ་རྒྱུད་དར་དཀར་འཕྱུར་འདྲའི་འདབས། །
ས་བཀྲ་ཤིས་གཡང་ཆགས་སྤུང་ལུག་བྲག །
ཡར་སྟེང་ན་ནམ་མཁའ་བླ་རེ་བྲེས། །

ལོགས་ཐམས་ཅད་སྤང་དང་ཤུག་པས་བརྒྱན། །
མདུན་བྲག་རི་རིན་ཆེན་སྤུངས་འདྲས་སྤྲས། །
ངོགས་ཀུན་ནས་རྫ་ཆབ་བསིལ་མ་འབབ། །
རྒྱབ་སྤང་རིའི་རྩེ་མོ་མཁའ་ལ་རེག །
ཕྱོགས་ཐམས་ཅད་རི་ཕྲན་རྣམས་ཀྱིས་བསྐོར། །
མདའ་ཆུ་བྲག་འཐབ་པས་སྒྲོ་སྨུང་བྱེད། །
དབྱིབས་ལྷ་ཡི་ཛ་ཆེན་ལྷ་བུར་རྨུས། །

I prostrate myself before lord lamas.
I take refuge in the three divine Precious Jewels.
Please bless me, that both I, a human,
And this solitary delightful grove may simultaneously exist.

Above the auspicious cave of prosperity at Pangluk
On the foothills of the clay range whose sides are like hoisted
    white flags
To the left of the great mountain deity, Seku Jakyung,
Which possesses the power to protect the area of Rebgong,
The slender canopy of sky is stretched out.

All sides of my hermitage have been decorated with meadows
    and juniper trees.
In front of it, rocks like heaps of jewels adorn a rock mountain.
From all the slopes, cool spring water cascades.
Behind it, peaks of grass-covered mountains touch the sky.
And in all directions, it is surrounded by small mountains.
Since waters in the lower parts of the valleys do battle with rocks,
They guard the entrances to my dwelling place.
Shapes wind together like a big divine drum.

བྱ་གོང་མོས་དབྱངས་སྙན་ཀུར་ཀུར་ལེན། །
བྱི་ཨུ་འཛོལ་མོས་སྐད་རིགས་སྣ་ཚོགས་སྒྱུར། །
ཀང་དྲུག་ལྡན་བུང་བས་དིར་དིར་ཟེར། །
ལུས་རབ་མཛེས་རི་དྭགས་བག་ཡེབས་རྒྱུ། །
ཤིང་སྣ་ཚོགས་ལྡེམ་ལྡེམ་གར་གྱིས་རོལ། །
ཟྭ་སྔོག་སོགས་ཚོད་མས་ཁོར་ཡུག་གང་། །
གཞི་ནེ་ཨུ་གསིང་མེ་ཏོག་ཚོགས་ཀྱིས་བརྒྱན། །

ཁ་ལྗོར་ལྷ་དགུན་དུས་ཉི་འོད་འཁྱིལ། །
དབྱར་སོས་དུས་བསིལ་ཞིང་རིག་པ་དྭངས། །
དུས་ཀུན་ཏུ་སྤྲོ་ཞིང་བག་ཡེབས་སྐྱིད། །
གྲོང་ཐག་རིང་འར་ཨུར་མེད་ཅིང་འགོལ། །

གནས་དེ་ལྟར་ངོ་མཚར་ལྡན་པ་ན། །
མདོག་རབ་མཛེས་རང་བྱུང་བྲག་ཕུག་ཡོད། །

ཕུག་དེ་ན་སྐལ་ལྡན་རས་པ་ང་། །
ལུས་ཧུར་སྒྲིག་གོས་ཀྱིས་གཡོགས་པས་བདེ། །
ངག་གླུ་དབྱངས་ལྷང་ལྷང་བླངས་པས་བདེ། །
སེམས་སྡུག་བསྔལ་མེད་པར་གནས་པས་བདེ།

Grouse murmur *kyur kyur* pleasantly.
Small thrushes trade a medley of calls back and forth.
Six-legged bees say "buzz buzz."
Beautiful hoofed animals roam carefree.
Trees enchant with supple dances.
The surroundings are full of herbs, such as nettles and garlic.
The splendid pastures are dotted with bouquets of flowers.

Since my dwelling faces south, in winter sunbeams converge on it.
In the summer, it is cool, and my cognition is clear.
At all times, I am joyful and relaxed.
There is no clamor of distant towns, and my life is easy with no distractions.

In such a wondrous place,
There is a colorful rock cave, naturally formed.

In that cave, because I, Kälden Repa,
Have covered my body with a saffron robe, I am happy.
Because I have sung a sonorous song, I am happy.
Because I have lived without mental suffering, I am happy.

ཉིན་ཆོས་སྤྱོད་ཅི་ནུས་བགྱིས་པས་བདེ། །
མཚན་གློ་ཕབ་བདེ་བར་ཉལ་བས་བདེ། །
དཔོན་དབང་ཆེས་གཉའ་གནོན་མེད་པས་བདེ། །
འཁོར་ཉེ་འབྲེལ་སྐྱོང་དགོས་མེད་པས་བདེ། །
གྲོགས་བྲ་ཙིག་གཉིས་ལ་བྲུས་པས་བདེ། །
དཔེ་རྣམ་ཐར་མང་དུ་བལྟས་པས་བདེ། །
དུས་རེས་འགའ་རི་རྩེར་འཁྱམས་པས་བདེ། །
སྐབས་ཕལ་ཆེར་མལ་སར་བསྡད་པས་བདེ། །
འཕྲལ་ཁ་ཊོམ་གྲོད་པ་འགྲངས་པས་བདེ། །
ཕུགས་བློ་རྩེ་ཆོས་ལ་གཏད་པས་བདེ། །
སྒོམ་དམ་ཚིག་ཅི་ནུས་བསྲུངས་པས་བདེ། །
ཆོས་ཕུན་དྲུག་རྣལ་འབྱོར་བསླུགས་པས་བདེ། །
སྤྲིན་ཤ་ཁྲེར་ཁྲག་ཁྲེར་བྲུས་པས་བདེ། །

གླུ་བདེ་བ་བཅུ་དྲུག་འདི་བླངས་པས། །
སྤྱིར་ཁམས་གསུམ་སེམས་ཅན་བདེ་བ་དང་། །
སྒོས་ཆོས་མཛད་སྐྱེས་བུ་ཀུན་བདེར་ཤོག

ཅེས་པ་རྫོང་བོའི་སྐལ་ལྡན་རས་པས་སྒྱུར་བའོ། ། ། །

Because by day I have performed whatever Dharma practices I could,
I am happy.
Because at night I have lain down comfortably on my side, I am happy.
Because I've not been put into the stocks by a powerful lord, I am happy.
Because I have no need to care for people around me or kinsmen,
I am happy.
Because I have made friends with both pikas and mice, I am happy.
Because I have read many stories of spiritual realization, I am happy.
Because I have occasionally wandered on mountain peaks, I am happy.
Because I have stayed for the most part near my dwelling place,
I am happy.
Because I have been free from hunger and thirst for a while, I am happy.
Because I have focused with my innermost mind on the Dharma,
I am happy.
Because I have preserved my vows and commitments as much as
possible, I am happy.
Because I have read the *Chö Tündrug Näljor*, I am happy.
Because I have made gifts to others, holding back neither flesh
nor blood, I am happy.

By means of my having sung this song of the sixteen happinesses,
May sentient beings of the three realms,
And in particular all humans who practice the Dharma, be happy.

Kälden Repa of Rongbo composed this.

ཨོཾ་སྭ་སྟི། །

བདེ་མཆོག་གི་ངོ་བོ་བླ་མ་དང་། །
བདེ་ཆེན་གྱི་དཔལ་སྟེར་ཧེ་རུ་ཀ །
བདེ་ལྡན་གྱི་གནས་ནས་རྟག་ཏུ་གཟིགས། །
བདེ་ཉམས་ཀྱི་གླུ་དབྱངས་འདི་ལྟར་འཐེན། །

བདེ་ལེགས་ཀྱི་རྩ་བ་བླ་མ་ལ། །
བདེ་བླག་ཏུ་གསོལ་བ་འདེབས་པ་འདི། །
བདེ་སྐྱིད་ཀྱི་ཉི་མ་འཆར་ཐབས་སུ། །
བདེ་གཤེགས་ཀུན་མཐུན་པར་ཡང་ཡང་གསུངས། །

བདེ་སྟེར་གྱི་ཐབས་མཆོག་དམ་པའི་ཆོས། །
བདེ་ལེགས་ཀྱི་ལམ་རྟེན་དལ་འབྱོར་ལུས། །
བདེ་མེད་ཀྱི་འཁོར་བར་རྙེད་དཀའ་བས། །
བདེ་སྡུག་ལ་མ་ལྟ་སྙིང་པོ་ལོངས། །

Oṃ swa sti!

The lama, essence of Cakrasaṃvara
And Heruka, who bestow the splendor of great bliss—
Please look upon me always from Sukhāvatī.
I'm going to sing a song about blissful experiences.

This easy-going petition to the lama, source of well-being,
Has been made over and over
In accordance with the realizations of all who have entered
into eternal bliss,
As a means for the sun of happiness to shine.

It is difficult to obtain a free and well-favored human birth,
a good foundation—
The path for the holy Dharma, the path of well-being,
And the most supreme means for giving happiness
To all beings in samsara, where there is no real happiness.
So without regard for your own happiness and suffering,
take advantage of it.

བདེ་བ་ནས་བདེ་བར་འགྲོ་བསམ་ན། །

བདེ་མཆོག་སོགས་ཡི་དམ་བསྙེན་སྒྲུབ་དང་། །

བདེ་སྡུག་སོགས་ཆོས་བརྒྱད་མགོ་སྙོམས་དང་། །

བདེ་བ་ལ་འགྲོ་ཀུན་འགོད་འདོད་སོགས། །

བདེ་ལྷག་ཏུ་བསྒྲུབས་ན་ཅིས་ཀྱང་ལེགས། །

ཞེས་པ་འདི་ཡང་སྐལ་ལྡན་རྒྱ་མཚོས་མེ་ཕག་གི་ལོར་སྦྱར་བ་བཀྲ་ཤིས། ། །།

If you are concerned with going from one happy state to another,
Recite mantras and propitiate *yidams* such as Cakrasaṃvara,
And equalize the distinctions of the eight worldly concerns—
Happiness and suffering, and so forth.

But if you have become spontaneously happy
By desiring to transfer all beings into a happy state, and so on,
By all means your happiness is good.

Kälden Gyatso composed this in the year 1647. Happiness!

Appendices

AIB	Harvey, Peter. *An Introduction to Buddhism: Teachings, History and Practices*. 2d ed. Cambridge, UK: Cambridge University Press, 2013.
B	Mitchell, Donald W., and Sarah H. Jacoby. *Buddhism: Introducing the Buddhist Experience*. 3d ed. Oxford: Oxford University Press, 2014.
BT	Tsepak Rigzin. *Tibetan-English Dictionary of Buddhist Terminology*. 2d ed., rev. and enl. Dharamsala, India: Library of Tibetan Works and Archives, 1993.
CL	Chris Leahy of the Massachusetts Audubon Society, interviews by author, e-mails, winter, 2006–2007; and fall, 2016.
DD	Dge 'dun Don grub, scholar in Rong bo Dgon chen, Reb gong, A mdo, interviews by author, notes, summers, 2015, 2016.
DL	Dan Lusthaus, Research Associate at Harvard University, interviews by author, notes, fall, 2016; and e-mails, winter, 2017.
EB	Buswell, Robert E., Jr., ed. *Encyclopedia of Buddhism*. 2 vols. New York: Macmillan Reference USA, 2004.
Geshe TC	Geshe Tsultrim Chopel of the Kurukulla Center in Malden, MA, interviews by author, notes, spring, 2008.
GK	Tenzin Gyatso, H. H. the Dalai Lama & Alexander Berzin. *The Gelug/ Kagyü Tradition of Mahāmudrā*. Ithaca, N.Y.: Snow Lion Publications, 1997.

IB	Prebish, Charles S., and Damien Keown. *Introducing Buddhism*. 2d ed. Abingdon, UK: Routledge, 2010.
IW	Waldo, Ives. Entries in *The Rangjung Yeshe Gilded Palace of Dharmic Activity*. http://rywiki.tsadra.org.
JV	Valby, Jim. Entries in *The Rangjung Yeshe Gilded Palace of Dharmic Activity*. http://rywiki.tsadra.org.
LC	Lobzang Chödrag, scholar in Rong bo Dgon chen, Reb gong, A mdo, interviews by author, notes, summers, 2006, 2015, 2016.
Ngag dbang, *Skal ldan gyi rnam thar*	Byang chub mi la Ngag dbang bsod nams. *Grub chen skal ldan rgya mtsho'i rnam thar yid bzhin dbang gi rgyal po*. Xining: Mtsho sngon mi rigs dpe skrun khang, 1990.
PDB	Buswell, Robert E., Jr., and Donald S. Lopez, Jr. *The Princeton Dictionary of Buddhism*. Princeton: Princeton University Press, 2014.
RJ	Jackson, Roger R. "The *dGe ldan-bKa' brgyud* Tradition of *Mahāmudrā*: How Much *dGe ldan*? How Much *bKa' brgyud*?" In *Changing Minds: Contributions to the Study of Buddhism and Tibet in Honor of Jeffrey Hopkins*, edited by Guy Newland. Ithaca, New York: Snow Lion Publications, 2001; interviews by author, e-mails, fall, 2016.
RY	Rangjung Yeshe. Entries in *The Rangjung Yeshe Gilded Palace of Dharmic Activity*. http://rywiki.tsadra.org.

S of SH	Sujata, V. *Songs of Shabkar: The Path of a Tibetan Yogi Inspired by Nature.* Cazadero, Calif.: Dharma Publishing, 2011.
SH	Zhabs dkar Tshogs drug rang grol, 1781–1851. *The Life of Shabkar: The Autobiography of a Tibetan Yogin.* Translated by Matthieu Ricard, et al. Albany: State University of New York Press, 1994.
Skal ldan, *Gsung 'bum* (1987)	Skal ldan rgya mtsho. *Gsung 'bum*. Carved at Rong bo monastery, Reb gong, Amdo in the *me yos* year, 1987.
Skal ldan, *Gsung 'bum* (1999)	Skal ldan rgya mtsho. *Yab rje bla ma skal ldan rgya mtsho'i gsung 'bum*. 4 vols. Xining: Kan su'u mi rigs dpe skrun khang, 1999.
Skal ldan, *Mgur 'bum* (1994)	Skal ldan rgya mtsho. *Shar skal ldan rgya mtsho'i mgur 'bum.* Xining: Mtsho sngon mi rigs dpe skrun khang, 1994.
TBRC	Buddhist Digital Resource Center (formerly Tibetan Buddhist Resource Center). http://www.tbrc.org.
TG	Tenzin Gyatso, the Fourteenth Dalai Lama. *A Flash of Lightning in the Dark of Night: A Guide to the Bodhisattva's Way of life*. Boston & London: Shambhala, 1994.
TSR	Sujata, Victoria. *Tibetan Songs of Realization: Echoes from a Seventeenth-Century Scholar and Siddha in Amdo.* Leiden: Brill, 2005.

TTC — *Bod rgya tshig mdzod chen mo.* Beijing: Mi rigs dpe skrun khang, 1993.

VDK — Leonard W.J. van der Kuijp, Professor of Tibetan and Himalayan Studies, Harvard University

ZH — Zhabs dkar Tshogs drug rang grol. *Rje zhabs dkar tshogs drug rang grol gyi gsung 'bum.* Vol. 1. Xining: Mtsho sngon mi rigs dpe skrun khang, 2002. (This is the biography of Shabkar. Please see my bibliography for its full title.)

Languages

T	Tibetan
S	Sanskrit
C	Chinese

While I have paraphrased definitions from my sources, or chosen certain terms from their lists, any errors are my own.

Notes

Preface

x **gur** (T: mgur) is a song of spiritual realization or experience. For a brief description of the development of gur up through the middle of the seventeenth century, as well as an explanation of how it was a means of expression for Kälden Gyatso, see *TSR*, 77–93.

Chapter 1. Homages to My Lamas

5 **[You who are] skilled in causing a soft rain**
of eloquent explanations to fall...

Rain is frequently used as a metaphor or simile in gur from Amdo, where water is scarce. In the positive sense, rain is equated with desirable things that one's lama grants in abundance, such as spiritual powers, teachings, and blessings. For the metaphor of rain, see *TSR*, 206, 207–208, 213.

Precious lord, lama who possesses the three [kindnesses],
[I] am calling out to you from afar, crying fiercely
[for your help]

rje gsum ldan bla ma rin po che/ /
khyod 'o dod drag pos rgyang nas 'bod/ /

I have interpreted the unexpressed object of "lama, possessed of the three," to be kindnesses. There are two sets of **three kindnesses**, and the reference refers ambiguously to either (LC). Within the context of the sutras (T: mdo phyogs), they are giving precepts (sdom pa), reading authorizations (lung), and teachings of the sutra tradition (khrid). Within the context of the tantras (T: sngags phyogs) they are conferring initiations or empowerments (dbang bskur), explaining the tantras, and giving concise instructions of the tantric tradition (man ngag gnang ba).

All the Victorious Ones and [their] sons, the bodhisattvas,
Who dwell in the realms of the ten directions,
Have taken your form, my spiritual guide,
Causing a rain of sutras and tantras—whatever I,
[your] subject, have desired—to fall

zhing phyogs bcur bzhugs pa'i rgyal ba dang/ /
sras byang chub sems dpa' mtha' dag gis/ /
'bangs bdag bshes khyod kyi tshul bzung nas/ /
rang gang 'dod mdo sngags chos char phab/ /

I thank LC for pointing out to me that bdag bshes is short for bdag gi dge ba'i bshes gnyen (T), my spiritual friend, teacher, guide.

ten directions (T: phyogs bcu) are north, south, east, west, southeast, southwest, northeast, northwest, up, and down. This basically means everywhere.

7 **At this time when the sun, the lord Buddha along with [his spiritual] sons,**

Has passed beyond the western mountain of another realm…

Western mountain does not specify the direction of their realms. It is merely in the direction of the setting sun. This passage refers to the **Degenerate Age** (T: snyigs dus). *See* Degenerate Age in the glossary.

Metaphors that involve the **sun** usually have to do with the Buddha, his teachings, the wisdom of one's lama, or his compassion. The sun can also refer to the nature of mind, or to happiness. For a discussion of the metaphor **sun rising**, see *TSR*, 206, 211–213.

[You], lord, who possess the three [kindnesses],
Are [in essence] inseparable from Vajradhara…

rje gsum ldan dbyer med rdo rje 'dzin/ / …

rje gsum ldan (T) = the lord who confers initiations or empowerments, explains the tantras, and gives oral instructions (LC). These are the three tantric kindnesses, explained above. *See* Vajradhara in the glossary.

11 **Such as jumping into a fiery pit, being pierced by one thousand iron nails…**

These are references to a series of five Jātakas, or rebirth tales, that deities tell the Buddha Śākyamuni in order to dissuade him from thinking that it is hopeless to try to help others, and that he should just enter final Nirvana without giving teachings. The deities tell the Buddha that in former lives, he allowed his body to be pierced by one thousand nails, burnt his body in a pit of fire, and so on, in order each time to receive just one stanza of the Dharma. After hearing the stories, the Buddha goes on to Deer Park, and gives his first teaching. For the karmic lessons that the stories entail, the respective stanzas that the Buddha is granted, his spontaneous healing after each mutilation, and so on, see Stanley Frye, trans., *The Sutra of the Wise and Foolish (Mdo dbzangs blun), or, The Ocean of Narratives (Üliger-ün dalai)* (Dharamsala, Distt. Kangra, H.P., India: Library of Tibetan Works & Archives, 1981), 1–12. I thank Jann Ronis for pointing out this source to me.

13 **Gendun Sherab** (T: Dge 'dun Shes rab), who requested this gur, does not seem to have played a frequent role in Kälden Gyatso's life. He is not mentioned anywhere else in this collection of gur, in any other colophon in Kälden Gyatso's *Collected Writings* (T: Gsung 'bum), in the main biography of Kälden Gyatso by Byang chub mi la Ngag dbang bsod nams, or in the main history of Rongbo Monastery by 'Jigs med theg mchog.

17 **Oh father, the one who holds the teachings, ocean**
[of] intelligence,
Whose kindness is so hard to repay,
Omniscient one in the great community of glorious Gönlung...

dpal dgon lung chos kyi sde chen na//
drin 'khor bar dka' ba'i thams cad mkhyen//
pha bstan 'dzin blo bzang rgya mtsho ba// ...

Kälden Gyatso refers to a revered teacher of his, Tendzin Lobzang Gyatso (1593–1638; T: Sde pa Chos kyi rje Bstan 'dzin blo bzang rgya mtsho) with a 'ba' (T) after his name, signifying that the words in the name should be understood individually rather than collectively as a name. Translating the words in his name renders the phrase as follows: the one who holds the teachings (T: bstan 'dzin), ocean (rgya mtsho) [of] intelligence or comprehension (blo bzang).

Depa Chökyije Tendzin Lobzang Gyatso (1593–1638; T: Sde pa Chos kyi rje Bstan 'dzin blo bzang rgya mtsho) was one of Kälden Gyatso's lamas in Amdo. Kälden Gyatso received many teachings from him, and wrote his biography, which is in Kälden Gyatso's *Collected Writings*. For this, see Skal ldan rgya mtsho, *Rje btsun thams cad mkhyen pa bstan 'dzin blo bzang rgya mtsho dpal bzang po'i zhal snga nas kyi rnam par thar pa dad pa'i sgo 'byed* in Skal ldan, *Gsung 'bum* (1987), vol. Ka-6; and Skal ldan, *Gsung 'bum* (1999), vol. 1, 180–255. He is sometimes referred to by his title, **Depa Chökyije.**

Gönlung Jampaling (T: Dgon lung byams pa gling) is considered one of the four great monasteries in the north of Amdo, along with Sku 'bum dgon pa (T), Gser kog dgon, and Bya khyung dgon (TBRC). For Gönlung, see maps 1 and 2.

the fifteenth day of the first month…

The Tibetan calendar is lunar, and the full moon falls on the fifteenth day of any month. The number of months can vary from year to year. The designation of a year involves two main components. The first is one of five elements: fire, earth, iron, water, and wood (T: me, sa, lcags, chu, shing). The second is one of twelve animals: elephant, tiger, rabbit, dragon, snake, horse, sheep, monkey, bird, dog, pig, and mouse (glang, stag, yos, 'brug, sbrul, rta, lug, sprel, bya, khyi, phag, byi). Combining the two lists, there are sixty possibilities, which correspond to the names of the respective years in the sixty-year cycle upon which the Tibetan calendar is based.

21 **Noble Nāgārjuna and disciples,**
The unrivalled Lobzang Dragpa,
And Lobzang Chökyi Gyältsen—
I beseech you with [all my] heart

Kälden Gyatso supplicates some of the most important philosophers and teachers of his lineage. It was Lobzang Chökyi Gyältsen who gave Kälden Gyatso full ordination. *See* Lobzang Chökyi Gyältsen (the first or fourth Panchen Lama), Nāgārjuna, Tsongkhapa (for Lobzang Dragpa) in the glossary.

Although the [eagle] of my nonconceptual mind
Longs to fly to the *dharmadhātu*...

rang sems spros med kyi rgod po/ /
chos dbyings su 'phur snying 'dod kyang/ / ...

I would like to be able to translate rgod (T) literally as **vulture**. However, in this case, I have followed M. Ricard's example in translating rgod as **eagle** rather than vulture, because of the negative connotation of the vulture in the West.

The term '**dharmadhātu**' here is being used in the sense of ultimate reality, the reality of the true nature of phenomena—lack of any inherent existence. By depending on the dharmadhātu, Kälden Gyatso wishes to "fly" to the state of enlightenment (Geshe TC). *See also* dharmadhātu in the glossary.

I thank Dharma Publishing for contractual permission to reuse any notes in my book, *Songs of Shabkar: The Path of a Tibetan Yogi Inspired by Nature* (2011).
For more about translating vulture (T: rgod) as eagle, please see *S of SH*, 290.

23 **the six levels of sentient beings—[my] fathers and mothers...**

All sentient beings are believed to have been one's **mothers in former lives**. Hence one should have compassion for all beings and a desire for their enlightenment, just as one would for one's biological mother. *See also* sentient beings of the six realms in the glossary.

But because [I] hope for [both] compensation and ripening,
[I] have been bound by my desires to the lower path

By lower path, Kälden Gyatso is referring to the path of the śrāvaka practitioners, within Hīnayāna. He is criticizing himself for seeking the śrāvaka's enlightenment, which he associates with self-serving motivations. *See* Hīnayāna, śrāvaka in the glossary.

For more about this song within the context of Kälden Gyatso's religious aims, see *TSR*, 73–74, and the entire chapter on the Ganden (T: Dga' ldan) tradition of Mahāmudrā in general, pp. 60–74. The translation I provide here has been updated.

25 **[Please lift] the *bindu*, the light of my mind,**
With [your] sharp, iron hook of compassion...

rang sems 'od kyi ni thig le/ /
thugs rje'i lcags kyu ni rnon pos/ / ...

For more, see bindu in the glossary.

27 **Sharp iron hook of compassion,**
Please hook onto and lift [me—this vase—]by [its] handle, [my] faith.
May I become inseparable from you, lama

thugs rje'i lcags kyu ni rnon po/ /
dad pa'i mgul long la thob cig /
bla ma khyed dang dbyer med du gyur cig /

I thank LC for having helped me with this difficult passage. Mgul long (T) is the correct spelling, but the meaning in the dictionaries is not helpful.
mgul = ske (T), throat (i.e. the throat of a vase); long = a long (T), a round handle; thob (T) = to hook onto and lift (here)
His vision is for Lobzang Chökyi Gyältsen to use his hook of compassion to hook onto the round handle at the throat of a vase and lift it up. The vase (with handle) is a metaphor for Kälden Gyatso, his disciple. The handle is a metaphor for Kälden Gyatso's faith (LC).

I am grateful to Brill, the publisher of *Tibetan Songs of Realization*, for contractual permission to reuse the songs in Appendix A of *TSR*. I present four texts from the Brill publication here because they have something significant to add to their respective chapters. The translations of those four texts appear here in updated versions. My objective in the 2005 translations was to make them very literal. Now I wish to make them a bit looser—while at the same time getting still closer to the intent of the songwriters. For my earlier translation of this song, see *TSR*, 364–69.

31 ....
...............is/ was your kindness.
Thank you, precious lamas.
Still now, [my] joy and sorrow are in your hands

....
.... khyod kyi drin/ /
bka' drin che'o bla ma rin po che/ /
da dung bdag gi skyid sdug khyed rang mkhyen/ /

This gur consists of quatrains, and, except for the first and last stanzas, there is stanza external repetition throughout. The lines quoted above are repeated in each stanza throughout the body of the song.

The last line khyed rang mkhyen would be more literally translated, "You know / understand / perceive [my] joy and sorrow." This phrase is sometimes also translated as '… is / am / are in the lama's hands'. This makes reference to the belief that one's lama in tantric Buddhism is one's main place of refuge, since he is the essence of the Buddha, teachings, community, and deities. *See also* refuge in the glossary.

Although due to the power of karma [I] was born
in the borderlands,
[I] came across the Buddha's teachings [anyway—this]
was your kindness

One of the ten favorable conditions for having a so-called free and well-favored human birth is to be born in a place where the Dharma flourishes. Here Kälden Gyatso expresses doubt that he would have come across the Dharma around his birth place in the borderlands of Amdo, had it not been for his lama's kindness. For more, see free and well-favored human birth in the glossary.

Here Kälden Gyatso's household is being compared to a **fiery pit**. Elsewhere in his songs, fiery pit is used as a simile for the dangers of samsara, since they need to be watched like a fiery pit. *See TSR*, 199.

33 **Respectfully touching the feet of whatever fine lamas**
[to my head],
[I] receive whatever [I] desire of the holy Dharma—[this]
is your kindness

There is a custom of a disciple touching the feet of his lama to his head with faith and good thoughts.

[I] have met many manifestations of Buddhas whose mere names if heard
[Could] protect [one] from all dangers—[this] is your kindness

mtshan tsam thos pas 'jigs pa kun skyob pa'i/ /
sangs rgyas sprul sku mang mjal khyod kyi drin/ /

He met many high lamas who are emanations of Buddha and bodhisattvas (LC).

35 **Although [I] did not fasten a protective mandala around [my] neck,**
[My] body and mind were not harmed by demons—[this] was your kindness

mgul du srung ba'i 'khor lo ma btags kyang/ /
lus sems gdon gyis ma gtses khyod kyi drin/ /

A **protective mandala** / protection circle around one's neck (T: mgul du srung ba'i 'khor lo) is made of cloth, is various sizes, has a mandala (S: maṇḍala) on it, is folded up, and is put on a thread for the neck (LC). *See* mandala in the glossary.

demon, evil / harmful spirit (T: gdon) is a type of demon, negative force, or evil spirit who causes madness (IW, RY), disease, possession (JV), and so forth.

Although death has devoured [the lives of] many youths…
'chi bas rang las gzhon pa mang zos kyang/ / …

Here food is a metaphor for life-force, the one who eats or devours the food is a metaphor for the Lord of Death (T: 'chi bdag), and the devouring of the food by the Lord of Death is a metaphor for death (LC). For more, see Lord of Death in the glossary.

37 **Although it is difficult to be in accord with the Dharma because of the [negative] power of the times...**

This is a reference to a time of decline, the Degenerate Age. *See* Degenerate Age in the glossary.

Although transgressions are falling continually like rain...

Here rain is used as another metaphor, this time in a negative sense.

41 **Although it is difficult to pursue antidotes for taming [my] mindstream,**
[I] make a pretense of striving toward the Dharma—[this] is your kindness

zhe rgyud 'dul ba'i gnyen por 'gro dka' yang/ /
chos la 'bad lo byed 'di khyod kyi drin/ /

'bad lo (T) is like 'bad khul (T), pretense at striving. Kälden Gyatso attributes that he is striving even just a little bit to his lama's kindness (LC).

zhe rgyud (T) = sems kyi rgyun, sems rgyud (LC)

Not giving my nose rope to others,
I continually grasp it myself—[this] is your kindness

This is a reference to a ring being put through the nostrils of a member of the yak family and then a rope tied to the ring, in order to control it better when one is leading it or riding it.

This couplet in my chapter on renunciation has a similar theme:

Kinsmen and relatives are a leading rope which entangles me.
When I practice the Dharma, I must show them the nape of my neck

Please bless [me], that my mind may proceed towards the Dharma.
Please bless [me], that [I] may progress along the path of the holy Dharma.
Please bless [me], that [I] may have no obstructions to the Dharma.
Please bless [me], that [I] may be like you, lamas

bdag blo chos su 'gro bar byin gyis rlobs/ /
dam chos lam du 'gro bar byin gyis rlobs/ /
chos la bar chad med par byin gyis rlobs/ /
bla ma khyed rang lta bur byin gyis rlobs/ /

As opposed to the stanza external repetition of the quatrains I discussed above, here in the last stanza of the gur there is stanza internal repetition. In Tibetan, the same three syllables are repeated at the end of each of the four lines. In English, the repetition of the three words works better at the beginning of each line.

Chapter 2. Dreadful Defects

45 **[I] bow at the feet of my father, Tendzin Lobzang…**

This is a reference to Kälden Gyatso's lama, Depa Chökyije Tendzin Lobzang Gyatso, identified above.

[It] has been said that...

It is insinuated that the Buddha said these three things.

47 **[Scores of] ferocious birds such as eagles and hawks...**
glag khra sogs bya tshogs ma rungs dang/ / ...

Eagles and hawks typically hunt alone and do not group together in flocks (CL). Hence, it would be problematic to translate bya tshogs (T) literally as 'flocks' of birds, and instead I have interpreted it as 'scores' of birds. Eagles and hawks fit the context of the passage well because they have a bad reputation in Tibet for killing live prey, as opposed to vultures, who only eat dead animals.

Mongols who engage in evil...
sdig spyod pa'i hor sog...

At Kälden Gyatso's time various tribes of Mongols (T: Hor sog) supported different sides of a civil war that had been going on for several centuries. Hence, Kälden Gyatso's relationship with Mongols was multifaceted, since he regarded some Mongol tribes as evil, and others as helpful. Here he expresses the danger of being born among evil Mongols, but on the other hand he was the personal lama of both the Tümed Mongol governor Qoloci (T: 'Kho lo che) and another great Mongol governor, the Junang (T), who patronized his school. For more about Qoloci and the Junang, including conjectures about whether Qoloci was the famed Tümed governor by that name or someone in his line, see *TSR*, 374, nn. 31, 32. For more about the Tümed Mongol governor Qoloci, see Ngag dbang, *Skal ldan gyi rnam thar*, 35. For more about the Junang, see Ngag dbang, *Skal ldan gyi rnam thar*, 46, 55, 56, 58, 60, 61, 65, 82, 104.

49 **[And if you] are born as a god, [you] will fight with demigods,**
And [if you] are born in the realms of demigods, [you] will fight with gods

This describes the battle between two types of gods—the gods proper (S: deva) and the jealous demigods (S: asura). The gods do not mind demigods, but since demigods want to fight with gods, the gods fight back (LC). For more, see sentient beings of the six realms, demigods, gods in the glossary.

For another song about **anger** and its destructive qualities, this time by Shabkar (1781–1851; T: Zhabs dkar Tshogs drug rang grol), see *SH*, 301; *ZH*, 606–607.

53 **Desire's actions are growing cruder.**
[Contemplations of] the repulsive, which swamp did you fall into?

'dod chags kho sku spyod je rtsing red/ /
mi sdug khyod gang gi 'dam du 'gyel/ /

Contemplation of the repulsive (T: mi sdug pa bsgom pa) is a technique for helping one renounce concerns for this world.

Anger's brute force is always increasing.
Loving kindness, where have you fled?

zhe sdang kho sku brjid je che red/ /
byams pa khyod sa cha gang du bros/ /

LC points out a meaning of brjid that does not appear in some main dictionaries:
sku brjid (T) = lus stobs, stobs shugs (LC), physical strength / power / force. Here physical strength or brute force is a metaphor for anger.

55 **Funeral repasts are more and more delicious to the mouth.
Spiritual practice, you are on the verge of dwindling
into emptiness**

'dad zas kho kha la je zhim red/ /
dge sbyor khyod stong yal 'gro la khad/ /

Kälden Gyatso frequently criticizes monks who enjoy eating **funeral repasts** (T: 'dad zas) in his *Collected Songs*.

**Spiritual practice, you are on the verge of dwindling
into emptiness**

In this clever line that reveals Kälden Gyatso's humor, he playfully distorts the meaning of emptiness. But emptiness is actually considered to be compatible with the way one sees the world. This compatibility is spelled out in the following lines in my chapter on emptiness and Mahāmudrā:

**Nevertheless, the view of emptiness
In terms of everyday appearances is free of contradictions—
So-called emptiness is not elsewhere,
[And] the view of [it] is not like [some] vision of the sky
One [mistakenly] hopes to have by looking at [one's] hand**

See also emptiness in the glossary.

Kälden Gyatso was born in **Rongbo** (= T; C = Tongren), within **Rebgong** (= T), an area in eastern Amdo where many if not all of Kälden Gyatso's main hermitages are located. Rebgong's boundaries have changed over time. **Rongbo Monastery** is a large monastery in Rongbo. For Rebgong and Rongbo, see maps 1 and 2.

Once again I am grateful to Brill, the publisher of *Tibetan Songs of Realization*, for contractual permission to republish the songs in my appendix. My translation here is the second of four updates of translations I made some fifteen years ago. For my earlier translation of this song, see *TSR*, 326–29.

57 **Phu Seku** (= T) refers to the **(Seku) Jakyung** mountain (T: Se ku bya khyung), a clay mountain about fifty to sixty kilometers to the west of Rongbo. It is not actually a range, but there are lots of foothills around it (DD). Jakhyung is also considered a great mountain deity who suppresses malevolent forces. Kälden Gyatso wrote a text on how to offer juniper leaves to this local deity. For this, see Skal ldan rgya mtsho, *Rje skal ldan rgya mtsho'i gsung las dkar phyogs skyong ba'i yul lha gnyan chen po se ku bya khyung la bsang mchod 'bul tshul*, in Skal ldan, *Gsung 'bum* (1987), vol. Nga-24; and Skal ldan, *Gsung 'bum* (1999), vol. 3, 441–43. For the location of Jakyung just to the west of Rongbo behind Rongbo Monastery, see maps 1 and 2 (DD).

Gyesum (T: Sgyed gsum) are three small peaks about five to six kilometers to the south of Rongbo. One can probably can see Phu Seku from there (DD). For the general vicinity of Gyesum, see Rongbo on map 2.

Depa Chökyi Gyälpo (T: Sde pa Chos kyi rgyal po), literally Dharma king, Sovereign of the Dharma, is another respectful way of referring to Depa Chökyije Tendzin Lobzang Gyatso.

59 **[I came to] know how to apply the essential meanings**
of teachings
In sutras and tantras to benefit [my] innermost mind,
But because [I] was unable to practice,
The fruits of experience and realization have not yet matured

chos mdo sngags kyi gnad don du ma zhig /
nang sems nyid steng du skor tshul shes/ / ...

Here LC points out a meaning for skor (T) which is not apparent in some dictionaries:
sems nyid steng du skor = to apply something to one's mind itself (in order to benefit it) (LC)
See sutras, tantras in the glossary.

Since Kälden Gyatso's theme of not having a chance to practice the Dharma appears often in his writings, it seems to have concerned him for many years. His main responsibilities were administering and supporting his two schools, and leading his hundreds of disciples to Buddhahood. At the same time, he was also able to take retreats in many mountain hermitages, holy places around the Yellow River (T: Rma chu), and caves. In spite of the intermittent retreats he was able to make, he continued to seem bothered by the notion that he had not integrated his mind with the many teachings he had received. He finally was able to relieve himself of all responsibilities, and for the final seven years of his life he made Tashikhyil his principal hermitage so that he could devote himself more fully to Dharma practice. For more, see *TSR*, 371–74 and Ngag dbang, *Skal ldan gyi rnam thar,* 19–20, 66.

The blessing of the deity Cakrasaṃvara is great
[And I] have taken him as [my] sole deity for many years.
But since [I] have not been able to do the recitations
for inducing [the presence of his] enlightened mind,
The merest sign [of him] in [my] dreams has not yet emerged

lha bde mchog byin rlabs che na yang / /
thugs skul byed kyi bzlas pa ma nus pas/ /
lha gcig pur bzung nas lo mang yang / /
dus da dung rmi ltas tsam ma byung / /

61 **[I] have been going through the motions of relying on mountain retreats.**
But because there is no difference between [my own] behavior and [that of a] common, worldly [person]
And [I] have not [yet] grown disgusted with [the concerns of] this life,
[I] have not yet attained the rank of a Dharma practitioner

gnas ri khrod bsten lo byas na yang / /
'phral phal ba dang bya spyod khyad med cing/ /
tshe 'di la zhen pa ma log pas/ /
dus da dung chos pa'i gral ma thob/ /

(verb stem) + lo = pretense at doing (verb) (LC)
Here Kälden Gyatso is saying that he has given the impression to others that he was relying on the retreats, but internally he felt he was not doing so from the heart.

63 **Khargong** (T: Mkhar gong) is a small mountain below Gyesum (DD). For the general vicinity of Khargong, see Rongbo on map 2.

67 **cuckoo** (T: khu byug) is likely to be the Common (or Eurasian) Cuckoo (*Cuculus canorus*) (CL).

For bird songs and interpreting the lines that claim that they are singing pleasing songs with good voices, and so forth, see *S of SH*, 288. For more references to cuckoos in gur, see *S of SH*, 63, 157, 259, 288. For a reference to the blue cuckoo, see *S of SH*, 273, 297.

Kälden Repa (T: Skal ldan ras pa) is Kälden Gyatso, a name Kälden Gyatso also uses for himself in some of his colophons.

repa (T: ras pa) signifies one who wears cotton, and calls to mind yogis who wear cotton in the winter, keeping themselves warm with practices involving inner heat. The "repa" in Milarepa's name has this origin. *See* caṇḍālī in the glossary.

When relatives look [at me, they think I'm] crazy.
When monks look [at me, they think I'm] fickle.
When I look [at myself, I think I'm] deceitful

sha nyes bltas tshe smyon pa/ /
grwa pas bltas tshe blo mang / /
rang gis bltas tshe zog po/ /

This is one of my favorite stanzas.

69 **Kälden Repa—**
May this advice I have given you
Benefit yourself and all others
Through [the blessings of] the Three Precious Jewels

skal ldan ras pa khyod la/ /
nga yis btab pa'i gros 'di/ /
rang gzhan kun la phan par/ /
dkon mchog gsum gyis mdzod cig /

Kälden Gyatso is addressing himself here.

Chapter 3. Aspirations for Renunciation

75 **If [you] are able [to practice] the divine Dharma—Oh joy!**
If [you] are able to abandon [concern for] worldly things—Oh happiness!

lha chos shig nus na dga' ba la/ /
mi chos 'di dor na skyid pa la/ /

For another example of the pattern **...Oh joy! ...Oh happiness!** (T: ...dga' ba la// ...dkyid pa la//) see *TSR*, 320–21.

No matter what [you]'ve done, [you are still] a worldly person. [But] when [you] abandon the world—How wondrous!

gang ltar byas kyang 'jig rten pa/ /
'jig rten spangs na ngo mtshar che/ /

This gur is not about a particular person. It is advice for Dharma practitioners of little experience. Kälden Gyatso tells them that no matter what spiritual practices they have done, if they have not renounced worldly concerns, the benefit will be small (LC).

Some of the main translations of the conjunction na (T) are 'if' and 'when'. Na (T) appears in the first two lines of the gur, cited in the previous note, and the last line of the gur, cited here. I have translated it as 'if' in the first two lines, and as 'when' in the last line. My choices take advantage of the nuances in English to express a progression from neutrality to optimism. 'If' implies neutrality in result, but 'when' insinuates optimism on Kälden Gyatso's part that the practitioners he is addressing will in fact abandon the world once they have heard his advice.

There is an interesting **change of meter** in this song. The meter is consistently 3+2+3 up to the last two lines. The change of meter for the conclusion of the song (No matter what..., cited above) to 2+2+3 further strengthens the message Kälden Gyatso is giving here.

The **colophon**, literally zhes pa 'di gnyis kyang…(T), refers to the two preceding gur together.

79 **May [I] strive continually day and night**
To follow the enlightened example of [my] lama.

I, an old man on the mountain peak at Tashikhyil
In this northern part of Amdo,
Am roaring boastfully like thunder

bla ma sangs rgyas kyi rnam par thar ba la/ /
nyin mtshan khor yug tu legs par 'bad par shog /

yul byang phyogs a mdo'i sa phyogs 'dir/ /
gnas bkra shis 'khyil gyi ri rtse na/ /
nga rgad pos kha pho 'brug bzhin ldir/ /

Here we have another interesting **change in meter** within a song. The first two lines are in the meter 2+3+2+3. The rest are in 1+2+2+3. The introduction or homage of a gur is usually separate from the rest in language and theme, and the change in meter here emphasizes that difference.

Tashikhyil, here, is **Rongbo Tashikhyil** (T: Rong bo Bkra shis 'khyil), Kälden Gyatso's main hermitage high above Rongbo valley, to the west. The reader is cautioned not to confuse Rongbo Tashikhyil (Kälden Gyatso's main hermitage) and **Yama Tashikhyil** (T: G.ya ma Bkra shis 'khyil, Shabkar's main hermitage). They are to the west and to the east of Rongbo valley, respectively.

Kälden Gyatso founded a school of tantric studies in 1648 at (**Rongbo**) **Tashikhyil** (Ngag dbang, *Skal ldan gyi rnam thar*, 31). Gendun Tenpai Nyima (T: Rgyal Mkhan chen Dge 'dun Bstan pa'i nyi ma), born perhaps in 1758, founded **Yama Tashikhyil** (*SH*, 12 n. 22; TBRC). Jamyang Shepai Dorje ('Jam dbyangs bzhad pa'i rdo rje) founded the very famous **Ladrang Tashikhyil** (T: Bla brang Bkra shis 'khyil) in 1709, between the foundings of Rongbo Tashikhyil and Yama Tashikhyil. It is located beyond Yama Tashikhyil, farther to the east. Because of the geographical proximity of the three sites, it seems that the names for Yama

Tashikhyil and Ladrang Tashikhyil are related to the name of Kälden Gyatso's hermitage. For the locations of the three, see map 2.

I…
Am roaring boastfully like thunder

Kälden Gyatso describes himself as roaring out boastfully because he thinks he is speaking with a very large voice for such an unimportant man (LC).

In the Amdo region, horses and yaks abound.
I, a weak old man, am alone,
So it would be difficult to look after [animals].
[I] am not going far away for [their] sake

Much of the region is extremely steep, since it is on the northeastern edge of the Tibetan plateau where rivers have cut deep valleys. I have often seen people descending way down precipitous slopes in search of their livestock, in order to bring them home before dinner.

The term 'yak' in English is a loanword from Tibetan, but in that language it actually only refers to a male animal. There are various words in Tibetan for the females, the hybrids, and so on, which collectively seem to be referred to as 'yak' in English. My Tibetan friends always laugh at me when I enthusiastically ask if some yoghurt I am being offered is yoghurt from yaks. Of course males do not produce milk!

81 ***Dharmakāya*, [the realization of] enlightened essence,**
Resides on the mind's throne, beyond the two extremes

khams bde gshegs snying po chos kyi sku/ /
rgyud mtha' gnyis spangs pa'i khri rtser bzhugs/ / / /

It is believed that the nature of mind is Buddha-nature, that we all have it within us, and that on this basis we can all attain enlightenment. *See also GK*, 253, 302. Throne here is a metaphor for renouncing both extremes (LC). I thank Geshe TC and Erik Pema Kunsang for helping me with the translation of these difficult two lines.

83 **Oṃ swa sti!** (= S) is an auspicious expression found at the beginning of some gur. It is often left in Sanskrit, but could be translated 'may all be auspicious', and 'may all enjoy peace and prosperity' (*BT*).

Chöpa Rinpoche, formally known as **Lobzang Tenpai Gyältsen** (1581–1659; T: Chos pa Rin po che, Blo bzang bstan pa'i rgyal mtshan) is Kälden Gyatso's elder half-brother and first teacher. Kälden Gyatso refers to Chöpa Rinpoche as "father" here because Chöpa Rinpoche was one of his main teachers.

Protector, [I] have no means of repaying your kindness.
[I] have recalled [you] again and again, and prayed.
In order to fulfill [your] wishes [I] have attended to the duties
Of the schools of teaching and practice as much as [I] could.

Even though my body was aged, I did not abandon [those] responsibilities.
Do you realize this, lama imbued with kindness?
Yet this [cycle of] birth and death is inexhaustible.
When the Lord of Death arrives, what shall [I] do?

For a summary of some of the intricate ways in which the two brothers interacted, see *TSR*, 370–73. For Kälden Gyatso's account of taking care of the schools for as long as he could; how he finally relieved himself of these responsibilities; and his motivations for leaving behind his homeland, village temples, and monasteries in favor of places of solitude, see *TSR*, 24–44. *See also* Lord of Death, samsara in the glossary.

85 **It is now time to practice [in order to] experience the Dharma directly**
chos zang ma zhig byed na da ni ran/ /

Four of my six sources have the spelling zad ma (T), which does not seem to produce a coherent translation of this line. Another source, printed from woodblocks, has a spelling that is indistinct. My sixth source clearly has the spelling zang ma (T). I believe that the translation of zang ma can work here. LC only very tentatively acknowledged that this spelling is a possibility.

blissful realm (T: bde ba'i zhing) refers to Buddha-fields. *See* Buddha-fields in the glossary.

87 **scent eater** (T: dri za; odor-eaters) is a being who lives on scents.

91 **I pray to the father, Tendzin Lobzang Gyatso,**
Lord lama omniscient in the teachings of the three [vehicles]

There are various sets of **three vehicles**, but since Kälden Gyatso studied Vajrayāna practices with **Tendzin Lobzang Gyatso**, the set to which Kälden Gyatso is referring here is likely to be the three main divisions of Buddhism—Hīnayāna, Mahāyāna, and Vajrayāna. For more, see three vehicles in the glossary.

[I] was a bit sad one day...

He explains his sadness and disillusionment over the way he has been practicing the Dharma in this song. For sadness, nature, and singing, see *TSR*, 91–92.

This [human life] is even rarer than a wish-fulfilling jewel.
[But] now [I actually] have the nerve to waste [it—my] heart is [as hard as] iron!

Kälden Gyatso is speaking to himself, giving himself advice and scolding himself about wasting the rare opportunity of having a human body. By 'iron heart' he means he has no feelings about squandering his rare chance to proceed towards enlightenment.

There are no pronouns anywhere in the body of this gur after the homage except for one, and it is 'you' in this line about his heart. I have chosen to translate the rest of the gur in the first person, so I've changed this pronoun here from 'you' to 'I'. *See* free and well-favored human birth in the glossary.

Up to now [my] mind has not integrated with the Dharma.
[I] thought about this and regret arose from [my] depths

dus da dung sems dang chos ma 'dres/ /
'di bsams shing 'gyod pa gting nas skyes/ /

For Kälden Gyatso's concern over a lack of integration with the teachings he has received, and it being a motivation of his for becoming a hermit, see *TSR*, 32–33.

93 **At times when I was not relying on mountain hermitages,**
[I] would intend to / imagine [I could] do [my] practices like Milarepa.
But when [I actually] entered into practice,
[My] hopes were not fulfilled

sngon ri khrod ma bsten gnas skabs su/ /
dus nam zhig sgrub pa byed pa'i tshe/ /
rje mi la lta bur byed snyam yang / /
da sgrub la zhugs tshe re ma byung / /

The first line could loosely read, "At those times when [I] was living among householders…"

Milarepa (1040–1123; T: Mi la ras pa; the cotton-clad Mila, his clan name) was a fiercely tenacious and determined Tibetan yogi practitioner who became enlightened in one lifetime and is widely revered as a crucial forefather of the Kagyü lineage. For more, see Milarepa in the glossary.

Dismiss [the notion of practicing] like Milarepa!
Today's common siddhas [have set their aims too high.]
If [they] cannot bear comparison [with Milarepa],
How can the qualities of experience and realization arise?

rje mi la lta bu phar la zhog/
dus da lta'i sgom chen tha ma la'ang/ /
mig yar bltas 'gran par mi bzod na/ /
nyams rtogs pa'i yon tan ga la skye/ /

The second line would be translated more literally, "Today's common siddhas look up [to Milarepa] with [such enormous] respect."

Chapter 4. Setting Off for Solitary Hermitages

97 **[I] bow at the feet of the lord, [my] father Lobzang Tenpai Gyältsen,**
Ruler over the dominion of the Dharma,
[And] protector of beings who have transformed all desires

rje **blo bzang** chos kyi rgyal srid la/ /
dbang 'dod dgur bsgyur ba'i 'gro ba'i mgon/ /
pha **bstan pa'i rgyal mtshan** zhabs la 'dud/ /

Lobzang Tenpai Gyältsen (T: Blo bzang bstan pa'i rgyal mtshan), the formal name for **Chöpa Rinpoche**, is divided between the first and third Tibetan lines, with the first two syllables in the first line and the last four syllables in the third line. This is a poetic figure called the 'disjointed riddle' that dates back to *The Mirror of Poetics* (S: *Kāvyādarśa*), the circa sixth-century text of Indian poetics by Daṇḍin. What makes Kälden Gyatso's use of this disjointed riddle particularly clever is that the first Tibetan line up through the sixth syllable leads us to believe that he is paying homage to one of his lamas, Rje Blo bzang chos kyi rgyal mtshan, the first Panchen Lama. Suddenly, for the seventh syllable, he provides a 'srid' (T) instead of the expected 'mtshan' (T), leaving the Tibetan reader wondering to whom the homage is addressed until the third line, where the missing part of the name of Chöpa Rinpoche is revealed. For a discussion of the disjointed riddle, its roots in Indian classical verse, and another example of it, see *TSR* 182–84.

Now, so [I] will not waver for the sake of wealth,
I, Kälden, am going to a mountain hermitage

da mi mgo nor phyir mi skor ched/ /
bdag skal ldan ri khrod dgon par 'gro /

The first line would be translated more literally, "Now, so [I] don't turn [my] human head for the sake of wealth."

99 **Because [my] mind has been very far from the gentle Dharma,**
Like water [from the dry core of hollow] pebbles,
[I am anxious] not to stray from [my] intention to practice.
[I], Kälden, of poor fortune, am now going to a solitary place

rgyud zhi dul chos dang rgyang ring bas/ /
dus da lta chu dang chu rdo bzhin/ /
da chos sems rgyab 'gal mi gtong phyir/ /
ming skal ldan skal dman dben par 'gro /

Although a rock is in the water for a long time, a hollow in the rock is still dry (LC).

Kälden, of poor fortune (T: skal ldan skal dman), is a pun on his name, since 'kälden' means one with good fortune.

You nephew-[disciples, other] monks, and patrons...
khyed dbon po grwa pa yon bdag rnams/ / ...

Nephews are often disciples of their uncles in monasteries.

Go now to the upper region of Ütsang,
stod dbus gtsang phyogs su da song la/ / ...

Ütsang, or **Ü** and **Tsang** (T: Dbus gtsang) are the two main provinces of Central Tibet. *See* map 1.

Here the upper region (T: stod) of **Ütsang** is being mentioned in contrast to the lower region (T: smad) of Amdo and Kham (T: Khams) in the next stanza. Kälden Gyatso is using the terms upper and lower descriptively here, since stod (T) can more specifically refer to Western Tibet, to the west of the central provinces of Ü and Tsang.

101 **Domey** (T: Mdo smad) sometimes refers to Amdo, and sometimes refers to Kham, both in Eastern Tibet. It is in very general terms all of eastern Tibet.

Just as a cuckoo goes off to live in a distant place,
Grasping a stalk of grain in [its] beak...

To say that a **cuckoo** is **grasping a stalk of grain** going to a distant place is puzzling, since cuckoos don't eat grain or make nests, and would have no reason to carry food while migrating.

Before flying south, birds put on layers of fat, and stop to feed and rest along the way (CL).

Here Kälden Gyatso is probably referring to the famous ***Eloquent Explanations*** (T: *Legs bshad*) by Sakya Paṇḍita (1182–1251).

Just as an eagle skillfully flies higher and higher,
And goes wherever it desires...

rgod je mtho je mthor legs 'phur nas/ /
rang gang 'dod sa ru 'gro ba ltar/ / ...

I have substituted "**eagle**" for "vulture" in this song for the same reasons that I explained above.

I am going farther and farther from the gate of [my] home,
To whatever delightful grove of a hermitage

nga yul las je ring je ring ngos/ /
gnas dben pa'i dga' tshal gang dgar 'gro /

Unlike what is given in some main dictionaries, ngos = sgo nas, i.e. from [his] gate or door (LC).

For another translation of this song, see *Songs of Spiritual Experience,* selected and translated by Thupten Jinpa and Jaś Elsner, 64.

107 The names **Lobzang Ngawang Sherap** could have been divided either way: Lobzang Ngawang and Sherap, or Lobzang and Ngawang Sherap. Since neither appears in the biography of Kälden Gyatso, or elsewhere in his *Mgur 'bum,* I have tentatively divided them as I have.

until summer (T: dus dbyar sos bar du)

Dbyar sos is one of the six Tibetan seasons, each two months long. It is roughly like the beginning of our summer (LC).

109 There is a colophon here in editions A, B, and E which does not appear in editions C, D, or F:

rje skal ldan rgya mtsho'i gsung las lta ba'i glu 'phreng rdo rje'i sgra dbyangs zhugs so/ /

It is more formal than other colophons I have translated here and was more than likely written by someone else.

113 **Near the waters of Lake Trishor Gyälmo**
Live many communities of Mongols,
But they are always engaged in evil deeds

Lake Trishor Gyalmo (T: Mtsho khri shor rgyal mo) is the huge lake in Amdo commonly known today as **Tsho Ngönpo** (=T), **Lake Kokonor,** and Qinghai Hu (= C). *See* Lake Kokonor on maps 1 and 2.

These communities of **Mongols** (T: Hor sog po) Kälden Gyatso refers to here could easily be members of the Chogthu tribe, who resided around the Kokonor and had allied themselves on the side of the civil war against the Gelugpa school. The Chogthu branch at the Kokonor was defeated there in 1637 by Gushri Khan and the Qoshot tribe, strong supporters of the fifth Dalai Lama. After that the Chogthu were under the power of the Qoshots, whose administration was held by Gushri Khan (d. 1654) and after 1658 by his son. The latter and Mongols at the lake continued to have poor relations, and the Dalai Lama's government requested around 1660 that all Mongol leaders take a vow to resolve their differences. For more, see Tsepon Wangchuk Deden Shakabpa, *One Hundred Thousand Moons*: A*n Advanced Political History of Tibet* (Leiden: Brill, 2010), 335–38, 358, 362. If the Chogthu at the Kokonor needed to be dealt with by an enemy tribe for decades after their defeat, it seems that they were still thought to be troublemakers by the Qoshot and other sympathizers of the Gelugpas. *See also* Gelugpa school in the glossary.

There is a mountain island which rises in the center of that lake,
Now called Mahādeva,
About which the king of the Dharma, Songtsen Gampo,
And the glorious Pema of Ugyen made prophesies in former times

Mahādeva (= S) is another name for **Tshonying** (T: Mtsho snying), a mountain island in Lake Kokonor. *See* Tshonying Is. on map 2.

Mahādeva is also the name of the deity who is said to dwell there. I have not found out who it is. Although Mahādeva is a name for Śiva, I have been told that the deity at the Kokonor is not Śiva (LC).

They both are said to have prophesized that this island would have blessings.

Songtsen Gampo (ca. first half of the 7th century; T: Srong brtsan sgam po) was the king of Tibet when Buddhism came into the country.

Pema of Ugyen / Ogyen (T: U rgyan pad+ma / O rgyan pad+ma) is another name for **Padmasaṃbhava** (= S) or **Guru Rinpoche**, the tantric master who is said to have been invited to Tibet by its king in the eighth century in order to tame indigenous spirits who were opposing Buddhism. For more, see Padmasaṃbhava in the glossary.

nāga (= S; T: klu) is a snake-like being thought to live in the underworld and water. Nāga **Bodhisattva** (T: klu byang chub sems dpa') is the minister of the nāgas—in this context, a bodhisattva who lives in Lake Kokonor (T: Mtsho sngon). For the pre-Buddhist origin of nāgas as symbols of water and fertility in India, see *EB*, 466–67.

115 **[But] if [I] rise early in the morning**
[When the essence of my] divine lama and yidam appears most vividly,
The intention to cultivate virtue will clearly arise

nang snga bar yar la langs tsa na/ /
lha bla ma yi dam wa ler 'char/ /
dge sgrub 'dod kyi 'dun pa lhang lhang skye/ /

See yidam in the glossary.

117 **A la la, if [I] carry out [my] intention [to stay on Mahādeva, I] will rejoice.**
O na la, if [I] carry out this aspiration, [I] will be happy

a la la bsam pa 'di 'grub na dga' ba la/ /
'o na la 'dun pa 'di 'grub na skyid pa la/ /

The interjection **a la la** (=T) is discussed in *TSR*, pp. 232–33. There I have translated it as "Wow!" **O na la** (T: 'o na la) is an interjection that expresses something similar.

There is an interesting **change of meter** in this song. The meter had consistently been 1+2+2+3 up to the concluding couplet. In each of those last two lines there is unexpectedly an interjection of three syllables tacked on in front of eight beats, and the eight beats surprisingly now have the subdivisions 3+2+3. This results in the overall meter of 3+3+2+3 for the final couplet. The change in meter is a beautiful stylistic touch, along with the interjections, to conclude the song.

This was written by Kälden Gyatso in the hermitage, the center of good fortune, in accordance with whatever thoughts came to mind

dben gnas bkra shis 'khyil bar bris pa'o// //

Here he refers to the name of one of his main hermitages, **Tashikhyil**, with a ba (T) after it, signifying that the individual words in the name should be translated. Hence in this colophon Tashikhyil is called 'the center of good fortune'. *See* Rongbo Tashikhyil, above.

121 ***The Stages of the Path to Enlightenment*** (T: *Byang chub lam gyi rim pa, Byang chub lam rim*) is the famed book by Tsongkhapa. For this, see Tsongkhapa in the glossary.

In this gur, Kälden Gyatso calls himself **Jampel Dorje**. This may have been the name he received after tantric initiation into the practice of Guhyasamāja (= S; T: Gsang ba 'dus pa'i rgyud) (VDK). Monks and laypersons familiar with the science of language (T: sgra rig pa) would know that this name is related to his usual one by linguistic rules that have their origin in Sanskrit and India (LC).

123 **If [I] go to the juncture of slate crags and meadows…**

This would be a convenient, pretty, and solitary place to stay. Being on top of a mountain is not convenient because there is no water.

125 The **meter** of most of this song is 2+2+2. It has a markedly strong pulse and character, and is consistently used here, except for two places where there are interjections. In both cases the interjections are three syllables:

1)
A la la—Oh joy!
A la la—Oh happiness!

a la la dga' ba la/ /
a la la skyid pa la/ /

Here we have 3+3 for these two lines. The total number of beats is the same as before, though the feeling is now very different. After the brief duration of two lines, there is a return to the 2+2+2 meter.

2)
A la la! If a desire like this
O na la! is quickly fulfilled,
A la la! The madman of Rongbo will be joyful!
O na la! I will be happy

a la la 'di 'dra'i yid smon/ /
'o na la myur du 'grub na/ /
a la la rong smyon dga' ba/ /
'o na la nga yi skyid pa/ /

Here we have 3+2+2 for the last four lines of the song. The total number of beats has now unexpectedly changed to seven.

These two areas with markedly **different meters** serve to punctuate the otherwise disyllabic rhythms in this gur and emphasize the song's playful and informal nature. They provide pulses, one for a few lines towards the end and a stronger, final one at the very end, and give the song an interesting and striking overall rhythmic shape.

The 2+2+2 meter is not one frequently used by Kälden Gyatso. Only five percent of the gur in the *Collected Songs* are in it. For more about this meter and its relation to the Central Tibetan folksong the she (T: gzhas), see *TSR*, 116, 121–23.

The siddha or yogi, to whom no principles of conduct can apply, was frequently eccentric and lived outside the norms of acceptable behavior. Hence, siddhas often gave the appearance or were perceived as **madmen** or **insane ones** (T: snyon pa). This tantric ideal of the siddha was in marked contrast to the Mahāyāna ideal of the bodhisattva. For more, see siddha, bodhisattva in the glossary.

Chapter 5. Emptiness and Mahāmudrā

133 **Oh lama, [you] are aware that conditions**
Exist only just this much—in mere name.
[At the same time, you] realize that
None exist from the very beginning in ultimate truth—
Please grant me [the ability] to see what you yourself see.

don dam la ye nas med na yang/ /
ming tsam la 'di tsam grub pa yi/ /
gnas tshul tsho rig pa'i bla ma des/ /
rang nyid kyis gang gzigs bdag la stsol/ /

Kälden Gyatso wants his lama to bestow on him the ability to see that conditions exist in mere name, and that none exist from the very beginning in ultimate truth. *See* conventional truth; Madhyamaka; ultimate truth; ultimate truth and conventional truth, relationship between in the glossary.

Nevertheless, the view of emptiness
In terms of everyday appearances is free of contradictions—
So-called emptiness is not elsewhere,
[And] the view [of it] is not like [some] vision of the sky
One [mistakenly] hopes to have by looking at [one's] hand

'o na ni deng sang snang ba la/ /
mi gnod par stong nyid lta ba ni/ /
lag pa la mig gis phar bltas pas/ /
nam mkha' ni mthong bar re ba bzhin/ /
stong nyid ni zer ba gzhan nas med/ /

Emptiness is not in contradiction to the hand or other everyday appearances, though conceptualization does not understand it. LC points out that the sky is a metaphor for stong pa'i stong sang (T), clear emptiness, vacuum, nothingness (RY, IW). *See* emptiness in the glossary.

135 **An explanation of emptiness**
As that completely empty, deep vacuum
Through which [one] refutes the way things seem
in the present
Appears in the instruction manuals

da ltar gyi snang tshul 'di bkag pa'i/ /
stong sang de zab mo stong nyid du/ /
lta khrid kyi yig char bshad nas snang/ /

I thank LC for helping me understand this stanza.

Due to the kindness of the lama,
I have related this [song] as counsel to myself.
[I] dedicate [it] for the sake of looking freshly
At the genuine face of all virtue,
Which lacks [real existence] in ultimate truth
from the very beginning

This passage refers to the lack of any inherent existence of virtue on the ultimate level of truth (Geshe TC).

This also was composed by Kälden Gyatso, a demon in the body of a monk
zhes pa 'di yang ban gzugs kyi rgyal 'gong skal ldan rgya mtshos sbyar ba'o/ / / /

rgyal 'gong (= T), "monk-demon" (RY, IW), is the third demon mentioned in these songs.

137 **Although I was not a renunciant who meditates on *nāḍī*,**
prāṇa, and _bindu_,
I was indeed an old monk whose mind is turns to the Dharma.
I was not one who meditates on *Mahāmudrā*—
Born through the power of *caṇḍālī*—
But an intense desire to see the nature of mind arose [in me]

The first of the six yogas of Nāropa, the generation of **caṇḍālī** (= S; T: gtum mo), or inner heat, involves exercises with the channels, energies, and drops. The heat is thought to melt the drops, which then flow in the channels and induce great bliss.

The generation of caṇḍālī can be considered the basis for the entire collection of yogas, which themselves are supporting practices for the realization of the nature of the mind, Mahāmudrā. Tsongkhapa explains the relationship of the practice of the six yogas to the attainment of Mahāmudrā in this way:

> In this tradition [i.e., the Six Yogas of Nāropa] the main technique is to arouse the inner heat at the navel chakra. When these energies enter the central channel the four blisses are induced, and one cultivates meditation on the basis of these in such a way as to give rise to the innate wisdom of mahāmudrā.

For this see Glenn H. Mullin, ed., trans., *Tsongkhapa's Six Yogas of Nāropa* (Ithaca, New York: Snow Lion Publications, 1997), 139. *See also* Mahāmudrā; nāḍī, prāṇa, bindu; six yogas of Nāropa in the glossary.

The term 'Mahāmudrā' can refer to fundamental reality or the nature of mind, the awareness that can realize it, the experience of realizing it, various systems of teachings for realizing it, and so on. In the first part of the stanza, cited above, Mahāmudrā refers to fundamental reality, the nature of mind. In the last part of the stanza, cited in the next note, Mahāmudrā refers to the system of teachings for realizing it. For more, see Mahāmudrā in the glossary.

So [I] petitioned lamas and deities in small meditation huts
And applied the oral instructions to [my] mind again and again.
And [I] am [now] an old monk who practices [*Mahāmudrā*]

bsam gtan khang bur bla ma lha la gsol ba btab nas/ /
gdams ngag yang yang sems steng bskor nas nyams su len pa'i ban rgan lags so/ /

139 **[I] was led to *mudrā* friends**
phyag rgya grogs su khrid nas...

It seems that he met spiritual consorts, women as tantric consorts (T: phyag rgya ma, las kyi phyag rgya).

Although [I] was not a renunciant who opens a hundred doors of *samādhi*
And sees a variety of pure perceptions...

ting 'dzin sgo brgya phye nas dag pa'i snang ba sna tshogs mthong ba'i bya btang min yang/ / ...

See pure perception, samādhi in the glossary.

In this gur there are very novel **changes of meter.** All the subdivisions are made up of two beats, but there is a very wide range of beats per line from eight to twenty-two. Beats per line are generally on the rise within the four lines of each stanza, and beats per line also increase from stanza to stanza. Much of the song has unusually long lines in comparison to Kälden Gyatso's other gur. These long lines seem to emphasize the evolution of Kälden Gyatso's Dharma practices and his determination to explain that the changes he made were well thought out. The gradual lengthening of the lines seems to depict his long voyage of development from the past (when he was not...) to the present (when he now is...), and to emphasize his firm commitment to the outcome.

143 **The Kagyü forefathers have asserted that**
There is compatibility in general between the mind—
The basis of all things [in samsaric experience]—
and emptiness

lar kun gzhi'i sems dang stong pa nyid/ /
don mthun par bka' brgyud gong ma bzhed/ /

Saraha (ca. seventh through ninth centuries), **Nāgārjuna** (ca. seventh through ninth centuries), **Nāropa** (956–1040) (= nA ro pa, Tibetanized Sanskrit) and **Maitrīpa** (ca. 1007–1085; = mai trI pa, Tibetanized Sanskrit) were four of the eighty-four mahāsiddhas of India, and are considered the founding fathers of the Mahāmudrā lineage. The transmission of Mahāmudrā teachings to Marpa is traditionally associated with Nāropa and Maitrīpa, though the exact details of whatever connections are still under debate. For more, see Ronald M. Davidson, *Tibetan Renaissance: Tantric Buddhism in the Rebirth of Tibetan Culture* (New York, Colombia University Press, 2005), 142–148. I thank RJ for having recommended sources that deal with this complex issue of transmission. *See* Mahāmudrā, mahāsiddha, Maitrīpa, Nāropa, Saraha in the glossary.

Please note that Nāgārjuna here is the **mahāsiddha Nāgārjuna** (= S), possibly a disciple of Saraha, not to be confused with the much earlier, famed expounder of Madhyamaka with the same name. For some of the stories surrounding the mahāsiddha Nāgārjuna's life including his ordination and earlier studies at Nālandā, his departure from the traditional monastic way of life, his quest for meditational visions of deities, a twelve-year retreat, and his ensuing attempts to be of use to the world in various colorful ways, see K. Dowman, *Masters of Mahāmudrā*, 112–17.

145 **The glorious Candrakīrti, Atiśa, Dromtön, and Tsongkhapa and his chief disciples**
Wanted to sever the root of [the grasping] mind,
[And] sought [precisely] what was to be refuted

dpal zla grags jo 'brom rje yab sras/ /
sems gzhi rtsa gcod 'dod dgag bya 'tshol/ /

Zla grags (T) is Candrakīrti (S); Jo = Jo bo (T) is Atiśa (S); 'Brom = 'Brom ston pa (T), disciple of Atiśa; and rje yab sras = Tsongkhapa and his chief disciples.

Candrakīrti (= S; T: Zla ba grags pa; ca. 600–650) was an Indian philosopher, author, and commentator of the Madhyamaka school. His approach was made central to monastic education in Tibet by Tsongkhapa.

Atiśa (= S; T: Jo bo; 982–1054) was an Indian monk, foremost scholar, and author. He was abbot of Vikramaśīla (S), one of the great Indian monastic universities, and later became a missionary in Tibet, where he contributed greatly to the rejuvenation of Buddhism after a long period of decline.

Dromtön (T: 'Brom ston pa, 'Brom ston Rgyal ba'i byung gnas; 1008–1064), was a lay disciple of Atiśa's. He founded the first monastery of the Kadampa school (T: Bka' gdams pa), out of which the Gelugpa school grew. For more on Candrakīrti, Atiśa, and Dromtön, see the glossary.

Here Kälden Gyatso is making a distinction between the approach of the group in the former stanza—Saraha, the mahāsiddha Nāgārjuna, Nāropa, Maitrīpa, Marpa, and Milarepa—and those in this present stanza—Candrakīrti, Atiśa, Dromtön, and Tsongkhapa and his chief disciples. However, by tradition it is also claimed that Tsongkhapa practiced Mahāmudrā, having received it from Vajradhara either through the divine revelation of Mañjuśrī, or via a lineage of human sources, including Nāropa and Maitrīpa, Marpa and Milarepa. The Gelugpa transmission attributed to Tsongkhapa came to be called the **Ganden Oral Tradition of Mahāmudrā,** alternatively translated as the **Ganden / Kagyü Tradition of Mahāmudrā** (T: Dga' ldan phyag rgya chen po, Dga' ldan snyan brgyud phyag rgya chen po, Dge ldan bka' brgyud phyag rgya chen po).

Kälden Gyatso wrote at least three, if not four, texts on Mahāmudrā: *A petition to the Mahāmudrā Lineage* (T: Phyag chen brgyud 'debs); *Quotations from Dge ldan phyag chen zab khrid gdams ngag rgya mtsho* (T: 'Jam pa'i dbyangs skal ldan rgya mtsho'i gsung las dge ldan phyag chen zab khrid gdams ngag rgya mtsho nas btus pa); *An Experiential Manual of the Dge ldan Oral Tradition of Mahāmudrā* (T: *Rdo* rje 'chang skal ldan rgya *mtsho'i gsung las dge ldan bka' brgyud phyag rgya chen po'i nyams khrid rje blo bzang bstan pa'i rgyal mtshan dpal bzang po'i gsung gis bskul ba*). He also probably wrote *An Instruction Manual of Mahāmudrā* (*Phyag chen gyi 'khrid yig*) (LC).

For these, see Skal ldan, *Gsung 'bum* (1987), vol. Kha-5; and Skal ldan, *Gsung 'bum* (1999), vol. 2, 211-13; Skal ldan, *Gsung 'bum* (1987), vol. Kha-6; and Skal ldan, *Gsung 'bum* (1999), vol. 2, 214-35; Skal ldan, *Gsung 'bum* (1987), vol. Kha-7; and Skal ldan, *Gsung 'bum* (1999), vol. 2, 236-53; and lastly Skal ldan, *Gsung 'bum* (1987), vol. Kha-8; and Skal ldan, *Gsung 'bum* (1999), vol. 2, 254–65.

For a summary of what is traditionally claimed to be the transmission of Mahāmudrā from Marpa and Milarepa to Tsongkhapa; the reputed transmission of what came to be called the Ganden Oral Tradition of Mahāmudrā from Tsongkhapa down to the first Panchen Lama; and for Kälden Gyatso and Chöpa Rinpoche's involvement in the Ganden Oral Tradition, see *TSR*, 60–74 and *GK*, 169–70. For a discussion about whether the Ganden tradition as a systematic teaching goes back to Tsongkhapa or just back to the first Panchen Lama, see Roger R. Jackson, "The *dGe ldan-bKa' brgyud* Tradition of *Mahāmudrā*: How Much *dGe ldan*? How Much *bKa' brgyud*?" 158–165.

**When ascertaining [the conventional existence of something,
That existence] needs to be determined by valid reason.
However, in the case in which things are to be negated,
[One simply sees that they] have no inherent existence**

de nges tshe khyab dang phyogs chos dgos/ /
lar dgag bya ltar du med pa la/ / …

No concise way to translate these two short lines occurred to me. LC suggested to simplify "khyab dang phyogs chos" (T) with "rtags yang dag," (T) correct reason, correct proof (IW, RY).

**Through that [process], when peaceful calm is stable,
[One] sustains both analytic and resting meditations together**

de'i stobs kyis zhi gnas brtan pa'i tshe/ /
sgom dpyad 'jog gnyis ka spel mar sbyong / /

Those following the Tibetan will notice that the spelling of the final verb here is sbyong (T), the spelling in all five of my sources, yet in some main dictionaries sbyong is not defined in the sense that I use in my translation. LC says that sbyong is the correct spelling, and that the meaning of sbyong is quite like skyong (T), to maintain or sustain. Kälden Gyatso frequently uses skyong—even here it appeared just three lines before.

Resting meditation refers here to peaceful calm, and analytic meditation refers here to insight mediation. Insight meditation and peaceful calm are the two main types of meditation practice. For more, see these in the glossary.

147 **If [one] is able to meditate, [one's progress] will be quicker than through other blessings.
This is the view and meditation of all Yellow Hats**

Yellow Hat (T: zhwa ser) is a term for the Gelugpa school. Its monks wear yellow hats, in contrast to the red hats worn by monks of other schools. *See* Gelugpa school, Tsongkhapa in the glossary.

While there is certainly a meditation component to the Gelugpa school, it is best known for its focus on scholarship and debate. Kälden Gyatso is making a surprisingly sweeping statement when he says that 'all' Gelugpas believe that meditation is the fastest way to progress towards enlightenment.

[Someone] able to meditate is a warrior
[Who can] cleave right through the midst of an [enemy] army,
Divide them, [and fight them single-handedly]

sgom nus na dpa' bo khrom shog yin/ /

I thank LC for his explanation of this passage.

Ha ha, although I have no intrinsic existence, [I] am jestfully playing!
ha ha rang la med kyang ku re rtse/ / / /

It is a given to himself and other scholars around him that he has no intrinsic existence and that emptiness is not in contradiction to the way things seem in the world. However, in the case of this comical line, Kälden Gyatso has flippantly distorted the concept of emptiness by insinuating that since he has no intrinsic existence, he should not be able to play around. He creates this distortion through the use of the word 'although' (T: kyang).

This closing line is related to the one in Chapter Two upon which I commented above, since they both play with the meaning of emptiness:

Spiritual practice, you are on the verge of dwindling into emptiness

The introduction of an interjection is again accompanied by an interesting **change in meter**. The meter had consistently been in 1+2+2+3 until the last line. With the sudden addition of the two-syllable interjection ha ha, it now unexpectedly becomes 2+2+2+3. This single-line colophon is written in verse instead of the usual format of prose.

151 **Look at your own experiences!**
When [you] have examined closely whether [they] exist [independently] or not
Through the logic of [whether they are] single entities
[Or can] be separated into however many [parts],
[They] will appear as primordially non-existent,
Just as [there are no] lotuses [in] the sky

rang gi nyams la ltos shig /
gcig dang du bral rigs pas/ /
yod med legs par dpyad tshe/ /
nam mkha'i pad+mo ji bzhin/ /
ye nas med par 'char ro/ /

The metaphor of no lotuses in the sky is a common one in this genre, so Tibetans singing, listening to, or reading this gur do not need the negative (there are no lotuses) spelled out for them. The inherent restriction of a certain number of syllables per line grouped in certain subdivisions often makes lines in this genre very concise, and that is presumably the reason that the negative is not explicitly stated here. *See also* emptiness in the glossary.

Place [your] unwavering [attention] single-pointedly
On the nature of mind in its shining manner,
Which has no conceptual elaboration whatsoever.
[You] will quickly attain the [direct] view [of its nature]

This direct realization of the nature of mind, or Mahāmudrā, is one aspect within the wider Gelugpa context of the **view** (RJ).

153 **By means of the virtuous merit of this composition,**
May [everyone] quickly encounter
That knowledgeable youth, rational cognition,
Together with that beautiful woman, emptiness

rigs shes gzhon nu mig yangs/ /
stong nyid mdzes ma lhan cig / ...

Here is another set of lovely metaphors, a youthful male for rational cognition, and a beautiful woman for emptiness.

mig yangs = rnam dpyod yangs pa (LC)

This was composed by the manifestation as a monk, Kälden Gyatso

Here is another wonderful colophon. It is very fitting after a song about Mahāmudrā.

Chapter 6. Mountain Retreats and Happiness

159 **[I] bow to the guru, Hāsa Vajra**
Namo guru ha sa badz+ra ya/ /

Hāsa Vajra (= S; Tibetanized Sanskrit: Ha sa badz+ra; T: Bzhad pa rdo rje) is the Sanskrit form of a name of Milarepa—the Laughing Vajra. Tibetanized Sanskrit is sometimes used in the opening line of a gur to create a more formal homage to a deity or high lama.

Mila Shepai Dorje (T: Mi la Bzhad pa'i rdo rje; Mi la ras pa Bzhad pa'i rdo rje; Mila / Milarepa Laughing Vajra) is a name given to Milarepa by Marpa and ḍākinīs. *See The Hundred Thousand Songs of Milarepa* (Boston: Shambhala, 1989), 333.

A la la, as for me, an old monk who wanders around the country...

There is stanza external repetition throughout this gur, with this being the first line of each quatrain. For a discussion of **quatrains** and **stanza external repetition**, see *TSR*, 140–47.

lesser monks and laypersons

This refers to people at the bottom of society, unimportant monks and laypersons, as opposed to the people with power.

161 **Finally, almshouse—the country, without direction**

He is saying that his **almshouse** (T: ldom sa), normally considered to be a place where beggars can receive food (JV), is wherever in the country, impartial in direction.

First, [I] studied the scriptural tradition a lot.
Next, [I] examined and analyzed the meaning of the texts.
Ultimately, a fine understanding arose [in me]

These are three steps towards understanding oral teachings and the scriptures, variously described as **learning, contemplating, and understanding** (T: thos pa, brtags dpyad, go ba); learning, studying, and understanding; and learning, contemplating, and meditating.

When [others] look [at me] from the outside, [my] interest in desirable objects [seems] intense,
[But when I] look within, craving and attachment are weak...

phyi bltas 'dod yon snang ba che yang/ /
nang bltas 'dod sred chags zhen chung la/ / ...

From the outside, it seems he wants desirable objects because people are frequently giving him nice gifts in homage.

163 **When [I] practice [the Dharma], [I] can sustain [myself]**
sgrub pa byas na kha ni sos 'dug /

Since he is a lama, people bring him food and so on, and so he does not need to do other work.

165 **Desirable objects and wealth have fallen [upon me] like rain,**
[But I] have not been clutched in the death grip of material possessions [or] riches.
For the sake of virtue, [I] have gone to any [lengths]

'dod yon dngos po char bzhin babs byung/ /
zang zing nor la shi spar ma 'thams/ /
dge ba'i phyogs su gang 'gro byas so/ /

Again we have the simile of rain, here in the negative sense.

When the time [once] came [for me] to take on the responsibilities of a great lama,
Although [I] neither [fully] accepted that burden, nor fully let [it] go,
Even this pretense [I made of renouncing it] was still in harmony with the Dharma

bla chen khur de dus skabs bab kyang/ /
khur de ma bzung bya btang tshugs bzung/ /
rang tshugs 'di yang chos dang mthun byung/ /

Unlike the definitions in some main dictionaries, I am translating tshugs (T) here to indicate pretense (not as 'firmly' or 'stable'). He gave the appearance of having renounced the school, the world, and so forth, but on the inside he felt he had not done a good job of letting them go (LC).

167 **Because [I] studied as much as [I] could in Ü,**
And promoted the teaching in the region of [Do] Kham...

dbus su slob gnyer gang nus bgyis nas/ /
khams gyi phyogs su bstan pa spel bas/ / ...

LC suggests that he is using **Ü** in the sense of center, and Kham (T: Khams) in the sense of **Do Kham** (T: Mdo khams), the north-eastern and eastern periphery or edge of the center.

Now [my] "entourage" which roams the mountain hermitages is large.
Steer the prow [of their ship] to the Dharma!
[I] will eventually benefit myself and others

da lta ri khrod 'grim pa'i 'khor mang/ /
de kun kha lo chos la sgyur dang/ /
nam zhig rang dang gzhan la phan no/ /

Here we have metaphors of the helmsman of a ship (himself, the lama) guiding those riding the ship (his students) to the Dharma.

169 **Kachu** (T: Bka' bcu) is a title given to monks who have mastered ten texts. **Kachuwa** (T: Bka' bcu ba) is a monk who has received this title.

...in front of the deity with a coat of gold mail, Ribo Phendzang

Ribo Phendzang (T: probably Ri bo 'phan 'dzang; though another spelling in two sources is Ri bo 'phan 'dzing) (DD). I have not yet found out who this deity is.

173 **[I] became spontaneously happy**
Because cuckoos, grouse, thrushes,
Crows, cranes, partridges, and other birds,
Were uttering pleasing sounds [such as] ***kyur kyur***

bya khu byug ri skegs 'jol mo dang / /
byi'u 'dzin ma bya shang gong mo sogs/ /
skad kyur kyur snyan pa'i sgra 'byin pas/ /
sems rang dbang med par skyid du bcug /

In order for us to fit scant clues in dictionaries with actual names of birds that live in Amdo below the treeline (since trees are mentioned in the song), CL has drawn on his experience birding in that area. We were stumped when it came to finding birds that murmur "kyur kyur," but cuckoos, thrushes, and cranes fit Kälden Gyatso's description of making pleasing sounds; while grouse and partridges whistle, cluck, and chatter; and crow sounds are often harsh (CL).

Cuckoo (T: khu byug) is likely to be the Common (or Eurasian) Cuckoo (*Cuculus canorus*).

A species of **grouse** (ri skegs, ri skyegs) that lives below the treeline in Amdo is the Chinese Grouse (*Tetrastes sewerzowi*).

Thrushes for 'jol mo (T), if small (IW) would include the Siberian Rubythroat (*Luscinia calliope*) and the White-tailed Rubythroat (*L. pectoralis*). Larger thrushes such as Chestnut Thrush (Turdus rubrocanus), Kessler's Thrush (*T. kessleri*) and Eurasian Blackbird (*T. merula*) also occur in Amdo, as do Laughing Thrushes, which are similar in size to the *Turdus* thrushes noted above.

Byi'u 'dzin ma (T) is not in my dictionaries, but is literally translated as '[a bird] that seizes [other birds'] chicks', so **crow** has been chosen, a notorious nest robber. These are likely to be the Carrion Crow (*Corvus corone*) or Large-billed Crow (*C. macrorhynchos*).

Bya shang (T) was the most obscure bird name to translate. I used IW's clues for a shang shang (T), which can be a mythological, garuda-like bird (RY), or a crane (JV). We have chosen **crane** because the garuda is a bird of prey whose character does not seem to fit the passage.

For gong mo (T) we have chosen **partridges**, since these birds occur in Amdo below the treeline. Again, I thank CL, without whose help I would not have been able to make educated guesses about how to translate these birds.

175 **And because most of the time it was quiet**
skabs phal cher zim mer 'dug pa des/ / …

zim me (T) means quiet here, as opposed to the definitions given in some main dictionaries (LC).

177 **[I] became spontaneously happy**
Because [I] had no anxieties [about sitting on] the hard, wet ground,
[Having made the floor of the cave comfortable]
By arranging mats and cushions on top of sweet-smelling juniper bark

dri bzang po 'thul ba'i shug shun la/ /
stan sngas 'bol la sogs legs byas nas/ /
sa sra rlan 'jigs las bskyabs pa des/ /
sems rang dbang med par skyid du bcug /

There are various ways to translate the things he put on the floor of his cave to make it comfortable.

[I] became spontaneously happy
Because [I already] had both salt and butter for tea,
Which are like very white milk,
[And] did not need attendants for yaks

ja tshwa mar gnyis kyi sdor ldan pas/ /
bzhin rab dkar 'o ma'i don ched du/ /
nor mdzo 'dri'i sku g.yog mi dgos pas/ /
sems rang dbang med par skyid du bcug /

I translate the names of the cattle collectively as yaks, the common usage in English, but the names are spelled out in the text here: nor (T) = cattle or yaks, mdzo (T) = a cross between a yak bull and a cow, 'bri (T) = a female yak (English).

*the **cave of Dzongnyin*** (T: Rdzong nyin) is a cave inside Rongbo on the southeast side of town (DD). For the general vicinity, see Rongbo on map 2.

181 **Above the auspicious cave of prosperity [at] Pangluk**
[On] the foothills of the clay range [whose sides]
are like hoisted white flags
To the left of the great mountain deity, Seku Jakyung,
Which possesses the power to protect the area of Rebgong,
The [slender] canopy of sky is stretched out

yul reb gong srung ba'i mthu rtsal can/ /
gnyan chen po se ku bya khyung gi/
g.yas rdza rgyud dar dkar 'phyar 'dra'i 'dabs/ /
sa bkra shis g.yang chags spang lug brag /
yar steng na nam mkha' bla re bres/ /

For **Seku Jakyung** (T: Se ku bya khyung) see Phu Seku, above, and Jakyung on maps 1 and 2.

Pangluk (T: Spang lug), the site of Kälden Gyatso's cave in this song, is in Nyalung in a small valley on a foothill of Jakhyung, about thirty kilometers to the southwest of Rongbo. Since the walls of the valley above Panglug are very steep, he can only see a narrow strip of the sky from his dwelling place. Here he is comparing that bit of sky to a stretched-out canopy (DD). I thank Dge 'dun Don grub for pointing out that Pangluk (literally meadow(s) [and] sheep) is a place name, and for giving me its location, and description. He has personally visited Pangluk, as well as many other holy places around Rebgong. For the general vicinity of Pangluk, see Jakyung on map 2.

The text says that Pangluk is on the right of Seku Jakyung, but this would be our left. Directions in Tibetan are always given from the mountain's view, as if the mountain were looking out (LC).

All sides [of my hermitage] have been decorated
with meadows and juniper trees.
In front [of it], rocks like heaps of jewels adorn
a rock mountain.
From all the slopes, cool spring water cascades.
Behind [it], peaks of grass-covered mountains touch the sky.
And in all directions, [it] is surrounded by small mountains.

Since waters in the lower parts of the valleys do battle with rocks,
[They] guard the entrances [to my dwelling place]

This entire stanza refers to directions from Kälden Gyatso's dwelling place, his cave.

183 **Grouse murmur *kyur kyur* pleasantly**
bya gong mos dbyangs snyan kyur kyur len/ /

Although Kälden Gyatso makes it seem like the **grouse** are singing melodically, grouse whistle, cluck, and chatter (CL).

In that cave, because I, Kälden Repa,
Have covered [my] body with a saffron robe, I am happy.
Because [I] have sung a sonorous song, [I] am happy.
Because [I] have lived without mental suffering, [I] am happy.
Because... (etc.)

phug de na skal ldan ras pa nga/ /
lus ngur smrig gos kyis g.yogs pas bde/ /
ngag glu dbyangs lhang lhang blangs pas bde/ /
sems sdug bsngal med par gnas pas bde/ /

Here we have an extended stanza of sixteen lines that follow the pattern **Because... am happy** (T: pas bde / bas bde). For a discussion about the **continual repetition of a finite verb** as an indigenous poetic figure, an example from Gtsang smyon He ru ka's compilation of Milarepa songs, and the use of this pattern in Daṇḍin's circa sixth-century text of Indian poetics, see *TSR* pp. 224–26.

Note also that Kälden Gyatso begins this long pattern with references to body, speech, and mind.

185 **Because [I] have made friends with both pikas and mice,**
I am happy
grogs bra tsig gnyis la byas pas bde/ /

Pikas (T: bra ba) are a mountain species, and look like plump mice without tails. They resemble rodents, but are actually related to rabbits. They are usually quite tame (CL).

Chö Tündrug Näljor (T: *Chos thun drug rnal 'byor*) refers to meditation to be done in six stages within twenty-four hours. Kälden Gyatso himself wrote two small texts on this topic (T: *Rje skal ldan rgya mtsho dpal bzang po'i gsung las thun drug gi rnal 'byor nyams su len tshul gyi rim pa gnyis*). *See* Skal ldan, *Gsung 'bum* (1987), vol. Ga-12; and Skal ldan, *Gsung 'bum* (1999), vol. 3, 77–80. There are various books with this phrase in their titles.

Again I am grateful to Brill, the publisher of *Tibetan Songs of Realization,* for contractual permission to republish the songs in my appendix. My translation here is the third of four updates of the ones that I made some fifteen years ago. For my earlier translation of this song, see *TSR,* 346–51.

189 **It is difficult to obtain a free and well-favored human [birth],**
a good foundation—
The path for the holy Dharma, the path of well-being,
[And] the most supreme means for giving happiness
[To all beings] in samsara, where there is no [real] happiness.
So without regard for your own happiness and suffering,
take advantage of it

bde ster gyi thabs mchog dam pa'i chos/ /
bde legs kyi lam rten dal 'byor lus/ /
bde med kyi 'khor bar rnyed dka' bas/ /
bde sdug la ma lta snying po longs/ /

This entire song, in which **every line begins with the same Tibetan syllable**, is written in a style that has its roots in formal Indian classical verse. The syllable 'bde' (T) is combined with other syllables to make compounds whose meanings are related to happiness. Because the meanings of the compounds are different, the intricate Tibetan style is not apparent in English translation. For a discussion of this syllabic pattern, see *TSR*, 177–80.

191 **[But if you have] become spontaneously [happy]**
[By] desiring to transfer all beings into a happy state, and so on,
By all means [your happiness] is good

bde ba la 'gro kun 'god 'dod sogs/ /
bde blag tu bsgrubs na cis kyang legs/ /

This is the fourth of the four texts I have updated from my Brill publication. For my earlier translation of this song, see *TSR*, 310–11.

Table of Meters

FIRST LINE	BEATS	METER	EXCEPTIONS
		Chapter 1. Homages to My Lamas	
Father, lama, lord, omniscient one	8	1+2+2+3	3+2+3, random (~5%)
Oh father, the one who holds the teachings, ocean of intelligence	8	1+2+2+3	—
I prostrate myself before the lama	7	2+3+2	five consecutive lines and another: 1+2+2+2 (~2%) last line: 9 beats, 2+2+3+2
I bow to the guru. / When we pray clearly	9	2+2+2+3	—

Chapter 2. Dreadful Defects

I bow at the feet of my father, Tendzin Lobzang	8	1+2+2+3	7 beats, 3+2+2, random (~2%)
I prostrate myself before the guru	8	3+2+3	—
One day I went to view the clay range of Phu Seku	8	1+2+2+3	3+2+3, random (~4%). One line begins with a three-syllable place name.
Having bowed respectfully at the feet	6	2+2+2	—

Chapter 3. Aspirations for Renunciation

If you are able to practice the divine Dharma—Oh joy!	8	3+2+3	last two lines: 7 beats, 2+2+3. *See* my notes.
May I strive continually day and night	8	1+2+2+3	first two lines: 10 beats, 2+3+2+3. *See* my notes.
Oṃ swa sti! / When I think	8	1+2+2+3	—

I pray to the father, Tendzin Lobzang Gyatso	8	1+2+2+3	3+2+3, random (~6%). One of these lines begins with a three-syllable place name.

Chapter 4. Setting Off for Solitary Hermitages

I bow at the feet of the lord, my father Lobzang Tenpai Gyältsen	8	1+2+2+3	3+2+3, random (~6%)
Oh protector, lama—splendid deity of deities, blazing glory of goodness, Buddha	8	1+2+2+3	3+2+3, random (~3%)
Oṃ swa sti! / Near the waters	8	1+2+2+3	last two lines: 11 beats, 3+3+2+3 (~5%). Each begins with a three-syllable interjection, either *a la la* or *o na la*. *See* my notes.

The Stages of the Path to Enlightenment	6	2+2+2	consistent except in the two places where there are interjections. 1) 3+3. Each line begins with the three-syllable interjection *a la la*. 2) last four lines: 7 beats, 3+2+2. Each line begins with either *a la la* or *o na la*.

Chapter 5. Emptiness and Mahāmudrā

Oh lama, you are aware that conditions	8	3+2+3	1+2+2+3, random (~8%). *See* my notes.
Oṃ swa sti! / I have looked up to renunciants	8 to 22 (always even)	2+2+2+2+...	general increase from 8 to 22 beats. *See* my notes.
I bow to the guru, Lokeśvara	8	1+2+2+3	last line: 9 beats, 2+2+2+3, begins with the disyllabic interjection *ha ha*. *See* my notes.
Oh lama, who perceives clearly	6	2+2+2	—

Chapter 6. Mountain Retreats and Happiness

I bow to the guru, Hāsa Vajra	11 / 8	3+2+2+2+2 (1st line of each stanza) 2+2+2+2 (lines 2–4 of each stanza)	homage: 9 beats, 2+2+2+3 introduction: 1st line: 8 beats, 2+2+2+2. 2nd–4th lines: 10 beats, 2+2+2+2+2. The first line of each stanza of the body of the *gur* begins with the three-syllable interjection *a la la*. 2nd–4th lines of some stanzas: 2+2+2+2+2 and 2+2+2+2+2+2, random
I bow at the feet of the father Tendzin Lobzang	8	1+2+2+3	—
I prostrate myself before lord lamas	8	1+2+2+3	—
Oṃ swa sti! / The lama, essence of Cakrasaṃvara	8	3+2+3	1+2+2+3, random (~6%)

Glossary of Buddhist Terms in Common Usage

I am indebted to the following sources: *EB, PDB, IB, B, AIB, SH, TB, GK*, Geshe TC, RY, JV, and DL, from which I have paraphrased these definitions.

absolute truth. *See* ultimate truth.

altruistic aspiration to enlightenment (S: **bodhicitta**; T: byang chub kyi sems, byang sems). Absolute bodhicitta is an awakened or enlightened mind that sees the emptiness of phenomena. Conventional bodhicitta is a mind set on practicing the six perfections and achieving enlightenment so one can help other beings become liberated from samsara. This attitude is central to Mahāyāna and Vajrayāna, and is the widespread motivation of the bodhisattva path. *See also* bodhisattva path, perfections, samsara.

Amitābha (= S; T: 'Od dpag med), or the Buddha of Unlimited Light, is a celestial Buddha who inhabits and rules his purified western realm, Sukhāvatī, and acts to liberate beings in samsara from suffering. He appears in various early Mahāyāna sutras as an object of great devotion.

arhat (= S; T: dgra bcom pa), or Worthy One is a person who has completed the arhat path by ceasing to create karmic cause for any future rebirth, overcoming all obscuring emotions and belief in a self. Whether a śrāvaka, by following the instructions of the Buddha

Śākyamuni, or a pratyekabuddha, through his own efforts, an arhat has realized Nirvana in this life, and will attain final liberation (S: parinirvāṇa; T: yongs su mya ngan las 'das pa) when he dies. The status of arhat is the highest that practitioners of Hīnayāna can achieve. *See also* Hīnayāna, pratyekabuddha, śrāvaka.

Atiśa (982–1054; = S; T: Jo bo a ti sha) was an Indian monk, prominent scholar, and author. He was abbot of Vikramaśīla (S), one of the great Indian monastic universities, and is said to have been invited to Tibet by the king of Guge (T) in order to aid with the rejuvenation of Buddhism after the Period of Darkness. He arrived in Tibet in 1042 and was active there for the remainder of his life. Through his teachings, writings, and new translations of Sanskrit works made in collaboration with Tibetan scholars, he contributed greatly in Tibet toward the strengthening of monastic ethics and discipline, and a clearer understanding of both exoteric and esoteric Buddhism. He is retroactively considered the forefather of the Kadampa (T: Bka' gdams pa) school and has influenced all areas of Tibetan Buddhism. *See also* Kadampa school, Period of Darkness.

Avalokiteśvara (= S; T: Spyan ras gzigs) is the bodhisattva of compassion. One of the main celestial bodhisattvas, he appeared in literature as early as the first century C.E. He looks down from his mountain abode to help sentient beings in the world become free from suffering, and also takes emanation bodies to carry out this goal. He is the patron of Tibet, where the Dalai Lamas are thought to be emanations of him, and where the recitation of his mantra, Oṃ maṇi padme hūṃ (S), is widespread.

bardo (= T; S: antarābhava), or intermediate state, usually refers to the state where the mind goes after death, for a duration ranging from a split second up to 49 days. While the term 'bardo' most commonly refers to this state between death and one's next rebirth, the concept can refer to five other types of intermediate states as well.

bindu (= S; T: thig le) are drops of life-supporting energy, psychic energy, or vital essence including semen. In some Vajrayāna yogic practices they are visualized as moving in the body's channels, which can lead the practitioner to great bliss. *See also* nāḍī, prāṇa, bindu.

bodhicitta. *See* altruistic aspiration to enlightenment.

bodhisattva (= S; T: byang chub sems dpa') is a practitioner on the Mahāyāna path who develops compassion and the six perfections in order to attain Buddhahood for the benefit of all sentient beings. Sometime in the first century B.C.E. or C.E., new sutras emerged that claim that the arhat path is self-centered, and that the bodhisattva path is the superior path to follow since it leads to full Buddhahood and increased ability to aid other sentient beings. *See also* arhat, bodhisattva path.

bodhisattva path (S: Bodhisattvayāna; T: Byang chub sems dpa'i theg pa) begins with the altruistic aspiration to enlightenment, or bodhicitta (S), and taking the bodhisattva vow. Descriptions of the path vary, but a common one has ten stages (S: bhūmi; T: sa), each corresponding to the development of a particular virtue or perfection (S: pāramitā; T: pha rol tu phyin pa). The tenth stage is associated with the perfection of all-inclusive wisdom. The path, after a potentially vast number of lifetimes, can lead to the attainment of Buddhahood. *See also* altruistic aspiration to enlightenment, bodhisattva, perfections.

Buddha-field (S: buddhakṣetra; T: zhing, sangs rgyas zhing) is a cluster of world systems in the Mahāyāna vision of the universe. Each is ruled by a Buddha or bodhisattva, and has been purified, or is in the process of being purified. There are innumerable Buddha-fields since with the emergence of Mahāyāna also came the notion that there can be countless Buddhas at any one time. A Buddha or bodhisattva can reach out across the cosmos from the field in which he or she resides to help all beings become free from suffering and samsara. Moreover, practitioners can attain very auspicious rebirths right in Buddha-fields, where the conditions for becoming enlightened are extremely favorable.

cakra (= S; T: 'khor lo) is a psycho-physical center along the central channel of the body. Cakras are located at the crown of the head, throat, heart, navel, and "secret" place, or "tip of the jewel" (DL). This basic list can vary, according to the tantric system. They mark points where the left and right channels intertwine around the central channel (RJ). There are practices which loosen these constrictions, benefiting the practitioner both physically and spiritually. *See also* nāḍī, prāṇa, bindu.

Cakrasaṃvara (= S; T: 'Khor lo bde mchog) is a main tantric yidam of the Tibetan new schools (T: gsar ma): Kagyüpa (T: Bka' brgyud pa), Sakyapa (Sa skya pa), and Gelugpa (Dge lugs pa). The deity gives his name to the *Cakrasaṃvara Tantra*, an Indian text classified as a highest yoga tantra, the most important type of tantra for the new schools. *See* Heruka, yidam.

calm abiding. *See* peaceful calm.

caṇḍālī (= S; T: gtum mo). *See* inner heat.

Candrakīrti (ca. 600–650; = S; T: Zla ba grags pa) was an Indian philosopher, author, and commentator of the Madhyamaka school. Competing interpretations of Madhyamaka and the intentions of its founder, Nāgārjuna, had developed before Candrakīrti's time, and his *Prasannapadā* defends the side of Buddhapālita (ca. 470–540; = S; T: Sangs rgyas bskyang) by criticizing Bhāviveka's promotion of independent inferences and proposing instead a strategy for defeating opponents in debate that relies solely on showing the absurdity of their statements. The approach of Buddhapālita and Candrakīrti was retroactively called Prāsaṅgika (S; T: Thal 'gyur ba) in Tibet, where it was central to monastic education as early as the twelfth century (RJ). *See also* Madhyamaka.

clear light (T: 'od gsal) refers to one of the six yogas of Nāropa, clear light yoga, equivalent to the realization of emptiness in the Completion Stage of highest yoga tantra. In a Gelugpa context, subjective clear light is mind that realizes emptiness and objective clear light is emptiness itself (Geshe TC). *See also* six yogas of Nāropa.

Completion Stage (S: niṣpannakrama; T: rdzogs rim) is the second of the two main divisions of the highest yoga tantra, the other being the Generation Stage. In very simple terms, the Completion Stage involves yogic techniques related to the channels, energies, and drops, which ultimately lead to an experience of enlightenment. *See also* Generation Stage.

conventional truth, relative truth, or **relative reality** (S: saṃvṛtisatya; T: kun rdzob kyi bden pa) refers to all things one perceives in the world through ordinary experience, including objects, concepts, and so on (DL). While these things do exist conventionally, perception of them by the unenlightened implies deception tainted by ignorance. According to the Madhyamaka doctrine of the two truths (S: satya-dvaya; T: bden pa gnyis), one needs a realization of ultimate truth (S: paramārthasatya; T: don dam pa'i bden pa) in order to understand the true nature of things that are perceived conventionally, or they may be misunderstood as having true or intrinsic existence. *See also* two truths; ultimate truth; ultimate truth and conventional truth, relationship between.

ḍākinī (= S; T: mkha' 'gro ma), as referred to in this text, is a sky-going female wrathful or semi-wrathful tantric deity who protects all Buddhist teachings in general, and a practitioner's spiritual practices in particular. The ḍākinī is one of the three "inner" refuges, along with the guru and yidam. *See also* refuge.

Degenerate Age (S: saddharmavipralopa; T: snyigs dus) is a dark age or time of decline in the understanding of Buddhism. Consistent with the view of impermanence, there are periods in which Buddhism will be forgotten. Following an age of decline, a new Buddha is needed to revive a true understanding of the Dharma. There is no general consensus about the precise duration of this cycle of decline and rejuvenation, and it can vary from around five hundred to five thousand years or more.

demigods (S: asura; T: lha min) are one of the six levels of sentient beings. They are depicted as warlike, power-hungry, lustful, hateful, proud beings who feel driven to fight with the gods proper (deva). Because of their jealousy of the gods, they were expelled from their original realm in the heavens. This made them all the more aggressive. In traditions in which there are five levels of beings, demigods are not included. *See also* sentient beings of the six realms.

dependent arising. *See* interdependent origination.

Development Stage. *See* Generation Stage.

Dharma (= S; T: chos) is the teachings and doctrinal pronouncements of the Buddha, and in a wider sense all Buddhist teachings. Dharma is one of the three refuges of Buddhism, along with the Buddha and Saṅgha. *See also* refuge.

Dharma body. *See* dharmakāya.

dharmadhātu (= S; T: chos kyi dbyings) in Mahāyāna usually refers to all things perceived by the senses, and to the universe in general, including time and space. Dharmadhātu can also refer to ultimate reality (*PDB*, 244), the reality of the true nature of phenomena—lack of any inherent existence. It is in the latter sense that the term is used in this text. *See also* emptiness.

dharmakāya or **Dharma body** (= S; T: chos kyi sku, chos sku) is the first of the three bodies of the Buddha. In early Buddhism, it may have referred to the collection of the Buddha's teachings and to the Buddha's auspicious qualities. In Mahāyāna, it is the true nature of Buddhahood, the 'body' of enlightened qualities, devoid of constructs, like space; and the source of the other two bodies of the Buddha. In the Gelugpa school, wisdom Dharma body is the omniscient mind of the Buddha. Nature Dharma body is the emptiness of Buddha's mind (Geshe TC). *See also* three bodies of the Buddha.

dharmapāla (= S; T: chos skyong), in the present sense, is a spirit or other bodiless being who protects the Buddhist teachings and their followers. According to legend, they predated the Dharma in Tibet as demonic local deities and were converted to Buddhism by Padmasaṃbhava, the tantric master who had been invited to Tibet in the late eighth century to vanquish forces opposing the construction of the first monastery there.

Dorjechang (S: Vajradhara; T: Rdo rje 'chang). *See* Vajradhara.

Dromtön (1008–1064; T: 'Brom ston pa, 'Brom ston Rgyal ba'i byung gnas) was the primary Tibetan disciple of the Indian scholar Atiśa, who had come to western Tibet in 1042 to help rejuvenate Buddhism after a long period of decline. In 1056, two years after Atiśa's death, Dromtön established Reting Monastery (T: Rwa sgreng) north of Lhasa, and founded the Kadampa school. The Kadampa, famous for its monastic discipline and exhaustive education, continued to exist independently for about four centuries, and influenced all schools of Tibetan Buddhism, especially the Gelugpa school. *See also* Atiśa.

eight worldly concerns or **preoccupations** (T: 'jig rten chos brgyad) are attachment to pleasure and aversion to pain, attachment to gain and aversion to loss, attachment to praise and aversion to blame, and attachment to fame and aversion to disgrace (T: bde dang mi bde, rnyed dang mi rnyed, bstod dang smad, snyan dang mi snyan). Though on the conventional level, one of each pair seems good and the other seems bad, they are all to be transcended.

emanation body. *See* nirmāṇakāya.

empowerment. *See* initiation.

emptiness (S: śūnyatā; T: stong pa nyid) refers to the notion that all phenomena are empty of, or lack, any independent, intrinsic existence. This does not mean that things do not exist, but rather that they do not exist on their own, so grasping at their appearances will not yield lasting happiness. Realizing emptiness through higher wisdom is thought to bring one freedom and further one's path towards Buddhahood. The view of emptiness, a much-featured theme in early Mahāyāna literature and a key concept of Mahāyāna philosophy, extends the earlier, more narrow Buddhist doctrine of no self (S: anātman; T: bdag med) to include all aspects of existence. *See also* Mahāyāna.

enjoyment body. *See* sambhogakāya.

eternalism. *See* two extremes.

five realms of rebirth. *See* realms of rebirth.

four noble truths (S: catvāry āryasatyāni; T: bden pa rnam bzhi) are a set of four related assertions that the Buddha taught in his first sermon. In English, the group of four are usually called the 'four noble truths', but the name of the set would be more literally translated as 'four truths [known by the spiritually] noble' (*PDB*, 304). In them, the word 'duḥkha' (= S; T: sdug bsngal), often translated as 'suffering', can also mean unsatisfactoriness, sorrow, pain, and so on. The four noble truths are: (1) the truth of suffering, which asserts that life as ordinarily lived is ultimately unsatisfactory; (2) the truth of the origin of suffering, which asserts that suffering is caused by ignorance, craving, and attachment; (3) the truth of its cessation, which asserts that suffering can be ended (in Nirvana) by eliminating craving and attachment; and (4) the truth of the path, which provides an eightfold path that leads to the end of suffering. *See also* truth of suffering.

four sessions. *See* six sessions, four sessions.

free and well-favored human birth (T: dal 'byor mi lus). A human birth with the so-called eight freedoms and the ten favors is highly valued because one has all necessary conditions for Dharma practice. "First are the **freedoms from eight obstacles** to practicing the Dharma, which are 1) to be born in a hell realm, 2) among the pretas, or tormented spirits, 3) as an animal, 4) among savages, 5) as a long-living god, 6) holding totally erroneous views, 7) in a dark kalpa, during which no Buddha has appeared in the world, [and] 8) with impaired sense faculties" (*SH*, 602).

"Second, among the **ten favorable conditions**, there are five conditions that depend on ourselves (T: rang 'byor lnga): 1) to be born as a human being, 2) in a place where the Dharma flourishes, 3) with complete sense faculties, 4) without the karma of living in a way totally opposite to the Dharma, 5) and having faith in what deserves it. There are five conditions that depend upon others (gzhan 'byor lnga): 1) a Buddha should have appeared in the world, 2) and have taught the Dharma, 3) the Dharma should have remained until our days, 4) we should have entered the Dharma, 5) and have been accepted by a spiritual teacher" (*SH*, 602). *See also* karma, sentient beings of the six realms.

Ganden Oral Tradition of Mahāmudrā, alternatively translated as **Ganden / Kagyüpa Tradition of Mahāmudrā** (T: Dga' ldan bka' brgyud phyag rgya chen po) is a form of Mahāmudrā that is attributed to Tsongkhapa, who by tradition received it as part of an ear-whispered transmission (T: snyan rgyud) from Vajradhara, either through the divine revelation of Mañjuśrī or via a lineage of human teachers, including Nāropa, Maitrīpa, Marpa and Milarepa. It is said to have been passed down through the Gelugpa school from Tsongkhapa. The first Panchen Lama seems to have been the first to record its systematic teaching in writing (RJ), though it may have taken systematic form as an oral teaching before his time. *See also* Kagyüpa school; Lobzang Chökyi Gyältsen, the first Panchen Lama; Mahāmudrā; Tsongkhapa.

The **Gelugpa school** (T: Dge lugs) is one of the four main schools of Tibetan Buddhism, and the last to be established. Tsongkhapa (T), retroactively revered as Gelugpa school's founder, formed its main ideas and practices by bringing together a range of exoteric and esoteric aspects of the Buddhist tradition. He also initiated the Great Prayer Festival in Lhasa (T), and founded Ganden (T: Dga' ldan) Monastery near Lhasa in 1409. The other two main Gelugpa monasteries in Lhasa were founded by his direct disciples soon afterwards. The incarnation lineage of Dalai Lamas (from Mongol: Dalai + T: bla ma; T: Ta la'i bla ma, Rgyal ba Rin po che) belongs to the Gelugpa school. *See also* Tsongkhapa.

Generation Stage or **Development Stage** (S: utpattikrama; T: skyed rim) is a class of tantric meditational practices utilizing visualizations and mantras whereby one seeks to transform one's own appearance, sound, and wisdom into those of a particular deity, and become one with its nature. The Generation Stage and the Completion Stage are the two main groups of practices in the highest division of tantric texts. *See also* Completion Stage.

gods (S: deva; T: lha), as in worldly gods, are the highest level of sentient beings in samsara. Due to good karma or mastery of contemplation in previous lives, they have earned the most pleasant of abodes in which to dwell, one of the many heavens. Like the other levels of sentient beings, this status is temporary, and according to the gods' karma, they may be reborn in any of the other samsaric realms in future lives. *See also* karma, sentient beings of the six realms.

guru yoga (= S; T: bla ma'i rnal 'byor) is a tantric practice of visualizations and recitations, through which one's lama is ritually invoked. One sees one's lama as the Buddha, expresses devotion to him, gives him offerings, requests him not to forsake the world, receives his blessing, and merges one's mind with his.

hell beings are the inhabitants of the many hell realms, which generally include eight hot hells and eight cold hells (RJ). *See also* karma, samsara, sentient beings of the six realms.

hell realm (S: nāraka; T: dmyal ba'i gnas, dmyal ba) is the lowest and worst level for sentient beings in samsara. One's prolonged stay in this realm is because of truly evil deeds in past lives, and the suffering, which can be due to heat, cold, cutting, and other tortures is tremendous. Rebirth in this realm is not permanent, so eventually a hell being will attain a higher rebirth. *See also* realms of rebirth.

Heruka (= S; T: Khrag 'thung) is the general name for wrathful, male, tantric deities. In the Gelugpa school, Heruka is often an alternate name for Cakrasaṃvara (RJ), the deity of the highest yoga tantra. Heruka may have originally been a deity appropriated from forest tribes or a form of Śiva in cremation grounds.

Hīnayāna (= S, T: Theg pa dman pa), the first main division of Buddhism, refers to the literature, doctrines, practices, and institutions of all early non-Mahāyāna Indian Buddhist schools or sects. These schools typically did not accept Mahāyāna sutras as having come from the Buddha. They emphasized the paths of practitioners who are moving towards arhatship or Nirvana either by learning the Dharma from others (Śrāvakayāna) or having no significant external teachers (Pratyekabuddhayāna). Literally 'Lesser Vehicle', Hīnayāna is a pejorative term that Mahāyāna 'Greater Vehicle' writers coined to express their view that the followers of the early Buddhist schools could not attain full Buddhahood. *See also* arhat, pratyekabuddha, śrāvaka, three vehicles.

human body complete with the freedoms and endowments. *See* free and well-favored human birth.

hungry ghosts or spirits of the dead (S: preta; T: yi dwags) are beings who are perpetually frustrated by hunger and thirst because of having been selfish and greedy in past lives. They inhabit the hungry-ghost realm. *See also* samsara, sentient beings of the six realms.

hungry-ghost realm (T: yi dwags kyi gnas) is the second-lowest level for sentient beings in samsara. Rebirth in the realm of hungry ghosts is temporary. This realm is said to be on the fringes of the human world or overlapping with it, a place that hungry ghosts haunt because of strong attachment to this earth. They are usually not seen by humans. *See also* realms of rebirth.

initiation or **empowerment** (S: abhiṣeka; T: dbang bskur) is a tantric rite whereby a lama empowers his or her disciple to invoke and identify with a tantric deity. The lama is considered to be a conduit for the teachings, and the rite is considered to be the gateway into the tantric path and realization of the common and supreme siddhis. *See also* siddhi, tantric Buddhism.

inner-calm meditation. *See* peaceful calm.

inner heat or **caṇḍālī** (= S; T: gtum mo). The first of the six yogas of Nāropa (T: Na ro chos drug), the generation of inner heat involves exercises with the channels, energies, and drops. The heat is thought to melt the drops, which then flow in the channels and induce great bliss. *See also* nāḍī, prāṇa, bindu; six yogas of Nāropa.

insight into emptiness. *See* insight meditation.

insight meditation or **penetrating insight** (S: vipaśyanā; T: lhag mthong) is a Buddhist meditational practice in which one single-pointedly analyzes self and phenomena in order to develop insight into their ultimate nature. In the case of Mahāyāna and Vajrayāna, this means the emptiness of all phenomena. It is often performed after the state of peaceful calm is attained. Peaceful calm and insight meditation are two main types of Buddhist meditation. *See also* emptiness, peaceful calm.

interdependent origination, **dependent origination**, or **dependent arising** (S: pratītyasamutpāda; T: rten cing 'brel bar 'byung ba, rten 'brel, rten 'byung) is a fundamental Buddhist theory that describes interdependent links of causal connections that bind a being to samsara and suffering, each following the previous one. It is commonly thought that the theory dates back to its realization by the future Buddha Siddhārtha Gautama under the Bodhi tree, and that his realization of it enabled his enlightenment. Important consequences of interdependent origination are that nothing can come into being by itself, and all phenomena are empty of intrinsic existence. A group of twelve links is commonly identified: "ignorance, habitual tendencies, consciousness, name and form, the six sense fields, contact, feeling, craving, grasping, coming into being (existence), birth, and old age and death" (*TG*, 135). The links can be followed in both directions. The forward order shows the progression from ignorance to birth and death, i.e. samsara. The reverse direction shows the progression from death down to ignorance. *See* emptiness.

The **Kadampa school** (T: Bka' gdams) was the first new school to arise in Tibet after the Period of Darkness, inspired in the eleventh century by the Buddhist renaissance of new translations, new translators, and new teachers. Based on the reforms and teachings of the Indian missionary and scholar, Atiśa, it was founded in the mid-eleventh century by Atiśa's disciple, Dromtön (T: 'Brom ston). Its followers were known for their monastic discipline, austere practice, and rigorous study. It survived only a few centuries, but influenced all other schools, especially the Gelugpa school. *See also* Atiśa, Dromtön, Period of Darkness.

The **Kagyüpa school** (T: Bka' brgyud), one of the four main schools of Tibetan Buddhism, was introduced in Tibet by Marpa (T) in the eleventh century. The roots of the lineage of instructions and meditation practices that he brought back from India are said to go back to the primordial tantric Buddha Vajradhara and various Indian mahāsiddhas. Marpa's main disciple was the famed Milarepa (T: Mi la ras pa), and Milarepa's disciple Gampopa (T: Sgam po pa Bsod nams rin chen) formally founded the Kagyüpa school by synthesizing Kadampa (T: Bka' gdams) principles of monastic education with particular tantric practices, and by establishing the first Kagyüpa monasteries. Vajradhara, Tilopa, Nāropa, Marpa, and Milarepa form the lineage that remains highly venerated today by all extant subsects of the Kagyüpa school. *See also* Maitrīpa, Marpa, Milarepa, Nāropa, Vajradhara.

karma (S: karman; T: las) is a moral law of causality central to Buddhism. According to the doctrine of cause and effect, every intentional action determines one's future conditions, whether in this or future lives, so that a wholesome action leads to better circumstances, and an unwholesome action leads to negative consequences.

Khorlo Demchog (S: Cakrasaṃvara; T: 'Khor lo bde mchog). *See* Cakrasaṃvara.

Lobzang Chökyi Gyältsen, **first Panchen Lama**, or **fourth Panchen Lama** (1570–1662; T: Blo bzang chos kyi rgyal mtshan; S: Paṇ + T: chen bla ma) was the teacher of the fourth and fifth Dalai Lamas (from Mongol: dalai + T: bla ma; T: Ta la'i bla ma). The fifth Dalai Lama appointed him abbot of Tashilhunpo (T: Bkra shis lhun po) Monastery in west central Tibet and gave him the title of Panchen Lama, out of gratitude for the role he had played in bringing to an end a vicious and lengthy civil war and helping make the fifth Dalai Lama the theocratic leader of Tibet. The title Panchen (short for Paṇḍita chenpo), or great scholar, predated Lobzang Chökyi Gyältsen. However, in this case, the fuller title of Panchen Lama was bestowed on him with the intention to honor him as an important Gelugpa lineage holder. Each reincarnation in the Panchen Lama lineage is considered an emanation of Buddha Amitābha and has had secular and spiritual powers second only to those of the Dalai Lamas. Most sources refer to Lobzang Chökyi Gyältsen as the first Panchen Lama. Three earlier reincarnations were named posthumously, also making him the fourth Panchen Lama. Either enumeration can apply to his position in the lineage.

Lobzang Dragpa. *See* Tsongkhapa.

Lokeśvara (= S; Tibetanized Sanskrit: Lo ke shwa ra ya), in this context, is a title of respect for the Buddha that means "Lord of the World."

Lord of Death, Yamarāja or **Yama** (= S; T: 'Chi bdag Gshin rje) is the lord of death and the king of hell. He interrogates the dead to determine their karma, and assigns the worst offenders to various hells. He is a god (deva) who threatens humans with karmic consequences in order to remind them to live virtuous lives.

lower realms (S: apāya, durgati; T: ngan song) are those of hell beings, hungry ghosts, and animals. *See also* hell realm, hungry-ghost realm, realms of rebirth.

Madhyamaka (= S; T: Dbu ma), or the Middle Way System, is a Mahāyāna Buddhist philosophical school. It is considered to have been founded by the Indian philosopher Nāgārjuna (ca. 2nd century), and was derived from his writings, especially his main treatise, *Verses on the Middle Way* (S: *Mūlamadhyamakakārikā*). Madhyamaka emphasizes the emptiness of all phenomena due to (a) their unfindability under ultimate analysis and (b) the fact that they are interdependently originated. It takes the middle way between pairs of extremes such as eternalism and nihilism, and Nirvana and samsara, recognizing each one to be empty of inherent existence. Besides emphasizing emptiness and interdependent origination, the school is much focused on the nature of ultimate truth, and the relationship between conventional truth and ultimate truth. Interpretations of Madhyamaka developed in the generations of philosophers following Nāgārjuna, sometimes with much disagreement between them. Madhyamaka was a central feature of Tibetan Buddhism predating the Period of Darkness (RJ). *See also* conventional truth, emptiness, Nirvana, Period of Darkness, two extremes, ultimate truth.

Mahāmudrā (= S; T: Phyag rgya chen mo) is a system of teachings for directly apprehending the nature of mind, one's Buddha nature, and the unity of luminosity (or phenomenal appearance) and emptiness. Meditating on the nature of mind can lead the practitioner to a state of enlightened awareness, whereby he or she sees every rising thought as empty of intrinsic existence. The term 'Mahāmudrā' is also used to refer to fundamental reality, the awareness that can realize fundamental reality, and the experience of realizing fundamental reality. Most Tibetan schools accept the mahāsiddha Saraha as the initiator of Mahāmudrā lineages in India (RJ). Kagyüpa traditions also specify that the Buddha Vajradhara gave Mahāmudrā instructions to the mahāsiddha Tilopa, and that he and the mahāsiddhas Nāropa and Maitrīpa developed a Mahāmudrā lineage that the Tibetan translator Marpa brought to Tibet, and passed on to his main disciple, Milarepa. The teachings are particularly important to the Kagyüpa school, and are also sometimes practiced in the Sakyapa and Gelugpa schools. *See also* Ganden Oral Tradition of Mahāmudrā, Maitrīpa, Marpa, Milarepa, Nāropa.

mahāsiddha (= S: T: grub thob chen po), essentially meaning the same as siddha, is the honorary title accorded a group of Indian tantric masters, both male and female, often eighty-four or eighty in number, many of whom were historical figures, and who came from all walks of society, including the most despicable. "If the power of the monk derives from the purity he acquires through abstaining from the things that laymen do, the power of the tantric yogin derives from his transgression of purity, engaging in acts that both violate monastic vows as well as the prescriptions regarding purity and pollution of traditional Indian society" (*PDB,* 508). Some important Tibetan practices, such as Mahāmudrā, trace their development back to one or more of the eighty-four mahāsiddhas in India, from whom the teachings were transmitted into Tibet. A number of them have retroactively been considered founders of important tantric lineages. *See also* Mahāmudrā, siddha.

Mahāyāna (= S; T: Theg pa chen po), literally the 'Greater Vehicle', is the second major division in Buddhism. Based on literary developments, it seems to have emerged around the beginning of the first century C.E. when a new wave of sutras with new ideals and clear differences in style from earlier sutras appeared in India. Like the earlier sutras these sutras still claimed to be the discourses of the Buddha, and those accepting them as genuine were considered to be devotees of Mahāyāna. Mahāyāna sutras feature the bodhisattva ideal of staying in samsara in order to help other beings attain Buddhahood, in contrast to the pre-Mahāyāna ideal of the arhat departing samsara and attaining Nirvana for himself or herself. Other innovative features of Mahāyāna are the simultaneity of countless celestial Buddhas, the doctrine of the three bodies of Buddha, and a view of emptiness that now includes every aspect of existence.

Much about the emergence of this movement that called itself 'Mahāyāna' in contrast to 'Hīnayāna' (the 'Lesser Vehicle', a pejorative term) is at present still a mystery. Based on the current dearth of archeological and inscriptional evidence, and the virtual absence of art historical evidence for it until the fifth century C.E., Mahāyāna appears to have been a religious movement that remained in the minority in India for some centuries. Mahāyāna is the main religion of Tibet. *See also* bodhisattva, emptiness, Nirvana, sutra, three vehicles.

Maitrīpa (ca. 1007–1085; = mai trI pa, Tibetanized Sanskrit; S: Maitrīpāda) was one of the famed eighty-four mahāsiddhas of India and by tradition is considered one of the great masters of Marpa (T), a translator and Sanskrit scholar from Tibet who had gone to India to seek practice instructions. Maitrīpa had been a successful scholar in several important Buddhist monasteries in India, where he also may have clandestinely practiced tantra on the side. According to some stories, he was expelled for violating prohibitions of alcohol and women. However, at the same time, it seems he felt inspired to leave monastic life to seek the guru Śavaripa for practice instructions. The guru, in turn, first tested him very harshly, and only eventually accepted him as a disciple. It is sometimes said that Maitrīpa gave

Marpa the Mahāmudrā teachings and songs of realization (S: dohā). Marpa disseminated the teachings in Tibet, where Mahāmudrā later became a central practice of the Kagyüpa school. Maitrīpa is retroactively considered one of the founding fathers of the Mahāmudrā lineage. *See also* Kagyüpa school, Mahāmudrā, mahāsiddha, Marpa.

mandala (S: maṇḍala; T: dkyil 'khor) is a diagram of the cosmos with complex symbolism for ritual use. First developed in India, it became a feature of tantric Buddhism. There are many kinds of mandalas. The most common are two-dimensional paintings or murals of three-dimensional structures viewed from above. Usually there is a circle marking off a sacred space, in which there is a grand palace with four elaborate gates in the cardinal directions. This is the residence of a central Buddha-deity and entourage—such as Buddhas, bodhisattvas, and guardian deities carefully placed to reflect their relationship with the main deity. In meditation one can use a mandala to visualize the realm of the main deity. *See also* tantric Buddhism.

Mañjuśrī (= S; T: 'Jam dpal dbyangs) is one of the principal celestial bodhisattvas in Mahāyāna, symbolizing wisdom or transcendent knowledge. He carries a blazing wisdom sword in his right hand, and a lotus upon which rests a book in his left. These symbolize his mission of using his great power to protect beings in need by cutting through their delusion and awakening their spiritual knowledge. He is thought to be a protector of scholars, and to help beings by appearing in dreams and visions. *See also* Mahāyāna.

mantra (= S; T: sngags) is a Sanskrit syllable or short string of syllables that symbolizes the nature of a specific meditational deity. The use of mantras in India dates back to the Vedas, and they were used in Mahāyāna before becoming a fundamental aspect of tantric Buddhism. The sound of the syllables, which often have no clear, translatable meaning, is endowed with great potency, and is recited with the aim of invoking the deity. *See also* tantra, tantric Buddhism.

Mantrayāna (= S; T: sngags kyi theg pa), or Mantra Vehicle; and the **secret Mantrayāna** (S: Guhyamantrayāna; T: gsang sngags kyi theg pa), or secret Mantra Vehicle, are synonymous with Vajrayāna. The use of these terms to refer to Vajrayāna reflects the strong role the recitation of mantras plays in Vajrayāna. *See also* mantra, Vajrayāna.

Marpa (~1011–1090s; T: Mar pa Chos kyi blo gros) was a Tibetan tantric practitioner and famous translator of Sanskrit who, according to later accounts, went to India three times to receive tantric instruction. There, he received important teachings from Indian tantric siddhas for practices such as Mahāmudrā and the six yogas of Nāropa (T: Na ro chos drug). He brought these and the tradition of songs of realization (S: dohā) back to Tibet with him and gave them to his main disciples, including the famed Milarepa (T: Mi la ras pa). Mahāmudrā and the six yogas of **Nāropa** became central teachings of the Kagyüpa school, soon to be formally founded by Gampopa (T: Sgam po pa), a disciple of Milarepa's. Marpa is retroactively considered the founding father of the Kagyüpa school, which begins its Tibetan lineage with him. *See also* Kagyüpa school, Mahāmudrā, Milarepa, six yogas of Nāropa, tantra, tantric Buddhism.

meditational deity. *See* yidam.

Milarepa (1028/40–1111/23; T: Mi la ras pa; the cotton-clad Mila, his clan name) was a famed and much-loved yogi and creator of songs who is believed to have become enlightened in one lifetime as a result of intense dedication, perseverance, and mastery of meditations. Retrospectively considered a forefather of the Kagyüpa lineage, he was a crucial link in the transmission of teachings that his teacher, **Marpa** (T: Mar pa Chos kyi blo gros), brought from India, including Mahāmudrā and the practice of yogic inner heat (S: caṇḍālī; T: gtum mo).

From the early sixteenth century on, Milarepa's life (T: rnam thar) and songs (T: mgur ma) were generally known from Tsang Nyön Heruka's (T: Gtsang smyon He ru ka's) fifteenth-century compilation of each of them. For these, see Lobsang P. Lhalungpa, trans., *The Life of*

Milarepa (Boston: Shambhala, 1985); Gtsang smyon He ru ka, comp., *Rnal 'byor gyi dbang phyug chen po mi la ras pa'i rnam mgur* (Xining: Mtsho sngon mi rigs dpe skrun khang, 1999); and Mi la ras pa, *The Hundred Thousand Songs of Milarepa,* ed., trans. Garma C. C. Chang (Boston: Shambhala, 1989). *See also* Kagyüpa school, Mahāmudrā, Marpa.

mudrā (= S; T: phyag rgya), in this text, is a formalized hand gesture used extensively in tantric rituals. Mudrās play symbolic roles that are meant to aid practitioners to worship and transform themselves into the divine. *See also* tantric Buddhism.

nāḍī. *See* nāḍī, prāṇa, bindu.

nāḍī, prāṇa, bindu (= S; T: rtsa, rlung, thig le) are three interconnected components of a vajra body, often translated as channels, winds, and drops or vital essences. According to Tibetan anatomy, life-supporting energies and drops flow through the channels. Meditating on these allows a yogi to remove whatever knots there may be in the channels, so that the winds flow smoothly. In Tibetan tantric traditions, the interconnected system of channels, winds, and drops is the site of advanced meditative practices—those of the Completion Stage—that enable the practitioner to attain blissful Buddhahood (RJ).

Nāgārjuna (ca. 2nd century; = S; T: Klu sgrub) was an Indian Buddhist monk and philosopher who is traditionally regarded as the founder of the Madhyamaka school of Mahāyāna. Most details of his life are at present a mystery, and he is best known through his writings. His major work, *Verses on the Middle Way* (S: *Mūlamadhyamakakārikā*), became the foundational document of Madhyamaka. In it he explains a view of emptiness in which everything lacks inherent existence, and shows that view to be consistent with the early Buddhist teachings. He examines the relationship between conventional and ultimate truth. He also proposes that negative mental dispositions that arise in people are a result of the faulty way they conceive of the world, and the way they use language about it. Hence their misconceptions are what ultimately lead them to be bound to samsara and suffering, whereas a clear realization of emptiness leads to the cessation of suffering and the attainment of Nirvana. *See* Madhyamaka; ultimate truth and conventional truth, relationship between.

Nāropa (956–1040; = nA ro pa, Tibetanized Sanskrit; S: Nāḍapāda) was a Vajrayāna practitioner, disciple of Tilopa (= Tibetanized Sanskrit; S: Tilopāda), and one of the famed 84 mahāsiddhas of India. Prior to being a siddha, he had been married and divorced, and had studied at the prestigious monastic university of Nālandā, where he served as abbot and senior instructor. According to legend, he was inspired by visions to leave all of that behind to seek the siddha, Tilopa. After many trials and much duress, he finally received instructions from Tilopa, which he compiled and codified, and transmitted to his students. Marpa became aware of Nāropa's teachings, took them to Tibet, and disseminated them there. Nāropa is retroactively considered one of the Indian founding fathers of the Kagyüpa lineage. *See also* Kagyüpa school, mahāsiddha, Marpa, siddha, Vajrayāna.

nature of mind (T: sems kyi rang bzhin, sems nyid) refers to mind's deepest nature of lucidity, clarity, and voidness. The ultimate nature of mind, the foundation of all good qualities, is pure because it is unstained by confusion and disturbing emotions. We all have it within us, and on this basis we can all attain omniscient awareness and enlightenment. "'Seeing the actual nature of mind'... refers to directly understanding voidness itself" (*GK*, 111).

nihilism. *See* two extremes.

nirmāṇakāya or **emanation body** (= S; T: sprul pa'i sku) is one of the three bodies of a Buddha in Mahāyāna—an earthly manifestation by a particular Buddha. An emanation of the Dharma body, it takes the form of what is needed to support the progress of a being along his or her Buddhist path. The forms of projection may vary from a human

Buddha to other person, divinity, animal, ghost, and even inanimate objects such as bridges and breezes. *See also* three bodies of the Buddha.

Nirvana (S: Nirvāṇa; T: mya ngan las 'das pa) is the state that one attains after eliminating false ideas and conflicting emotions. The term is understood differently according to Hīnayāna and Mahāyāna. For the former, whose highest ideal is the level of arhat, Nirvana during life entails the cessation of attachment, hatred, and delusion, and after death the arhat is free from any future rebirth in samsaric existence. This end of involvement with samsara is alluded to in the third Noble Truth of the Buddha's first sermon. For the Mahāyāna practitioner, Nirvana is freedom from the extremes of either samsara or the Nirvana of an arhat. *See also* arhat, Hīnayāna, Mahāyāna, samsara.

Padmasaṃbhava (= S) or **Guru Rinpoche** (S: Guru + T: Rin po che) was an Indian Buddhist mahāsiddha who is said to have been invited to Tibet by its king in the eighth century in order to tame indigenous spirits who were opposing Buddhism as a foreign religion and blocking the construction of its first Tibetan monastery, Samye (T: Bsam yas). After Padmasaṃbhava converted the local spirits into protectors of Buddhism, Samye was established without mishap. Besides playing a crucial role in Buddhism's establishment in Tibet, he gave many Vajrayāna teachings, some of which have been passed down orally, and others of which were hidden as treasures (T: gter ma) to be discovered later. He is considered the second Buddha by the Nyingmapa school (T: Rnying ma pa), and its founder. He is said to have been born in Uḍḍiyāna / Oḍḍiyāna, an area probably in the northwest of India. Another of his names, **Pema of Ugyen / Ogyen** (T: U rgyan pad+ma / O rgyan pad+ma), makes reference to this place. *See also* Vajrayāna.

Panchen Lama, first or fourth. *See* Lobzang Chökyi Gyältsen.

peaceful calm, inner-calm meditation, or **calm abiding** (S: śamatha; T: zhi gnas) is single-pointed, effortless focus on an object of meditation, accompanied by calmness and physical and mental ecstasy. It is achieved through repeated concentration on a chosen object. It is said to have many healing and integrating benefits, and also serves as preparation for insight meditation and the careful observation that the latter entails. Peaceful calm and insight meditation are the two main types of Buddhist meditation practice. *See also* insight meditation.

perfections (S: pāramitā; T: phar phyin, pha rol tu phyin pa) are special virtues or qualities of Buddhahood to be developed by practitioners in order to perfect themselves and benefit other beings. The most common list is of six perfections that are central to the bodhisattva path. They are generosity (S: dāna, T: sbyin pa), morality (S: śīla, T: tshul khrims), patience (S: kṣānti, T: bzod pa), diligence (S: vīrya, T: brtson 'grus), contemplation (S: dhyāna, T: bsam gtan), and transcendental knowledge or insight (S: prajñā, T: shes rab). Unlike ordinary generosity, and so on, they are pure actions untainted by attachment and free from dualistic concepts. The bodhisattva's ideal of compassion embraces the first five perfections. The last one is the bodhisattva's wisdom, and with this profound view of emptiness, he or she is able to practice the previous five in a pure, direct way. There is also a group of ten perfections in Mahāyāna, made by adding four more to the standard six. The Śrāvakayāna has a list of ten perfections that help one attain the śrāvaka's ideal of Nirvana, some of which overlap with the Mahāyāna perfections. *See also* bodhisattva path, Nirvana, Śrāvakayāna.

Period of Darkness or **Dark Period** was a time of decline in institutionalized Dharma in Tibet from around the mid-ninth century into the eleventh century.

Practice Lineage (T: sgrub brgyud) is the lineage of lamas and their disciples who mainly do meditation practices and focus on their experience of the teachings, often in solitary places. It is often contrasted with the scholastic lineage (T: bshad brgyud).

Prajñāpāramitā (= S; T: sher phyin), or the **Perfection of Wisdom sutras**, is a genre of texts that date back to sometime around the first century B.C.E. or C.E. and are among the earliest writings of Mahāyāna Buddhism. One of the earliest extant texts of this genre is the *Perfection of Wisdom Discourse in 8,000 Lines*. The texts focus on the wisdom insight into the empty nature of all things, and depict the emerging bodhisattva path as being motivated by the six perfections and altruistic aspiration to enlightenment (S: bodhicitta). They also present a new understanding of Nirvana, and depict arhats as selfish for forsaking the suffering beings in samsara. The Perfection of Wisdom sutras' main themes of wisdom and emptiness were an inspiration for the development of a new philosophical school, that of Madhyamaka. Prajñāpāramitā is also the name of the sixth perfection (S: pāramitā), the perfection of wisdom; and the name of a goddess personifying that perfection. *See also* arhat, bodhisattva path, Madhyamaka, Nirvana, perfections, samsara.

prāṇa. *See* nāḍī, prāṇa, bindu.

Prātimokṣa (= S; T: So sor thar pa) is probably the oldest section of the Vinaya, the Code of Discipline for regulating an ordered and peaceful way of behavior among monks and nuns. It does not address conformity to doctrine. The rules, several hundred in number, are arranged in seven categories according to the severity of the punishment or reprimand for a rule's infringement, and range from expulsion from the monastery down to mere acknowledgement of the transgression. Monks and nuns who are at least twenty years old and have taken full ordination are responsible for following the rules, which they recite in monasteries twice a month. The Prātimokṣa also includes rules for novices, laymen, and laywomen. One of the Prātimokṣa lineages, the Mūlasarvāstivāda-vinaya, is still used in Tibet today. *See* Vinaya.

pratyekabuddha (= S; T: rang sangs rgyas) is a self-made Buddha, someone who becomes an arhat and attains enlightenment and Nirvana by him or herself. One does this without relying on a Buddha for instruction in one's last lifetime, in contrast to the śrāvaka's way of hearing and following the Buddha's teachings. Someone on the path of pratyekabuddhas does not tend to teach others, other than by example.

Pratyekabuddhayāna (S: Pratyekabuddhayāna; T: Rang sangs rgyas kyi theg pa) is the vehicle of the pratyekabuddhas, who seek to be arhats by themselves. The path of pratyekabuddhas is one of two main aspects of Hīnayāna, along with Śrāvakayāna, the path of śrāvakas. *See* pratyekabuddha, Hīnayāna.

protectors of the Dharma. *See* dharmapāla.

pure perception (T: dag snang) is the Vajrayāna principle of regarding everything around one, whether beings, sounds, or thoughts, as divine. Hence beings are seen as deities; sounds are heard as mantras; and thoughts are perceived as displays of wisdom (RY). Pure perception can also come through dreams and visions (JV). *See also* Vajrayāna.

reading transmission. *See* textual transmission.

realms of rebirth (S: gati; T: 'gro ba). These are the realms where sentient beings of various levels reside. Beings wander in samsara among these realms, always subject to the possibility of suffering. They can be reborn in any of the realms—such as the hell realm, the realm of hungry ghosts, the heavens, and so forth—according to their good and bad karma, and/ or the expiring of good or bad karma. Life in none of the realms is permanent. If five in number, the realms are those of hell beings, hungry ghosts, animals, humans, and gods. If six, the realm of demigods is included. *See also* free and well-favored human birth, hell realm, hungry-ghost realm.

One takes **refuge** in the three refuges (S: triśaraṇa; K: skyabs gsum)—the Buddha, the Dharma, and the Saṅgha—to attain safe haven from the suffering of samsara. The rite is an important part of many rituals, and is performed by reciting the formula, "I go to the Buddha for refuge. I go to the Dharma for refuge. I go to the Saṅgha for refuge," repeated three times. The act of taking refuge is one way to define oneself as a Buddhist. With the advent of Mahāyāna, taking refuge in the Buddha means taking refuge in all the celestial Buddhas. In tantric Buddhism, three "inner" refuges are added to the standard "outer" refuges—the guru, meditational deities (T: yidam), and ḍākinīs—and the guru is regarded as the essence of teachings and Buddhist community, as well as the essence of all the deities. *See also* ḍākinī, Dharma, samsara, Saṅgha, yidam.

relative truth. *See* conventional truth.

samādhi (= S; T: ting nge 'dzin, ting 'dzin) is a state of deep, unwavering concentration, attained by a family of techniques that develop one-pointedness of mind (S: cittaikāgratā; T: sems rtse gcig pa) on a specific object of meditation.

samaya (= S; T: dam tshig), or commitments, are sacred pledges made by practitioners to do certain practices. They existed in earlier forms of Buddhism and became a prominent feature of tantric Buddhism, where they are taken as part of an initiation rite performed by a guru. Keeping the vows is considered necessary for doing the practices, and breaking the vows can lead to severe karmic consequences. *See also* initiation, karma.

sambhogakāya or **enjoyment body** (= S; T: longs spyod rdzogs pa'i sku), the second body in Mahāyāna doctrine of the three bodies of the Buddha, is a body of subtle materiality that a celestial Buddha takes on for his or her own enjoyment or for the enjoyment of bodhisattvas who can perceive it. It can only be seen by bodhisattvas in Buddha-fields. A sambhogakāya "will always teach Mahāyāna doctrine, it will always last until the end of samsara, it will always be surrounded exclusively by bodhisattvas who have reached the bodhisattva bhūmis (S), and it will always be endowed with the thirty-two major and eighty minor marks of a great person" (*PDB*, 750). The enjoyment body, the source of which is the Dharma body (S: dharmakāya), also attains the Buddha's supernatural powers to further his or her mission to care for beings suffering in samsara. *See also* bodhisattva path, Buddha-field, samsara, three bodies of the Buddha.

samsara (S: saṃsāra; T: 'khor ba), in contrast to Nirvana, or liberation, is the cycle of rebirths within the six realms—those of gods, jealous gods, human beings, animals, hungry ghosts, and hell beings. Beings in the lower realms of samsara mainly experience suffering because of having committed unvirtuous deeds. Beings in heaven mainly experience happiness because of their past virtuous deeds. Humans experience a mixture of suffering and happiness. The arhat's final Nirvana entails no further rebirths in samsara. *See also* arhat, Nirvana.

Saṅgha (= S; T: dge 'dun) is the community of followers of the Buddha's teachings, and usually refers to monks and nuns. Broader interpretations of 'Saṅgha' also include laymen and laywomen. *See also* Hīnayāna, Three Jewels.

Saraha (ca. seventh through ninth centuries; = S; T: Mda' snun) was one of the famed eighty-four mahāsiddhas of India, and is well known for the role he played in spreading the teachings of Mahāmudrā. He had initially been a monk, and then abandoned the monastery for the life of a siddha, where he maintained the unconventional attitude that one can progress spiritually while at the same time being married and enjoying the pleasures of life. He was guided by a vision to a particular teacher, a female fletcher, and according to some stories became a very powerful siddha who could do amazing feats such as drinking molten metal. He realized Mahāmudrā and the nature of mind, and later helped spread the teachings. He is considered one of the founding fathers of the Mahāmudrā lineage, and is also known for his songs of realization (dohā). *See also* Mahāmudrā, mahāsiddha, siddha.

secret Mantrayāna. *See* Mantrayāna.

sentient beings of the six realms, six levels of sentient beings (T: 'gro drug sems can, 'gro ba rigs drug gi sems can) are hell beings, hungry ghosts, animals, humans, demigods, and gods. They are caught within cycles of rebirth among the corresponding six realms due to karma and defilements, such as attachments, aggression, and ignorance. *See also* demigods, free and well-favored human birth, gods, hell beings, hell realm, hungry ghosts, karma, realms of rebirth.

sentient beings of the three realms (T: khams gsum sems can) is a threefold classification of all beings in samsara according to which of the three realms they inhabit—the sensuous realm, the realm of pure form, or the formless realm. *See* three realms.

siddha (= S; T: grub thob) is a tantric practitioner who is considered to be enlightened or very nearly so, and to have accomplished the siddhis. Tantric Buddhism made the siddha its ideal, replacing the Mahāyāna ideal of bodhisattva, which had itself replaced Hīnayāna's ideal of the arhat. The siddha is very different from both the arhat and bodhisattva, since he or she is powerful and eccentric, beyond the usual standards of behavior, and can attain enlightenment very quickly. Siddhas most often lived outside the context of monasteries or even lay Buddhist life, sometimes working at common jobs, sometimes living in cremation grounds, and sometimes staying in solitary retreats where they focused on their practices. The concept of siddha goes back at least to the fifth century in India, where it may have arisen in Hindu communities that worshiped Śiva. *See also* arhat, bodhisattva, mahāsiddha, siddhi.

siddhi (= S; T: dngos grub) is an accomplishment associated with tantric practice. The siddhis are divided into two groups: The eight mundane, or **common accomplishments** (T: thun mong gi dngos grub) are the development of supernatural powers, variously enumerated and described. One list describes eight: the siddhis of the sword, of invisibility pills, of eye medicine, of swift walking, of partaking of essences or alchemy, of being able to go to a celestial realm, of invisibility, and of finding underground treasure (ral gri'i dngos grub, ril bu, mig sman, rkang mgyogs, bcud len, mkha' spyod, mi snang ba, sa 'og) (JV). Some of these yogic accomplishments can be explained in general terms as "clairvoyance, clairaudience, flying in the sky, becoming invisible, everlasting youth, or powers of transmutation" (RY). The development of these powers is a byproduct of concentration meditation. They are not meant to be goals in themselves. The **supreme accomplishment** (S: uttamasiddhi; T: mchog gi dngos grub) is complete enlightenment. *See also* siddha.

six levels of sentient beings. *See* sentient beings of the six realms.

six perfections. *See* perfections.

six realms of rebirth. *See* realms of rebirth.

six sessions (T: thun drug); **four sessions** (thun bzhi). These are sessions within a twenty-four-hour period that are used to measure or regulate one's Dharma practice. There are several ways of defining these periods: the six sessions can be three hours each; or can be spaced in various ways such as two in the morning, two in the afternoon, one in the evening, and one at night; or three in the day and three at night. The four sessions can be at dawn, in the morning, afternoon, and evening (RY).

six yogas of Nāropa or **six Dharmas of Nāropa** (T: Na ro chos drug) are a set of six Vajrayāna instructions attributed to Nāropa, who received various instructions from his teacher, the mahāsiddha Tilopa, and later compiled and codified them. Marpa may have received them from some of Nāropa's disciples, and brought them to Tibet, where the set of practices was given its name. Though lists vary, the six yogas usually are inner heat (T: gtum mo), illusory body (sgyu lus), dreams (rmi lam), clear light ('od gsal), intermediate state (bar do), and transference ('pho ba). The six yogas became especially important for the Kagyüpa school, but also are known within the Gelugpa school. *See also* caṇḍālī; Kagyüpa school; Marpa; nāḍī, prāṇa, bindu; Nāropa.

spiritual friend (S: kalyāṇamitra; T: dge ba'i bshes gnyen) is an advisor or companion who gives one encouragement and helps one focus on one's spiritual path. A spiritual friend might be an instructor, fellow practitioner, lay supporter, and so on. In Mahāyāna, the guru can be the spiritual friend or guide.

śrāvaka (= S; T: nyan thos, nyan thos pa) was initially anyone who heard the Buddha's teaching directly and strove to become an arhat. In more general terms, a śrāvaka is a practitioner of Hīnayāna, whose highest ideal is the arhat and who has received Dharma instruction from others. Śrāvakas seek to attain enlightenment for themselves by studying the four noble truths and the twelve links of interdependent origination, eliminating emotional obscurations or defilements and realizing the nonexistence of a permanent, independent personal self. With the attainment of Nirvana they free themselves from cycle of rebirth in samsara. Those following Mahāyāna later used the term 'śrāvaka' in a disparaging way, stating that śrāvakas are selfish for forsaking the needs of other beings suffering in samsara in order to attain their own Nirvana, and that the śrāvakas' enlightenment is an imperfect state. *See also* arhat, four noble truths, Hīnayāna, interdependent origination, Nirvana.

Śrāvakayāna (= S; T: nyan thos kyi theg pa) is the vehicle of the disciples or śrāvakas, who seek to be arhats. *See* śrāvaka.

state of peaceful calm. *See* peaceful calm.

Sukhāvatī (= S; T: Bde ba can) is the western pure Buddha-field of Buddha Amitābha. It is believed that Amitābha and his bodhisattva helpers will appear before any dying person who keeps Amitābha in mind, and lead him to Sukhāvatī. The inhabitants of Sukhāvatī have great facility in spiritual progress, are free of defilements, and know only beauty and bliss. *See also* Amitābha.

sutra (S: sūtra; T: mdo, mdo sde) is a discourse by or said to be by the Buddha. The collection of these teachings of Buddhism for the general public, the Basket of Discourses (S: sūtra piṭaka), in contrast to the much later esoteric, tantric teachings, is one of three major parts of the two earliest extant Buddhist canons—the Pāli Canon of the Theravāda, and the Āgama collections, found only in Chinese translation. Besides the teachings supposedly committed to the oral record by the Buddha's major disciples at the time of the First Council, convened shortly after the Buddha's passing, other teachings remembered later were added to the Pāli Canon if they fit well in style and content with the others. Tradition says that this collection of sutras was passed down orally for centuries, and finally written down around the first century B.C.E.

Later, Mahāyāna texts claiming to be original discourses of the Buddha were added to this collection. The inclusion of these Mahāyāna texts, though with some marked differences in style and message, was justified on the grounds that they had been hidden away at the time of the Buddha and only emerged centuries later, sometimes via meditations and dreams, when practitioners were able to embrace their messages. This continual adding to sutras as authoritative teachings of the Buddha continued in India for centuries, and paved the way for later claims that the tantras, too, had been taught by the Buddha (RJ). *See also* Mahāyāna.

tantra (= S; T: sngags) is a category of literature usually made up of esoteric teachings thought to have been given by the Buddha in his sambhogakāya form. In contrast to sutras, texts classified as tantras often include ritual manuals about meditation and power (S: siddhi) that involve mantras, mandalas, mudrās, secrecy, the central role of a guru, initiations, fire sacrifices, feasts, and much symbolism. In some cases, they present the new ideal of the siddha and typically hold out the prospect of a much quicker path to enlightenment than the bodhisattva path. Although tantras did not proliferate in India until around the late seventh and early eighth centuries C.E. (*PDB*, 894)—and continued to be written down there until the thirteenth century—tradition claims that most tantras are traceable to the historical Buddha, who taught them to a select few disciples to be handed down secretly. Other tantras were revealed in visions or dreams by the Buddha Vajradhara. In Tibet, some tantras were buried in the earth, to be found when the time was right by treasure masters (T: gter ston). *See also* mudrā, siddha, three bodies of the Buddha.

tantric Buddhism (S: Tantrayāna, more frequently called Mantrayāna) is Buddhism based on the tantras. *See* tantra.

textual transmission or **reading transmission** (T: lung) is a ceremony that occurs when a teacher reads a text for his or her students out loud, often very rapidly. This imparts authorization to the disciple to read and practice it, and blessings to comprehend it. A textual transmission sometimes accompanies an initiation or is given at the outset of a teaching. *See also* initiation.

thigle (= T; S: bindu). *See* nāḍī, prāṇa, bindu.

three bodies of the Buddha (S: trikāya; T: sku gsum) is a doctrine central to Mahāyāna that describes three aspects or bodies of a Buddha: the Dharma body (S: dharmakāya); the enjoyment body (sambhogakāya); and the emanation body (nirmāṇakāya). It arose among followers of the Yogācāra school in India. The Dharma body is considered "the true nature of Buddhahood, ultimate reality itself, an abstract resolution of all dualities, beyond any conceptualization or designation" (*IB*, 115). With the Dharma body perpetually still, different Buddhas—emanation bodies and enjoyment bodies—manifest it, and through those manifestations, the Dharma body brings aid and relief to beings suffering in samsara. This doctrine is in contrast to the belief in pre-Mahāyāna texts that there can only be at most one Buddha at a time, and provides sentient beings with three ways to experience Buddhahood. Any one way will fit best for a particular being's level of spiritual development at a particular time. Emanation bodies are accessible to ordinary, worldly people. Enjoyment bodies are accessible to those beings high on the bodhisattva path. *See also* dharmakāya, Mahāyāna, nirmāṇakāya, sambhogakāya.

Three Jewels or **Three Precious Ones** (S: ratnatraya; T: dkon mchog gsum) are the three objects of refuge, the Buddha, Dharma, and Saṅgha. *See also* Dharma, refuge, Saṅgha.

three realms of existence (S: traidhātuka; T: khams gsum) is a threefold classification of realms where rebirth can take place. These three samsaric realms are the sensuous realm (S: kāmadhātu; T: 'dod pa'i khams), the realm of pure form or subtle materiality (S: rūpadhātu; T: gzugs khams), and the formless realm (S: arūpyadhātu, arūpadhātu; T: gzugs med kyi khams). The desire realm is inhabited by hell beings, hungry ghosts, animals, humans, demigods, and some of the lower gods proper (deva). They all have five senses and strong propensities for liking and disliking objects of the senses. The realm of [pure, elemental] form is inhabited by higher gods, humans in their last lifetime before enlightenment, or humans who have attained enlightenment. These beings have two senses—sight and hearing—and lack sensuous desire for the objects around them. The third realm is the formless realm for the most refined types of rebirth, that of the gods whose "existence is entirely mental, no longer requiring even a subtle material foundation for their ethereal states of mind" (*PDB*, 63). They have no body or senses at all, and "existence is characterized by pure and rarified forms of consciousness" (*EB*, 184). *See also* samsara, sentient beings of the six realms.

three trainings (S: triśikṣā; T: bslab pa gsum) are three types of Buddhist practices that a practitioner is to develop. The three are: the training in higher morality (S: adhiśīlaśikṣā; T: lhag pa tshul khrims kyi bslab pa), the training in higher concentration (S: adhisamādhiśikṣā; T: lhag pa ting nge 'dzin gyi bslab pa), and the training in higher wisdom (S: adhiprajñāśikṣā; T: lhag pa shes rab kyi bslab pa).

three vehicles (S: triyana; T: theg pa gsum). There are several sets of three 'vehicles', or means, taught for beings to move towards liberation. A grouping commonly found in Mahāyāna sutras is made up of the vehicle of śrāvakas, or those who have been taught the Dharma (S: Śrāvakayāna; T: Nyan thos kyi theg pa), the vehicle of pratyekabuddhas, or self-made Buddhas (S: Pratyekabuddhayāna; T: Rang sangs rgyas kyi theg pa), and the vehicle of bodhisattvas (S: Bodhisattvayāna; T: Byang chub sems kyi theg pa). In this set, the first two are vehicles used by Hīnayāna, and the last is a Mahāyāna vehicle. Another set of three vehicles is made up of the three main divisions of Buddhism—Hīnayāna, Mahāyāna, and Vajrayāna. Yet another set is comprised of Hīnayāna, Pāramitāyāna, and Vajrayāna, where the last two are viewed as two forms of Mahāyāna, one esoteric and one exoteric. *See also* bodhisattva, bodhisattva path, Hīnayāna, Mahāyāna, perfections, pratyekabuddha, śrāvaka, Vajrayāna.

truth of suffering (S: duḥkhasatya; T: sdug bsngal gi bden pa) is the first of a set of four realizations the Buddha taught in his first sermon in Deer Park. It states that "existence in the realms that are subject to rebirth, called samsara, is qualified by suffering (duḥkha)" (*PDB*, 304). The truth of suffering does not say that there is no happiness in life. However, beings' habit of grasping at things and mental processes in search of lasting happiness will bring dissatisfaction, because everything is impermanent and always subject to change. *See also* emptiness, four noble truths.

Tsongkhapa or **Lobzang Dragpa** (1357–1419; T: Blo bzang grags pa, Tsong kha pa) was a great Tibetan scholar, a prolific writer, teacher, religious leader, and innovator, and is revered as the founder of the Gelugpa school of Tibetan Buddhism. He was inspired by Atiśa and the Kadampa school, with whom he shared an insistence on monastic discipline and rigorous study along with debate, and he received teachings from a variety of scholars and schools of his day. It is said that he had visions of such exalted philosophers as Nāgārjuna (regarded as the founder of Madhyamaka), Buddhapālita (retroactively considered the founder of Prāsaṅgika), and the bodhisattva deity Mañjuśrī (bodhisattva of wisdom), all of whom guided him toward a fuller understanding of Buddhism. Tsongkhapa's most prestigious work is the *Great Treatise on the Stages of the Path to Enlightenment* (T: *Lam rim chen mo*), which outlines a progressive path a practitioner can follow through successive motivations and goals as developed in both pre-Mahāyāna and Mahāyāna, culminating in a coupling with Vajrayāna techniques. *See also* Atiśa, Candrakīrti, Gelugpa school, Kadampa school, Mañjuśrī, Nāgārjuna, Vajrayāna.

tummo (T: gtum mo). *See* inner heat

two accumulations (T: tshogs gnyis) are the collections of merits (S: puṇyasaṃbhāra; T: bsod nams gyi tshogs) and the collections of knowledge (S: jñānasaṃbhāra; T: ye shes kyi tshogs). They are gathered by a bodhisattva over countless lifetimes, and are needed to attain Buddhahood. The accumulation of meritorious deeds is associated with the first three of the six perfections: giving, morality, and patience. The accumulation of knowledge is associated with the last two perfections: meditative absorption and wisdom. The fourth perfection, effort, contributes to both collections. *See also* bodhisattva, perfections.

two extremes (T: mtha' gnyis) are **eternalism** (S: śāśvatānta; T: rtag pa'i mtha') and **annihilationism** (S: ucchedānta; T: chad mtha'). Eternalism takes various forms, but invariably involves the belief that there exists a permanent, independent self in persons and phenomena. Annihilationism is the belief that there is no such self because it is destroyed at death (DL), and that there are no effects of karma, no rebirth, and no liberation. Beyond these generalities, various schools of Buddhist philosophy differ in the precise details of how these two terms are defined (*PDB*, 931). *See also* Madhyamaka.

two truths (S: satyadvaya; T: bden pa gnyis) are conventional truth and ultimate truth. These are key concepts in Buddhist philosophy. The distinction between the two and their relationship are crucial for understanding existence. The specifics with which they are defined differed in India from school to school. *See also* conventional truth; ultimate truth; ultimate truth and conventional truth, relationship between.

ultimate truth, **ultimate reality**, or **absolute truth** (S: paramārthasatya; T: don dam pa'i bden pa, don dam pa), in a Madhyamaka sense, is emptiness of inherent existence. The realization of ultimate truth through insight into interdependent origination aids one in becoming detached from the world, and can lead to Nirvana. Ultimate truth, along with conventional truth, make up the doctrine of the two truths. *See also* conventional truth; two truths; ultimate truth and conventional truth, relationship between.

ultimate truth and conventional truth, relationship between, was much discussed by Madhyamaka philosophers, such as Nāgārjuna. He explained that ultimate truth does not contradict the relative existence of what one can perceive at the conventional level of truth (i.e. that fire is hot). It is the realization of ultimate truth that allows one to see the true nature of what one sees conventionally, and conventional truth makes it possible for us to express the ultimate truth (*B*). *See also* conventional truth, Nāgārjuna, two truths, ultimate truth.

Vajradhara (= S; T: Rdo rje 'chang) is the lord of the Buddha families, the primordial Buddha of the Gelugpa and Kagyüpa schools, and the source of various tantric teachings, such as Mahāmudrā. *See also* Gelugpa school, Kagyüpa school, Mahāmudrā.

Vajrayāna (= S; T: Rdo rje theg pa) is an esoteric path that vastly shortens the time to Buddhahood. Though usually esoteric in form, it shows many similarities to Mahāyāna in goals and philosophy, and accepts earlier Buddhist scriptures as genuine. However, the tantric ritual techniques in its esoteric ritual manuals distinguish it from other forms of Buddhism: they are faster and more powerful, and are believed to put Buddhahood within one's reach in one lifetime. This is in contrast to the countless lifetimes it may take someone to complete the bodhisattva path. In Vajrayāna, initiations, the support of a guru, tantric vows, mantras, mudrās, mandalas, visualizations, and various yogas are used to identify one's body, speech, and mind with those of a Buddha. In Tibet, the terms Vajrayāna, tantric Buddhism, and (the secret) Mantrayāna are often used interchangeably. *See also* bodhisattva path, initiation, Mantrayāna, tantric Buddhism.

Victorious One (S: jina; T: rgyal ba) is a title that was given to Śākyamuni Buddha after he attained enlightenment, and is an epithet for Buddhas in general. It may refer to the Buddha's conquest of the demon Māra (= S; T: bdud), personification of evil, who had tried to prevent his awakening under the bodhi tree. More broadly, the epithet can also refer to any Buddha's conquest of impurities such as sensual desire, desire for continued existence, false views, and ignorance. It also can refer to their victory over unwholesome activities that lead to lower rebirths (*IB*, 295; *PDB*, 388).

victory banner (S: ketu; T: rgyal mtshan) is one in a set of eight Indian symbols of good fortune (S: aṣṭamaṅgala; T: bkra shis rtags brgyad). It represents the triumph of a Buddha's teachings over Buddhism's opponents (*PDB*, 431). The eight symbols are the lotus, the endless knot, the pair of golden fish, the parasol, the victory banner, the treasure vase, the white conch shell that whorls to the right, and the wheel of doctrine.

Vinaya (= S; T: 'dul ba) is the collection of rules for proper monastic discipline and etiquette for monks and nuns that evolved around the time of the Buddha. There are also rules for novices, laymen, and laywomen. Many of the rules aim to support harmony within Buddhist institutions and with lay people. The term 'vinaya' also refers to the texts that put forth those rules. The Vinaya is one of the Three Baskets of the oldest extant Indian-language canon, the Pāli Canon, and contains the Prātimokṣa, as well as commentaries on each rule. The collection developed into a number of versions. The Mūlasarvāstivāda vinaya, used in Tibet, contains 253 rules for fully ordained monks and 364 rules for fully ordained nuns. *See also* Prātimokṣa.

yidam (= T), or **tutelary deity**, is one's personal meditation deity, a Buddha or bodhisattva with whom a practitioner has a special relationship, and the object of one's meditation. One relies on one's yidam for guidance to enlightenment and protection for one's practice. In tantric Buddhism, the yidam is one of the three inner refuges, along with the guru and ḍākinī. *See also* ḍākinī, refuge.

Sources for the Songs

With Notes for My Critical Edition of the Tibetan Text

At present, there are at least six extant versions of Skal ldan rgya mtsho's *mgur 'bum* in Tibet.[i] These range in time from 1756 up to recent years, and include two woodblock prints; three bound volumes; and a print the shape and size of a traditional Tibetan book but with computer-generated letters. For each of the twenty-four songs translated in this book, referred to by its first line of translation, I give the page numbers in these six sources:

A) *Gsung mgur*. Carved at Thos bsam gling, Rong bo monastery, Reb gong, Amdo, in the *me pho byi* year, 1756.[ii] Copied and published under the title *Rnam 'dren bla ma skal ldan rgya mtsho'i gsung mgur* (*The Collected Songs of Spiritual Experience of Rong bo Grub chen Skal ldan rgya mtsho*). New Delhi: A lags 'Jam dbyangs, 1977.

B) *Gsung mgur chen mo*. In *Gsung 'bum* by Skal ldan rgya mtsho. Vol. Ca. Carved in Rong bo Monastery, Reb gong, Amdo in the *me yos* year, 1987.[iii]

C) *Shar skal ldan rgya mtsho'i mgur 'bum*. Xining: Mtsho sngon mi rigs dpe skrun khang, 1994.

D) *Yab rje bla ma skal ldan rgya mtsho'i mgur 'bum*. In *Yab rje bla ma skal ldan rgya mtsho'i gsung 'bum*, by Skal ldan rgya mtsho. Vol. 4, pp. 1–320. Xining: Kan su'u mi rigs dpe skrun khang, 1999.

E) *Rnam 'dren bla ma yab rje skal ldan rgya mtsho'i mgur 'bum*. [Gtsos grong khyer, Gansu]: Bod gna' deng rig gnas 'dzin skyong dar spel gling, [in or after the *me pho byi* year, 1996?].

F) *Chos phung brgyad khri bzhi stong gi yang snying gdams pa rnams glu dbyangs su mdzad pa gsung mgur chen mo*. In *Mdo smad sgrub brgyud bstan pa'i shing rta ba chen po phyag na pad+mo yab rje bla ma shar skal ldan rgya mtsho'i gsung 'bum*. Vol. 5. Rong bo: Rong bo dgon chen grwa tshang thos bsam rnam par rgyal ba'i gling gi slob gnyer 'dzin skyong tshogs pas 'grems spel, the *chu pho 'drug* year 2012.

The Tibetan text I provide is my critical edition (referred to below as VS). It is based on sources A through F. Spelling choices are listed below under any entry when the editions are different or when my spelling is different from all editions. My critical edition of all material quoted in this book largely relies on common usages listed in the *TTC*. I am gratef.ul to the Rong bo Monastery scholar, LC, for having made many suggestions, including the eight spelling choices listed below that are different from those in all six sources, and for having proofread my entire edition. Without his assistance, I would not have been able to bring my critical edition to its current level. Besides those choices in my critical edition, I have standardized all sets of *pa*/ *ba*s and *po*/ *bo*s according to customary orthographic rules, without listing the variants below. I accept responsibility for any shortcomings in the text.

Chapter 1. Homages to My Lamas

Father, lama, lord, omniscient one: 4–13; *mgur 'bum* A: 56.3–59.1, B: 20v.1–21v.1, C: 42–44, D: 38–40, E: 65.3–68.4, F: 34–36.

zim VS 4, line 3; *zim* CDEF; *sim* AB.
dod VS 4, line 10; *dod* BCDEF; *'dod* A.
rgyang VS 4, line 10; *rgyang* BCDEF; *rgyangs* A.
tam VS 8, line 1; *tam* BE; *ram* ACDF.

zim VS 8, line 8; *zim* CDEF; *sim* AB.
bstsal VS 10, line 7; *bstsal* ACDEF; *stsal* B.
sgos VS 10, line 15; *sgos* BDF; *dgos* ACE.
rgyang VS 12, colophon line 1; *rgyang* BCDEF; *rgyangs* A.

Oh father, the one who holds the teachings, ocean of intelligence: 16–17; *mgur 'bum* A: 399.2–5, B: 166v.2–5, C: 345, D: 306, E: 514.1–5, F: 273–74.

bco VS 16, line 6; *bco* BCDEF; *bcwo* A.
dkar VS 16, line 14; *dkar* ACDE; *dka'* BF.
bos VS 16, line 17; *bos* CDF; *bo* BE; *bo'i* A.

I prostrate myself before the lama: 20–27; *mgur 'bum* A: 258.2–259.4, B: 102v.2–103r.4, C: 223–24, D: 196–97, E: 331.2–333.2, F: 176–77.

rnyi VS 20, line 9; *rnyi* BDF; *snyi* ACE.
zab VS 20, line 11; *zab* ABCDF; *zam* E 86.3.
'thob VS 22, line 6; *'thob* BCDEF; *thar* A.
nga'i VS 24, line 7; *nga'i* ABEF; *ba'i* CD.
med (no "*du*") VS 24, line 12; *med* (no "*du*") CDF; *med du* ABE.
skyel ma VS 24, line 15; *skyel ma* ABDEF; *skye lam* C.

I bow to the guru. / When we pray clearly: 30–41; *mgur 'bum* A: 396.2–398.5, B: 165r.3–166r.5, C: 342–44, D: 303–305, E: 509.1–513.2, F: 271–73.

po'i VS 30, line 2; *po'i* ABCE; *por* DF.
srung VS 34, line 9; *srung* BE; *bsrung* ACDF.
rgyun VS 36, line 5; *rgyun* DEF; *rgyud* ABC. Either is fine. If I need to choose one, I'll choose *rgyun*.
bsdams VS 36, line 6; *bsdams* ACDEF; *sdom* B.
'jug VS 40, colophon line 1; *'jug* ACDEF; *'dug* B.

The following stanza on VS 36, lines 13-16, only appears in ABEF; not in CD. It was included in the texts BEF as usual, and was inserted into A above the top line of the page:

zhe sdang 'bar nas tshig rtsub smras na yang/ /
dge ba'i myu gu mi bsreg khyod kyi drin/ /
bka' drin che'o bla ma rin po che/ /
da dung bdag gi skyid sdug khyed rang mkhyen/ /

Chapter 2. Dreadful Defects

I bow at the feet of my father, Tendzin Lobzang: 44–49; *mgur 'bum* A: 253.5–255.2, B: 100v.1–101r.3, C: 219–20, D: 193–94, E: 325.1–327.2, F: 173–74.

sgos VS 44, line 6; *sgos* CDF; *dgos* ABE.
gzan VS 46, line 11; *gzan* BCDEF; *zan* A.

I prostrate myself before the guru: 52–55; *mgur 'bum* A: 159.3–160.2, B: 59v.4–60r.1, C: 130, D: 115–16, E: 196.5–197.4, F: 102–103.

co VS 52, line 2; *co* BCDEF; *ce* A.
rgyal VS 52, line 8; *rgyal* ACDEF; *rbyal* B.
'dad VS 54, line 3; *'dad* C; *dad* ABDEF.

One day I went to view the clay range of Phu Seku: 56–63; *mgur 'bum* A: 47.5–50.1, B: 17v.2–18r.5, C: 36–38, D: 33–34, E: 56.1–58.3, F: 29–31.

zhig VS 56, line 1; *zhig* BCDEF; *cig* A.
rgyud VS 56, line 2; *rgyud* AB; *brgyud* CDEF.
te VS 56, line 6; *te* BCDEF; *de* A.
sgos VS 56, line 15; *sgos* DF; *dgos* ABCE.
skul VS 58, line 10; *skul* BCDEF; *bskul* A.
bsten VS 60, line 2; *bsten* DF; *sten* ABCE.
rlabs VS 60, line 8; *rlabs* BCDEF; *brlabs* A.

sbun VS 60, line 9; *sbun* BCDEF; *spun* A.
bsten VS 60, line 13, against all readings in ABCDEF, which have *sten*.

Having bowed respectfully at the feet: 64–69; *mgur 'bum* A: 242.1–5, B: 94v. 6–95r.5, C: 207–208, D: 183, E: 308.4–309.5, F: 164.

lta VS 64, line 8; *lta* ABCEF; *ltar* D.
bzhi'i VS 64, line 9, against all readings in ABCDEF, which have *bzhis*.
nyes VS 66, line 13; *nyes* CDEF; *nyas* AB.

Chapter 3. Aspirations for Renunciation

If you are able to practice the divine Dharma—Oh joy!: 74–75; *mgur 'bum* A: 405.5–406.2, B: 169v.2–4, C: 350–51, D: 311, E: 522.3–5, F: 278.

bltas VS 74, line 3; *bltas* ACDEF; *bltos* B.
bltas VS 74, line 4; *bltas* ACDEF; *bltos* B.

May I strive continually day and night: 78–81; *mgur 'bum* A: 395.4–396.2, B: 164v.5–165r.3, C: 341–42, D: 302–303, E: 508.1–509.1, F: 270–71.

rgad VS 78, line 5; *rgad* ABCEF; *rgod* D.
pho VS 78, line 5; *pho* ABCDF; *bo*: E.
pur VS 78, line 7; *pur* ACDEF; *bur* B.
rtser VS 80, line 6; *rtser* ACDE; *rtsar* BF.

Oṃ swa sti! / When I think: 82–87; *mgur 'bum* A: 297.2–298.3, B: 120r.4–120v.5, C: 256–57, D: 227–28, E: 381.5–383.3, F: 203–204.

slebs VS 82, line 13, against all readings in ABCDEF, which have *sleb*.
zang VS 84, line 1; *zang* E (probably); *zad/ zang* A; *zad* BCDF. *zang* has been approved only tentatively by LC.
zhig VS 84, line 1; *zhig* BCDEF; *cig* A.

zhen (no *la*) VS 84, line 5; *zhen* (no *la*) CDE; *zhen la* ABF.
kyi VS 84, line 12; *kyi* ABCE; *pa'i* DF.
nas VS 84, line 14; *nas* BCDEF; *na* A.
'dod VS 84, line 15; *'dod* ABCD; *'dong* F.
gyis VS 84, line 15; *gyis* CDEF; *kyis* AB.
pa de VS 86, line 5; *pa de* BCDEF; *bde* A.

I pray to the father, Tendzin Lobzang Gyatso: 90–93; *mgur 'bum* A: 50.1–51.3, B: 18r.5–18v.4, C: 38, D: 34–35, E: 58.3–59.5, F: 31.

blangs VS 90, line 8; *blangs* CDEF; *blang* AB.
sgos VS 90, line 14; *sgos*: BDF; *dgos*: ACE.
gtam VS 92, line 3; *gtam* BCDEF; *gtams* A.

Chapter 4. Setting Off for Solitary Hermitages

I bow at the feet of the lord, my father Lobzang Tenpai Gyältsen: 96–101; *mgur 'bum* A: 192.3–194.1, B: 73r.5–74r.1, C: 161–62, D: 143–44, E: 241.4–243.5, F: 127–28.

lta VS 98, line 2; *lta* ABCE; *ltar* DF.
zhig VS 98, line 3; *zhig* B; *cig* ACDEF.
'thob VS 98, line 3; *'thob* CDF; *thob* ABE.
dbon VS 98, line 9; *dbon* ABE; *dpon* CDF.

Oh protector, lama—splendid deity of deities, blazing glory of goodness, Buddha: 106–109; *mgur 'bum* A: 195.5–197.1, B: 74v.5–75r.4, C: 164–65, D: 146, E: 246.2–247.4, F: 129–30.

bun VS 108, line 1; *bun* CDF; *'un* ABE.
'dun VS 108, line 10; *'dun* ABEF; *mdun* CD.
'dun VS 108, line 12; *'dun* ABEF; *mdun* CD.
legs VS 108, line 12; *legs* ABC; *lags* DF.
byes VS 108, line 13; *byes* BCDF; *byas* AE.

ABE have the following colophon. CDF don't have it. I didn't translate it because it is much more formal than the other colophons and seems to be by someone else:

rje skal ldan rgya mtsho'i gsung las lta ba'i glu 'phreng rdo rje'i sgra dbyangs bzhugs so/ /

Oṃ swa sti! / Near the waters: 112–17; *mgur 'bum* A: 188.3–189.5, B: 71v.3–72r.4, C: 157–58, D: 140–41, E: 236.3–238.2, F: 124–25.

shor VS 112, line 2, against the two readings in ABCDE: *shog* CD; *gshog* ABEF.
srong VS 112, line 8; *srong* ABCEF; *sron* D.
dbon VS 112, line 14; *dbon* CDEF; *dpon* AB.
bsrung VS 114, line 2; *bsrung* ACDEF; *srung* B.
bla VS 114, line 3, against all readings in ABCDEF, which have *sla*.
srung VS 114, line 11; *srung* BCDEF; *bsrung* A.

The Stages of the Path to Enlightenment: 120–25; *mgur 'bum* A: 177.1–178.2, B: 66v.6–67r.6, C: 146–47, D: 130–31, E: 219.5–221.3, F: 115–16.

'grog VS 120, line 18; *'grog* C; *'grogs* ABDEF.
bshes VS 124, line 1; *bshes* BCDEF; *gshes* A.
par VS 124, line 12; *par* ABCE; *pa* DF.

Chapter 5. Emptiness and Mahāmudrā

Oh lama, you are aware that conditions: 132–35; *mgur 'bum* A: 208.1–5, B: 80r.1–5, C: 175–76, D: 155–56, E: 262.2–263.2, F: 138–39.

nas VS 132, line 1 against all readings in ABCDEF, which have *ni*.
bstsal VS 132, line 8; *bstsal* ACDEF; *stsal* B.
bltas VS 132, line 15; *bltas* ABCEF; *blta* D.

Oṃ swa sti! / I have looked up to renunciants: 136–39; *mgur 'bum* A: 284.2–285.2, B: 114r.6–114v.5, C: 245–46, D: 216–17, E: 365.3–366.4, F: 193–94.

lta VS 136, line 3, against the two readings in ABCDEF: *blta* ABCEF; *bltas* D.
pa'i VS 136, line 9; *pa'i* ABEF; *lo'i* CD.
gsog VS 138, line 3; *gsog* CDF; *bsag* AB; *bsags* E.
gyong VS 138, line 6; *gyong* BCDEF; *gyod* A.
bskyangs VS 138, line 7; *bskyangs* BCDE; *skyong* A; *bskyongs* F.

I bow to the guru, Lokeśvara: 142–47; *mgur 'bum* A: 204.2–205.3, B: 78r.5–78v.5, C: 172–73, D: 152–53, E: 257.2–258.4, F: 136.

shva ra VS 142, line 1; *shva ra* ACDEF; *shvar* B.
dbyings VS 142, line 2; *dbyings* BCDEF; *dbyibs* A.
ngo VS 142, line 5, against all readings in ABCDEF, which have *so*.
gdal VS 142, line 14; *gdal* CDF; *bdal* ABE.
par VS 146, line 3; *par* ABCE; *pa* DF.
bo VS 146, line 8; *bo* ACDEF; *be* B.
shog VS 146, line 8; *shog* CD; *gshog* ABEF.

Oh lama, who perceives clearly: 150–53; *mgur 'bum* A: 214.3–215.2, B: 82v.4–83r.2, C: 181–82, D: 160–61, E: 270.4–271.4, F: 143.

dgag VS 150, line 6; *dgag* ABDEF; *dag* C.
mjal VS 152, line 12; *mjal* ACDEF; *'jal* B.

Chapter 6. Mountain Retreats and Happiness

I bow to the guru, Hāsa Vajra: 158–69; *mgur 'bum* A: 237.3–239.5, B: 92v.5–93v.5, C: 202–205, D: 179–81, E: 301.4–305.3, F: 160–62.

drin VS 158, line 9; *drin* CDEF; *bran* AB.
'khob VS 162, line 6; *'khob* BCDEF; *'khop* A.

na VS 162, line 8; *na* ABCDF; *nas* E.
'dun VS 162, line 8; *'dun* ABEF; *mdun* CD.
babs VS 164, line 2; *babs* CDEF; *bab* AB.
spar VS 164, line 3; *spar* CDE; sbar ABF.
skyongs VS 166, line 11; *skyongs* CDEF; *skyong* AB.
'dzang VS 168, colophon line 1; *'dzang* ACDE; *'dzing* BF. 'dzang has been suggested by DD as a likely possibility between the two choices.

I bow at the feet of the father Tendzin Lobzang: 172–77; *mgur 'bum* A: 165.1–166.4, B: 62r.2–62v.4, C: 136–37, D: 121–22, E: 204.1–206.2, F: 107–108.

zim VS 172, line 3; *zim* CDEF; *sim* AB.
skegs VS 172, line 9; *skegs* BCDF; *skeg* AE.
pas VS 172, line 15; *pas* BCDEF; *bya* A.
mgos VS 174, line 2; *mgos* BCDF; *'gos* AE.
bu'i VS 174, line 2; *bu'i* ABCDF; *pu'i* E.
las VS 176, line 3; *las* CDEF; *pas* AB.
pa'i VS 176, line 7; *pa'i* CDEF; *pas* AB.
sdor VS 176, line 9; *sdor* C; *rdor* ABDEF.
ched VS 176, line 10; *ched* ABCE; *chen* DF.

I prostrate myself before lord lamas: 180–85; *mgur 'bum* A: 181.5–183.4, B: 68v.6–69v.3, C: 152–53, D: 135–36, E: 228.1–230.2, F: 119–120.

srung VS 180, line 5; *srung* B; *bsrung* ACDEF.
re VS 180, line 9; *re* ABDEF; *bres* C.
ngogs VS 180, line 12; *ngogs* ACD; *dngos* BEF.
bsil VS 180, line 12; *bsil* CDEF; *sil* AB.
srung VS 180, line 15; *srung* BCDEF; *bsrung* A.
gsing VS 182, line 7; *gsing* BCDEF; *bsing* A.
lhor VS 182, line 8; *lhor* ACDEF; *lho* B.
tu VS 182, line 10; *tu* BCDEF; *du* A.

bra VS 184, line 5; *bra* BCDEF; *pra* A.
sgos VS 184, line 16; *sgos* CDF; *dgos* ABE.

Oṃ swa sti! / The lama, essence of Cakrasaṃvara: 188–91; *mgur 'bum* A: 126.5–127.4, B: 46r.5–46v.2, C: 100–101, D: 90, E: 153.5–154.4, F: 80.

la VS 188, line 6; *la* ABCEF; *las* D.
mgo VS 190, line 3; *mgo* CDEF; *'go* AB.

Notes

i There was also an edition published in India in 1994, made from a copy written out by hand by A khu Khri rgan tshang, the brother of the seventh Skal ldan rgya mtsho, during the former's stay in India sometime after 1958. There are supposed to be copies of Khri rgan tshang's handwritten copy in the libraries in Dharamsala and Varanasi. I have no information on which version of the *Mgur 'bum* Khri rgan tshang's copy was based. *See* Skal ldan rgya mtsho, *Grub dbang skal ldan rgya mtsho'i mgur 'bum*, ed. Rab gsal (Varanasi: Rig pa 'byung ba'i grong khyer dpe sgrig sde tshan, 1994).

ii In 1751 when Khri rgyan 'Jam dbyangs Dge 'dun bstan 'dzin was thirty-five, he is said to have heard the voice of Skal ldan rgya mtsho saying, "If you put my *Mgur 'bum* onto woodblocks, benefit will come to the teaching and sentient beings." He became the editor of the undertaking, which was completed in 1756. From 1778, the woodblocks were administered by the corporation (*bla brang*) of the lineage of Khri rgan. See *Chos kyi rgyal po yab rje skal ldan rgya mtsho'i bka' 'bum gyi dkar chag don ldan rin chen lnga yi do shal*, in Skal ldan, *Gsung 'bum* (1987), folios 8v.6–9r.4.

iii The next wood carving was done in 1843, and was administered by the corporation of Rong bo Khri chen. In 1935, the seventh incarnation of Skal ldan rgya mtsho, Blo bzang bstan 'dzin 'jigs med 'phrin las collected many donations (25, 549 in paper money) towards another printing, which was finally realized in 1987 in Rong bo. *See Chos kyi rgyal po yab rje skal ldan rgya mtsho'i bka' 'bum gyi dkar chag don ldan rin chen lnga yi do shal*, in Skal ldan, *Gsung 'bum* (1987), folios 9r.5–10v.3.

The unusual iconography with which Kälden Gyatso is commonly depicted shows him as a scholar and siddha. He wears a Gelukpa hat and his left hand holds a volume of his *Collected Writings*. His right hand is at his ear in the same *mudrā* as Milarepa, indicating that he is singing *gur*.

A statue of Kälden Gyatso, currently in the chapel of his eighth incarnation at Rongbo Tashikhyil

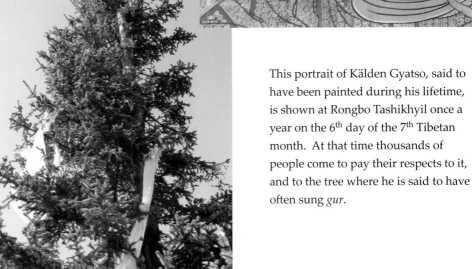

This portrait of Kälden Gyatso, said to have been painted during his lifetime, is shown at Rongbo Tashikhyil once a year on the 6th day of the 7th Tibetan month. At that time thousands of people come to pay their respects to it, and to the tree where he is said to have often sung *gur*.

Biography

Kälden Gyatso was born in the Rebgong region of Amdo in 1607, and studied for nine years at Ganden Monastery, during which time he received full ordination from the first Panchen Lama in the Jokhang. After returning to Amdo at age twenty-one, he founded Thösamling, a philosophical school, at Rongbo Monastery, and Kadam Phodrang, a school for tantric studies, at Rongbo Tashikhyil. He wrote sixty books, including a short history of the spread of Buddhism in Amdo, various biographies, eulogies, and works on *Mahāmudrā*.[1] He was the personal lama of several Mongol governors, and had hundreds of disciples, many of which founded Buddhist monasteries and schools in their own regions. His strongest desire was to retire from all obligations of the schools, and in the last seven years of his life, he lived principally in the hermitage Rongbo Tashikhyil,[2] where *gur* was his preferred means of expression for his experiences. He passed away there in 1677. Kälden Gyatso was the first in a lineage of which the eighth incarnation is alive today.

---

1 *See TSR*, Appendix E, 384–426, for a catalogue of Kälden Gyatso's *Collected Writings*.

2 *TSR*, Appendix B, 370–75. For more information about Kälden Gyatso's life, see Ngag dbang, *Skal ldan gyi rnam thar*.

A Tibetan-style book or *pecha*, the *Collected Songs of Milarepa,* which had a strong influence on Kälden Gyatso

Villagers still sing Kälden Gyatso's songs at funerals in courtyards of the deceased, as well as on mountaintops, and yearly in large tents for fifteen days over the summer solstice

Bibliography

Byang chub mi la Ngag dbang bsod nams. *Grub chen skal ldan rgya mtsho'i rnam thar yid bzhin dbang gi rgyal po.* Xining: Mtsho sngon mi rigs dpe skrun khang, 1990.

_____. *Grub chen skal ldan rgya mtsho'i rnam thar yid bzhin dbang gi rgyal po.* In *Gsung 'bum,* by Skal ldan rgya mtsho. Vol. Ka. Carved at Rong bo monastery, Reb gong, Amdo in the *me yos* year, 1987.

_____. *Grub chen skal ldan rgya mtsho'i rnam thar yid bzhin dbang gi rgyal po.* In *Yab rje bla ma skal ldan rgya mtsho'i gsung 'bum,* by Skal ldan rgya mtsho. Vol. 1, pp. 1–99. Xining: Kan su'u mi rigs dpe skrun khang, 1999.

Davidson, Ronald M. *Tibetan Renaissance: Tantric Buddhism in the Rebirth of Tibetan Culture.* New York: Colombia University Press, 2005.

Dge 'dun rab gsal. "Skal ldan mgur ma dang de'i khyad chos." In *Religion and Secular Culture in Tibet*: *Tibetan Studies II*. Edited by Henk Blezer. Pp. 97–112. Vol. 2/2 of Brill's Tibetan Studies Library: *PIATS 2000: Tibetan Studies: Proceedings of the Ninth Seminar of the International Association for Tibetan Studies, Leiden 2000,* edited by Henk Blezer. Leiden: Brill, 2002.

Don grub rgyal. *Bod kyi mgur glu byung 'phel gyi lo rgyus dang khyad chos bsdus par ston pa rig pa'i khye'u rnam par rtsen pa'i skyed tshal.* In *Dpal don grub rgyal gyi gsung 'bum*, by Don grub rgyal. Vol. 3, pp. 316–601. Beijing: Mi rigs dpe skrun khang, 1997.

Dowman, Keith, ed., trans. *Masters of Mahāmudrā: Songs and Histories of the Eighty-Four Buddhist Siddhas.* Albany: State University of New York Press, 1985.

Frye, Stanley, trans. *The Sutra of the Wise and the Foolish (Mdo bdzangs blun) or The Ocean of Narratives (Üliger-ün dalai).* Dharamsala, India: Library of Tibetan Works & Archives, 1981.

Gtsang smyon He ru ka, comp. *Rnal 'byor gyi dbang phyug chen po mi la ras pa'i rnam mgur.* Xining: Mtsho sngon mi rigs dpe skrun khang, 1999.

Jackson, Roger R. "The *dGe ldan-bKa' brgyud* Tradition of *Mahāmudrā*: How Much *dGe ldan*? How Much *bKa' brgyud*?" In *Changing Minds: Contributions to the Study of Buddhism and Tibet in Honor of Jeffrey Hopkins*, edited by Guy Newland. Ithaca, New York: Snow Lion Publications, 2001.

'Jigs med theg mchog. *Rong bo dgon chen gyi gdan rabs rdzogs ldan gtam gyi rang sgra.* Xining: Mtsho sngon mi rigs dpe skrun khang, 1988.

Lhalungpa, Lobsang P., trans. *The Life of Milarepa.* Boston: Shambhala, 1985.

Mi la ras pa. *The Hundred Thousand Songs of Milarepa.* Edited and translated by Garma C. C. Chang. 2 vols. Boston: Shambhala, 1989.

Mullin, Glenn H. *Tsongkhapa's Six Yogas of Nāropa.* Ithaca, N.Y.: Snow Lion Publications, 1997.

_____, ed., trans. *Readings on the Six Yogas of Nāropa.* Ithaca, N.Y.: Snow Lion Publications, 1997.

Nebesky-Wojkowitz, Réne de. *Oracles and Demons of Tibet: The Cult and Iconography of the Tibetan Protective Deities.* 1956. Reprint, Delhi: Book Faith India, 1996.

Paṇ chen Blo bzang chos kyi rgyal mtshan. *A Root Text for the Precious Gelug/ Kagyü Tradition of Mahāmudrā: The Main Road of the Triumphant Ones (Dge ldan bka' brgyud rin po che'i phyag chen rtsa ba rgyal ba'i gzhung lam).* Translated by Alexander Berzin. In *The Gelug/ Kagyü Tradition of Mahāmudrā.* Pp. 95–102, 352–55. Ithaca, N.Y.: Snow Lion Publications, 1997.

Roberts, Peter Allen, trans. *Mahāmudrā and Related Instructions: Core Teachings of the Kagyü schools.* Boston: Wisdom Publications, 2011.

Shakabpa, Tsepon Wangchuk Deden. *One Hundred Thousand Moons: An Advanced Political History of Tibet.* Translated by Derek F. Maher. 2 vols. Leiden: Brill, 2010.

Skal ldan rgya mtsho. *Chos phung brgyad khri bzhi stong gi yang snying gdams pa rnams glu dbyangs su mdzad pa gsung mgur chen mo.* In *Mdo smad sgrub brgyud bstan pa'i shing rta ba chen po phyag na pad+mo yab rje bla ma shar skal ldan rgya mtsho'i gsung 'bum.* Vol. 5. Rong bo: Rong bo dgon chen grwa tshang thos bsam rnam par rgyal ba'i gling gi slob gnyer 'dzin skyong tshogs pas 'grems spel, in the *chu pho 'drug* year 2012.

_____. *Gsung 'bum.* Carved at Rong bo monastery, Reb gong, Amdo in the *me yos* year, 1987.

_____. *Gsung mgur.* Carved at Thos bsam gling, Rong bo monastery, Reb gong, Amdo, in the *me pho byi* year, 1756. Copied and published under the title *Rnam 'dren bla ma skal ldan rgya mtsho'i gsung mgur* (*The Collected Songs of Spiritual Experience of Rong bo Grub chen Skal ldan rgya mtsho*). New Delhi: A lags 'Jam dbyangs, 1977.

_____. *Gsung mgur chen mo.* In *Gsung 'bum* by Skal ldan rgya mtsho. Vol. Ca. Carved in Rong bo monastery, Reb gong, Amdo in the *me yos* year, 1987.

_____. *'Jam pa'i dbyangs skal ldan rgya mtsho'i gsung las dge ldan phyag chen zab khrid gdams ngag rgya mtsho nas btus pa.* In *Gsung 'bum*, by Skal ldan rgya mtsho. Vol. Kha-6. Carved at Rong bo monastery, Reb gong, Amdo in the *me yos* year, 1987.

_____. *'Jam pa'i dbyangs skal ldan rgya mtsho'i gsung las dge ldan phyag chen zab khrid gdams ngag rgya mtsho nas btus pa.* In *Yab rje bla ma skal ldan rgya mtsho'i gsung 'bum,* by Skal ldan rgya mtsho. Vol. 2, pp. 214–35. Xining: Kan su'u mi rigs dpe skrun khang, 1999.

_____. *Phyag chen brgyud 'debs.* In *Gsung 'bum,* by Skal ldan rgya mtsho. Vol. Kha-5. Carved at Rong bo monastery, Reb gong, Amdo in the *me yos* year, 1987.

_____. *Phyag chen brgyud 'debs.* In *Yab rje bla ma skal ldan rgya mtsho'i gsung 'bum,* by Skal ldan rgya mtsho. Vol. 2, pp. 211–13. Xining: Kan su'u mi rigs dpe skrun khang, 1999.

_____. *Phyag chen gyi 'khrid yig.* In *Gsung 'bum,* by Skal ldan rgya mtsho. Vol. Kha-8. Carved at Rong bo monastery, Reb gong, Amdo in the *me yos* year, 1987.

_____. *Phyag chen gyi 'khrid yig.* In *Yab rje bla ma skal ldan rgya mtsho'i gsung 'bum,* by Skal ldan rgya mtsho. Vol. 2, pp. 254–65. Xining: Kan su'u mi rigs dpe skrun khang, 1999.

_____. *Rdo rje 'chang skal ldan rgya mtsho'i gsung las dge ldan bka' brgyud phyag rgya chen po'i nyams khrid rje blo bzang bstan pa'i rgyal mtshan dpal bzang po'i gsung gis bskul ba.* In *Gsung 'bum,* by Skal ldan rgya mtsho. Vol. Kha-7. Carved at Rong bo monastery, Reb gong, Amdo in the *me yos* year, 1987.

_____. *Rdo rje 'chang skal ldan rgya mtsho'i gsung las dge ldan bka' brgyud phyag rgya chen po'i nyams khrid rje blo bzang bstan pa'i rgyal mtshan dpal bzang po'i gsung gis bskul ba.* In *Yab rje bla ma skal ldan rgya mtsho'i gsung 'bum,* by Skal ldan rgya mtsho. Vol. 2, pp. 236–53. Xining: Kan su'u mi rigs dpe skrun khang, 1999.

_____. *Rje btsun thams cad mkhyen pa bstan 'dzin blo bzang rgya mtsho dpal bzang po'i zhal snga nas kyi rnam par thar pa dad pa'i sgo 'byed*. In *Gsung 'bum*, by Skal ldan rgya mtsho. Vol. Ka-6. Carved at Rong bo monastery, Reb gong, Amdo in the *me yos* year, 1987.

_____. *Rje btsun thams cad mkhyen pa bstan 'dzin blo bzang rgya mtsho dpal bzang po'i zhal snga nas kyi rnam par thar pa dad pa'i sgo 'byed*. In *Yab rje bla ma skal ldan rgya mtsho'i gsung 'bum*, by Skal ldan rgya mtsho. Vol. 1, pp. 180–255. Xining: Kan su'u mi rigs dpe skrun khang, 1999.

_____. *Rje skal ldan rgya mtsho dpal bzang po'i gsung las thun drug gi rnal 'byor nyams su len tshul gyi rim pa gnyis*. In *Yab rje bla ma skal ldan rgya mtsho'i gsung 'bum*, by Skal ldan rgya mtsho. Vol. 3, pp. 77–88. Xining: Kan su'u mi rigs dpe skrun khang, 1999.

_____. *Rnam 'dren bla ma yab rje skal ldan rgya mtsho'i mgur 'bum*. [Gtsos grong khyer, Gansu]: Bod gna' deng rig gnas 'dzin skyong dar spel gling, [in or after the *me pho byi* year, 1996?].

_____. *Shar skal ldan rgya mtsho'i mgur 'bum*. Xining: Mtsho sngon mi rigs dpe skrun khang, 1994.

_____. *Yab rje bla ma skal ldan rgya mtsho'i gsung 'bum*. 4 vols. Xining: Kan su'u mi rigs dpe skrun khang, 1999.

_____. *Yab rje bla ma skal ldan rgya mtsho'i mgur 'bum*. In *Yab rje bla ma skal ldan rgya mtsho'i gsung 'bum*, by Skal ldan rgya mtsho. Vol. 4, pp. 1–320. Xining: Kan su'u mi rigs dpe skrun khang, 1999.

Sujata, Victoria. "A Commentary on the *Mgur 'bum* (*Collected Songs of Spiritual Realization*) of Skal ldan rgya mtsho, a Seventeenth Century Scholar and Siddha from Amdo." Ph.D. diss., Harvard University, 2003.

_____. "*Nyams mgur* of Pha bong kha pa bDe chen snying po (1878–1941): An Analysis of His Poetic Techniques." In *Tibetan Literary Genres, Texts, and Text Types: From Genre Classification to Transformation*. Edited by Jim Rheingans. Pp. 197–228. Vol. 37 of Brill's Tibetan Studies Library, edited by Henk Blezer, Alex McKay, and Charles Ramble. Leiden: Brill, 2015.

_____. "Relationships between Inner Life and Solitary Places: The *Mgur* of Two *Siddhas* in Amdo." In *Contributions to Tibetan Buddhist Literature: Proceedings of the Eleventh Seminar of the International Association for Tibetan Studies, Königswinter 2006.* Edited by Orna Almogi. Pp. 549–69. Beiträge zur Zentralasiaenforschung. Halle: International Institute for Tibetan and Buddhist Studies, 2008.

_____. "Rong bo Grub chen Skal ldan rgya mtsho and Chos pa Rin po che." Paper presented at the VIIIth Seminar of the International Association for Tibetan Studies, Bloomington, Indiana, July 1998.

_____. "The Singing of Seventeenth-century *Mgur* in Amdo today: A Continuing Tradition." *Tibetan Studies: Proceedings of the Tenth Seminar of the International Association of Tibetan Studies, Oxford, 2003* (forthcoming).

_____. *Songs of Shabkar: The Path of a Tibetan Yogi Inspired by Nature.* Cazadero, Calif.: Dharma Publishing, 2011.

_____. *Tibetan Songs of Realization: Echoes from a Seventeenth-Century Scholar and Siddha in Amdo.* Vol. 7 of Brill's Tibetan Studies Library, edited by Henk Blezer, Alex McKay, and Charles Ramble. Leiden: Brill, 2005.

Tenzin Gyatso, the Fourteenth Dalai Lama. *A Flash of Lightning in the Dark of Night: A Guide to the Bodhisattva's Way of life.* Translated by The Padmakara Translation Group. Boston & London: Shambhala, 1994.

Tenzin Gyatso, H. H. the Dalai Lama & Alexander Berzin. *The Gelug/ Kagyü Tradition of Mahāmudrā.* Ithaca, N.Y.: Snow Lion Publications, 1997.

Thrangu Rinpoche. *Buddha Nature: Ten Teachings on the Uttar Tantra Shastra*. Translated by Erik Pema Kunsang. Kathmandu, Nepal: Rangjung Yeshe Publications, 1993.

Thupten Jinpa and Jaś Elsner, comps., trans. *Songs of Spiritual Experience: Tibetan Buddhist Poems of Insight & Awakening*. Boston: Shambhala, 2000.

Tsong kha pa. *A Book of Three Inspirations: A Treatise of the Stages of Training in the Profound Path of Nāro's Six Dharmas* (*Zab lam nāro'i chos drug gi sgo nas 'khrid pa'i rim pa yid ches gsum ldan*). Edited and translated by Glenn H. Mullin. In *Tsongkhapa's Six Yogas of Nāropa*. Pp. 109–226. Ithaca, N.Y.: Snow Lion Publications, 1996.

_____. *The Great Treatise on the Stages of the Path to Enlightenment*. Translated by Lamrim Translation Committee. Edited by Joshua W.C. Cutler and Guy Newland. 3 vols. Ithaca, N.Y.: Snow Lion Publications, 2014.

Willis, Janice D. *Enlightened Beings: Life Stories from the Ganden Oral Tradition*. Boston: Wisdom Publications, 1995.

Zhabs dkar Tshogs drug rang grol. [*Bya btang tshogs drug rang grol gyis rang dang skal ldan gdul bya la mgrin pa gdams pa'i bang mdzod nas glu dbyangs dga' ston 'gyed pa rnams*.] In *Rje zhabs dkar tshogs drug rang grol gyi gsung 'bum*. Vols. 3–4. Xining: Mtsho sngon mi rigs dpe skrun khang, 2002.

_____. *Bya btang tshogs drug rang grol gyis rang dang skal ldan gdul bya la mgrin pa gdams pa'i bang mdzod nas glu dbyangs dga' ston 'gyed pa rnams*. In *Zhabs dkar tshogs drug rang grol gyi bka' 'bum: The Collected Works of Zhabs dkar tshogs drug rang grol (1781–1851)*. Vol. 3 (Ga), vol. 4 (Nga), and vol. 5 (Ca): 1–402. New Delhi: Shechen Publications, 2003.

_____. *Snyigs dus 'gro ba yongs kyi skyabs mgon zhabs dkar rdo rje 'chang chen po'i rnam par thar pa rgyas par bshad pa skal bzang gdul bya thar 'dod rnams kyi re ba skong ba'i yid bzhin gyi nor bu bsam 'phel dbang gi rgyal po.*

In *Rje zhabs dkar tshogs drug rang grol gyi gsung 'bum* by Zhabs dkar Tshogs drug rang grol. Vol. 1. Xining: Mtsho sngon mi rigs dpe skrun khang, 2002.

Zhabs dkar Tshogs drug rang grol, 1781–1851. *The Life of Shabkar: The Autobiography of a Tibetan Yogin*. Translated by Matthieu Ricard, et al. Albany: State University of New York Press, 1994.

_____. *Rainbows Appear: Tibetan Poems of Shabkar.* Edited and translated by Matthieu Ricard. Calligraphy by Jigme Doushe. Boston: Shambhala, 2002.

Reference Texts

Bod rgya tshig mdzod chen mo. Beijing: Mi rigs dpe skrun khang, 1993.

Buswell, Robert E., Jr., ed. *Encyclopedia of Buddhism*. 2 vols. New York: Macmillan Reference USA, 2004.

Buswell, Robert E., Jr., and Donald S. Lopez, Jr. *The Princeton Dictionary of Buddhism*. Princeton: Princeton University Press, 2014.

Harvey, Peter. *An Introduction to Buddhism: Teachings, History and Practices*. 2d ed. Cambridge, UK: Cambridge University Press, 2013.

Mitchell, Donald W., and Sarah H. Jacoby. *Buddhism: Introducing the Buddhist Experience.* 3d ed. Oxford: Oxford University Press, 2014.

Prebish, Charles S., and Damien Keown. *Introducing Buddhism*. 2d ed. Abingdon, UK: Routledge, 2010.

Rvavec, Karl E. *A Historical Atlas of Tibet.* Chicago: The University of Chicago Press, 2015.

Tsepak Rigzin. *Tibetan-English Dictionary of Buddhist Terminology*. 2d ed., rev. and enl. Dharamsala, India: Library of Tibetan Works and Archives, 1993.

Websites

Hartley, Lauran. "Review of *Tibetan Songs of Realization: Echoes from a Seventeenth-Century Scholar and Siddha in Amdo*, by Victoria Sujata." *Journal of the International Association of Tibetan Studies* 3 (December 2007): 1–6. http://www.thlib.org/static/reprints/jiats/03/pdfs/rev_sujata JIATS _ 03_2007.pdf

Himalayan Art Resources. www.himalayanart.org

The Rangjung Yeshe Gilded Palace of Dharmic Activity: A Glossary of Buddhist People, Places, and Things. http://rywiki.tsadra.org

Buddhist Digital Resource Center (formerly Tibetan Buddhist Resource Center). https://www.tbrc.org

Discography

Sujata, Victoria, recorder, compiler, translator, and annotator. *Tibetan Songs of Realization: A Continuing Tradition from the Seventeenth Century*. CD. Brill, 2005. Available with Victoria Sujata, *Tibetan Songs of Realization: Echoes from a Seventeenth-Century Scholar and Siddha in Amdo* (Leiden: Brill, 2005).

Supplemental Bibliography

Additional Sources for Songs and Other Mystical Verse

'Brug pa kun legs. *The Divine Madman: The Sublime Life and Songs of Drukpa Kunley*. Translated by Keith Dowman and Sonam Paljor. Clearlake, Calif.: The Dawn Horse Press, 1980.

_____. *Vie et chants de 'Brug pa kun legs, le yogin*. Edited and translated by R. A. Stein. Paris: G.-P. Maisonneuve et Larose, 1972.

Chögyam Trungpa. *Mudrā: Early Poems & Songs*. Boston: Shambhala, 2001.

Guenther, Herbert V. *Ecstatic Spontaneity: Saraha's Three Cycles of Dohā.* Berkeley: Asian Humanities Press, 1993.

Jackson, Roger R., trans., annot. *Tantric Treasures: Three Collections of Mystical Verse from Buddhist India.* Oxford: Oxford University Press, 2004.

Jamgon Kongtrul, the Great. *The Spiritual Song of Lodro Thaye: Jamgon Kongtrul's Summary of Mahāmudrā.* Thrangu Rinpoche and Geshe Lharampa, commentary. Translated by Cornelia Weishaar-Gunter. Boulder, Colo.: Namo Buddha Seminar, 2001.

Kvaerne, Per. *An Anthology of Buddhist Tantric Songs: A Study of the Caryāgīti.* Det Norske Videnskaps-Akademi. II. Hist.-Filos. Klasse. Skrifter, Ny Serie, no. 14. Oslo: Universitetsforlaget; Irvington-on-Hudson, N.Y.: Columbia University Press, 1977.

Mi la ras pa. *Drinking the Mountain Stream: New Stories of Tibet's Beloved Saint, Milarepa.* Translated by Lama Kunga Rinpoche and Brian Cutillo. Boston: Wisdom Publications, 1995.

_____. *Milarepa: Songs on the Spot.* Translated by Nicole Riggs. Eugene, Oreg.: Dharma Cloud Press, 2003.

_____. *Miraculous Journey: New Stories & Songs by Milarepa.* Translated by Lama Kunga Rimpoche and Brian Cutillo. Novato, Calif.: Lotsawa, 1986.

Mullin, Glenn H. *Mystical Verses of a Mad Dalai Lama.* Wheaton, Ill.: The Theosophical Publishing House, 1994.

_____, comp., ed., trans. *Teachings of the Dalai Lamas: Selected Works of the Dalai Lama VII: Songs of Spiritual Change.* 2d ed. Ithaca, N.Y.: Snow Lion Publications, 1985.

Nālandā Translation Committee under the direction of Chögyam Trungpa, trans. *The Life of Marpa the Translator: Seeing Accomplishes All.* Boston: Shambhala, 1995.

_____. *The Rain of Wisdom: The Essence of the Ocean of True Meaning: The Vajra Songs of the Kagyü Gurus*. Boston: Shambhala, 1999.

Rabten, Geshe. *Song of the Profound View.* Edited and translated by Stephen Batchelor. London: Wisdom Publications, 1989.

Schaeffer, Kurtis R. *Dreaming the Great Brahmin: Tibetan Traditions of the Buddhist Poet-Saint Saraha*. New York: Oxford University Press, 2005.

Sørensen, Per K. *Divinity Secularized: An Inquiry into the Nature and Form of the Songs ascribed to the Sixth Dalai Lama*. Wiener Studien zur Tibetologie und Buddhismuskunde, heft 25. Wien: Arbeitskreis für tibetische und buddhistische Studien, Universität Wien, 1990.

Stearns, Cyrus. *Song of the Road: The Poetic Travel Journal of Tsarchen Losal Gyatso.* Boston: Wisdom Publications, 2012.

Stearns, Cyrus, ed., trans. *Hermit of Go Cliffs: Timeless Instructions from a Tibetan Mystic*. Boston: Wisdom Publications, 2000.

Thrangu Rinpoche. *Songs of Nāropa*. Translated by Erik Pema Kunsang. Hong Kong: Rangjung Yeshe Publications, 1997.

Thrangu Rinpoche, Khenchen. *A Song for the King: Saraha on Mahāmudrā Meditation.* Edited by Michele Martin. Translated by Michele Martin and Peter O'Hearn. Boston: Wisdom Publications, 2006.

Tsultrim Gyamtso Rinpoche, Khenpo. *Beautiful Song of Marpa the Translator.* Prajna Editions, inaugural issue. Auckland, New Zealand: Zhyisil Chokyi Ghatsal Publications, 2001.

Table of Tibetan Words

phonetics	*transliteration*
Amdo	A mdo
bardo	*bar do*
Chö Tündrug Näljor	*Chos thun drug rnal 'byor*
Chöpa Rinpoche	Chos pa Rin po che
Dalai Lama	Ta la'i bla ma
Demchog	Bde mchog
Depa Chökyi Gyälpo	Sde pa Chos kyi rgyal po
Depa Chökyije Tendzin Lobzang Gyatso	Sde pa Chos kyi rje Bstan 'dzin blo bzang rgya mtsho
Dewachen	Bde ba can
Do Kham	Mdo Khams
Domey	Mdo smad
Dorjechang	Rdo rje 'chang
Dromtön	'Brom ston
Dzongnyin	Rdzong nyin
Gampopa	Sgam po pa
Ganden	Dga' ldan
Geluk	Dge lugs
Gendün Sherab	Dge 'dun Shes rab
Gendun Tenpai Nyima	Dge 'dun Bstan pa'i nyi ma
Gönlung Jampaling	Dgon lung byams pa gling

gur	*mgur*
Gurbum	*Mgur 'bum*
gurma	*mgur ma*
Gyesum	Sgyed gsum
Jakyung	Bya khyung
Jampel Dorje	’Jam dpal rdo rje
Jamyang Shepai Dorje	’Jam dbyangs bzhad pa’i rdo rje
Kachu	*Bka' bcu*
Kachuwa	*Bka' bcu ba*
Kadam	Bka’ gdams
Kagyü	Bka’ brgyud
Kälden Gyatso	Skal ldan rgya mtsho
Kälden Repa	Skal ldan ras pa
Kham	Khams
Khargong	Mkhar gong
Khorlo Demchog	’Khor lo bde mchog
Ladrang Tashikhyil	Bla brang Bkra shis ’khyil
Lhasa	Lha sa
Lobzang	Blo bzang
Lobzang Chödrag	Blo bzang chos grags
Lobzang Chökyi Gyältsen	Blo bzang chos kyi rgyal mtshan
Lobzang Dragpa	Blo bzang grags pa
Lobzang Tenpai Gyältsen	Blo bzang bstan pa’i rgyal mtshan
lung	*rlung*
Marpa	Mar pa
Milarepa	Mi la ras pa
Mila Shepai Dorje	Mi la Bzhad pa’i rdo rje
Ngawang Sherap	Ngag dbang Shes rab
Nyalung	?
Nyingma	Rnying ma
Ogyen	O rgyan
o na la	’o na la
Pangluk	Spang lug

Pema	Padma
Phu Seku	Phu se ku
Rebgong	Reb gong
repa	*ras pa*
Ribo Phendzang (?)	Ri bo 'phan 'dzang (?)
Rong	Rong
Rongbo	Rong bo
Rongbo Tashikhyil	Rong bo Bkra shis 'khyil
Sakya	Sa skya
Samye	Bsam yas
Seku Jakyung	Se ku bya khyung
Shabkar	Zhabs dkar
she	*gzhas*
Songtsen Gampo	Srong btsan sgam po
Tashikhyil	Bkra shis 'khyil
Tashilhunpo	Bkra shis lhun po
Tendzin Lobzang Gyatso	Bstan 'dzin blo bzang rgya mtsho
thigle	*thig le*
Trishor Gyälmo	Khri shor rgyal mo
tsa	*rtsa*
Tsang Nyön Heruka	Gtsang smyon He ru ka
Tsho Ngönpo	Mtsho sngon po
Tshonying	Mtsho snying
Tsongkhapa	Tsong kha pa
tummo	*gtum mo*
Ü	Dbus
Ütsang	Dbus gtsang
Yama Tashikhyil	G.ya ma Bkra shis 'khyil
yidam	*yi dam*

Index

Maps

Beijing
Wutaishan
ng
shikhyil
N
0
500
0
500 km

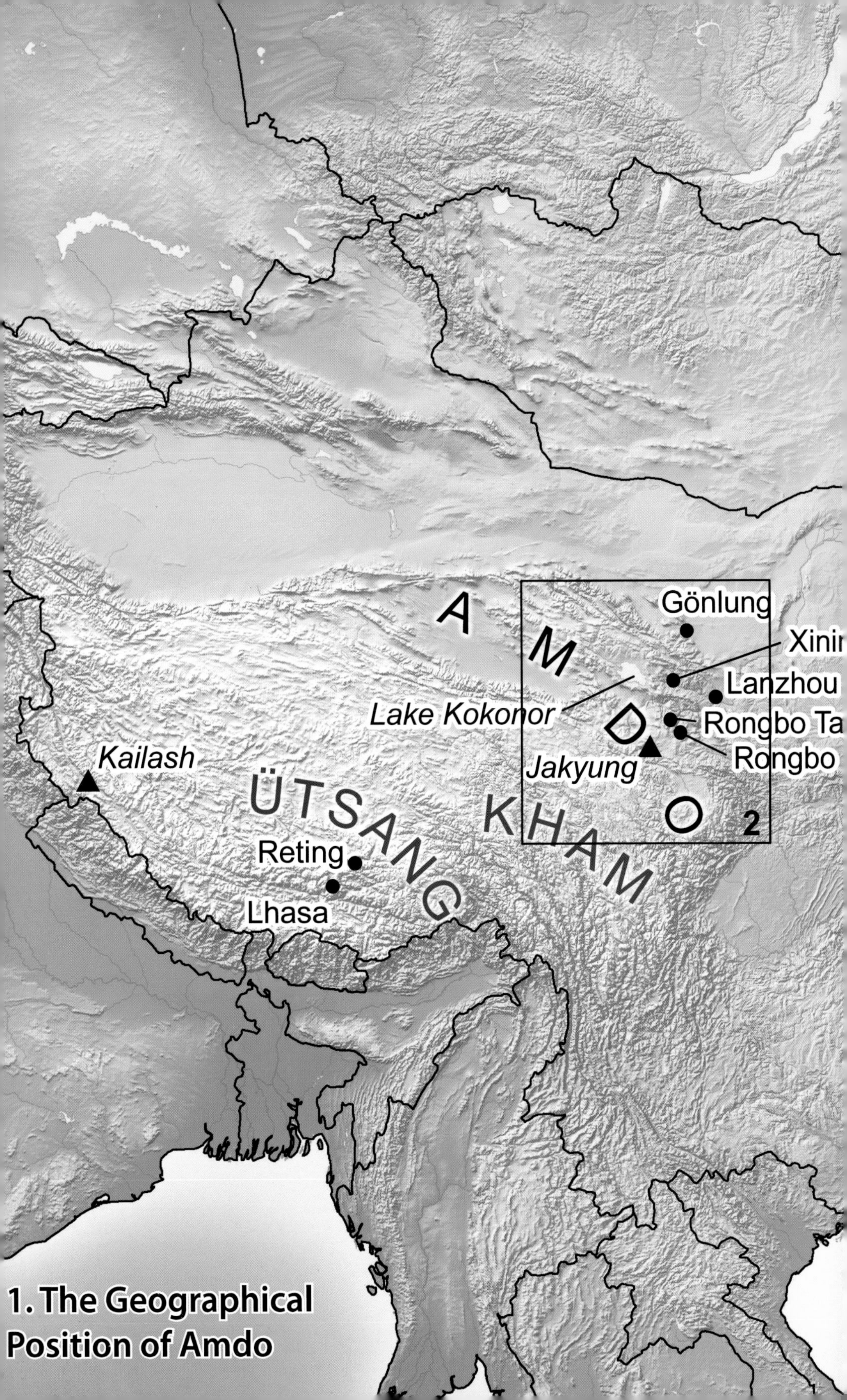

1. The Geographical Position of Amdo

Gönlung
Xining
Lanzhou
Tashikhyil
Yama Tashikhyil
Rongbo
Guchu
Ladrang Tashikhyil
REBGONG
N
0
0
50 km

2. Amdo, Showing Places Found in the Songs and Notes